WITH
LAWRENCE
IN ARABIA

COLONEL T. E. LAWRENCE

WITH
LAWRENCE
IN ARABIA

by

LOWELL THOMAS

WITH FRONTISPIECE AND 30 OTHER
ILLUSTRATIONS

105TH THOUSAND

HUTCHINSON & CO.
(*Publishers*) *Ltd.*
LONDON

MADE AND PRINTED IN GREAT BRITAIN
AT GAINSBOROUGH PRESS, ST. ALBANS
BY FISHER, KNIGHT AND CO., LTD.

TO EIGHTEEN GENTLEMEN OF CHICAGO
THIS NARRATIVE OF A MODERN
ARABIAN KNIGHT IS GRATE-
FULLY DEDICATED

The Publishers desire to state that Colonel Lawrence is not the source from which the facts in this volume were obtained, nor is he in any way responsible for its contents.

CONTENTS

CONTENTS

LIST OF ILLUSTRATIONS

LIST OF ILLUSTRATIONS

FOREWORD

SURELY no one ever offered a volume to the public who was quite so deeply indebted to others, and I have long looked forward to the opportunity of expressing my gratitude. To do this I must turn back the pages of time to the days when, accompanied by my photographic colleague, Mr. Harry A. Chase, and two other assistants, I left America to gather information and secure a pictorial record of the various phases of the struggle that was then in progress all the way from the North Sea to far off Arabia.

We had set forth early in 1917 and were expected to return at the end of a year or so to help in the work of stimulating enthusiasm for the Allied Cause. The late Mr. Franklin K. Lane, Secretary of Interior, had suggested that I resign from the faculty of Princeton University in order to undertake this. To Secretary Lane, Secretary of the Navy Daniels, and Secretary for War Baker, who were responsible for our becoming attached successively to the various Allied armies, I am indebted for the opportunities which enabled me to obtain the material for this volume. This was before a special appropriation had been set aside for such work, and as the result of Secretary Lane's suggestion, eighteen distinguished private citizens supplied the funds for the undertaking.

Mr. Chase and I have just concluded a three-year speaking tour of the world, during which I have shown the pictorial record and narrated to several million people the story which we brought back of Allenby's conquest of the Holy Land, and the hitherto unknown story of Lawrence and the War in the land of the Arabian Nights. The generous praise and innumerable courtesies which have been extended to us during this tour have been received by us on behalf of these eighteen nameless gentlemen. For it is to them that the credit is due. In Europe, Americans are commonly regarded as mere worshippers of Mammon; yet these financiers are typical American business men, and if this book proves to be a contribution of value because it happens to be the only written fragmentary record of the most romantic campaign in history, then the credit belongs to these unselfish, anonymous gentlemen of

Chicago. For had it not been for them, the story of Colonel
Lawrence's achievements in Arabia might never have been
told, and might never have become very widely known even
among his own countrymen.

To Colonel John Buchan, who in those days was one of
the mysterious high priests of the Ministry of Information, I
am indebted for the permit that got me out to Palestine at the
time when other missions were not allowed there, and at the
time when Allenby, Britain's modern Cœur de Lion, was leading his army in the most brilliant cavalry campaign of all
time. I also am deeply indebted to the great Commander-in-
Chief himself, and likewise to the chief of his Intelligence Staff,
Brigadier-General Sir Gilbert F. Clayton. It was they who
were responsible for our being the only observers attached
to the Shereefian forces in Holy Arabia.

During the time that Mr. Chase and I were in Arabia, I
found it impossible to extract much information from Lawrence
himself regarding his own achievements. He insisted on
giving the entire credit to Emir Feisal and other Arab leaders,
and to his fellow adventurers, Colonel Wilson, of the Sudan,
Newcombe, Joyce, Dawnay, Bassett, Vickery, Cornwallis,
Hogarth, Stirling, etc., all of whom did magnificent work in
Arabia. So to them I went for much of my material, and I
am indebted to various members of this group of brilliant men
whom General Clayton used in his Near Eastern Secret Corps.
Eager to tell me of the achievements of their quiet scholarly
companion, they refused to say much about themselves,
although their own deeds rivalled those of the heroes of "The
Arabian Nights."

To the Right Honourable Lord Riddell, and to Mr.
Louis D. Froelick, editor of *Asia Magazine*, I am grateful for
the encouragement which led me to believe that I should
attempt the delightful task of recording what little I know of
this romance of real life. I owe a special debt to Miss Elsie
Weil, former managing editor of *Asia Magazine*; also to
Captain Alan Bott, M.C., R.A.F. ("Contact"); to my
colleague, Mr. Dale Carnagey, the American novelist; and to
my wife—for it was their invaluable co-operation that finally
enabled me to prepare this volume.

There are others infinitely better qualified than I to give
the world a full account of the Arabian Revolution. For
instance, Commander D. G. Hogarth, the famous Arabian
authority who played a prominent advisory part, could easily
do this. It is to be hoped that his archæological work and
duties as curator of the Ashmolean Museum at Oxford will

not prevent him from preparing a final official history. But it is to Lawrence himself that we must look for the inside story of the War in the land of the Arabian Nights.

Unhappily, no matter how much unselfish work a man does for his country, and no matter how modest he is, there are always people hovering about on the side lines ready to tear his record to pieces. For instance, there are those who say that Lawrence has received altogether too much "publicity" through me. They piously declare that this is not in accordance with military ethics. There may be something in this, though I doubt it. But if there is, the blame should *all* be mine.

There is no question but what the praise I have given him has embarrassed him exceedingly. Indeed, had he realized when I was in Arabia that I one day would be going up and down the world shouting his praises, I have not the slightest doubt but what he would have planted one of his nitro-glycerine "tulips" under me instead of under a Turkish train!

However, not only did Lawrence little dream that I might one day be "booming him," as he describes it, but it had never even occurred to me that I should be so doing. The conspirators who were largely responsible for my coming to England were Sir William Jury, formerly of the Ministry of Information, and Major Evelyn Wrench, of the English Speaking Union, and more particularly, Mr. Percy Burton, the London impresario formerly associated with Sir Henry Irving, and Sir Johnston Forbes-Robertson. It was Mr. Burton who came to me in New York and inveigled me into agreeing to appear for a season at Covent Garden Royal Opera House, London, with my production, "With Allenby in Palestine and Lawrence in Arabia."

Another "bazaar rumour" that has been going the rounds is to the effect that Colonel Lawrence has renounced Christianity and turned Mohammedan. This also is the offspring of some feverish imagination! From what I saw of Lawrence I rather believe that he is a better Christian than the most of us. In his introduction to a new edition of Doughty's classic, "Arabia Deserta," he says of that great Arabian traveller: "He was book-learned, but simple in the arts of living, trustful of every man, very silent. He was the first Englishman they had met. He predisposed them to give a chance to other men of his race, because they found him honourable and good. So he broke a road for his religion. They say that he seemed proud only of being Christian, and yet never crossed their faith." The tribute he pays to Doughty might be applied equally appropriately to himself.

L. T.

———

The introduction by T. E. Lawrence to "Travels in Arabia Deserta," by Charles Montague Doughty, which the author quotes on page 249, is contained in the edition published in 1921 by Messrs. Jonathan Cape.

SOME OF LAWRENCE'S " DRINKERS OF THE MILK OF WAR "

LAWRENCE OF ARABIA

WITH LAWRENCE IN ARABIA

CHAPTER I

A MODERN ARABIAN KNIGHT

ONE day not long after Allenby had captured Jerusalem, I happened to be in front of a bazaar stall on Christian Street, remonstrating with a fat old Turkish shopkeeper who was attempting to relieve me of twenty piastres for a handful of dates. My attention was suddenly drawn to a group of Arabs walking in the direction of the Damascus Gate. The fact that they were Arabs was not what caused me to drop my tirade against the high cost of dates, for Palestine, as all men know, is inhabited by a far greater number of Arabs than Jews. My curiosity was excited by a single Bedouin, who stood out in sharp relief from all his companions. He was wearing an agal, kuffieh, and abba such as are worn only by Near Eastern potentates. In his belt was fastened the short curved sword of a prince of Mecca, insignia worn by descendants of the Prophet.

Christian Street is one of the most picturesque and kaleidoscopic thoroughfares in the Near East. Russian Jews, with their corkscrew curls, Greek priests in tall black hats and flowing robes, fierce desert nomads in goatskin coats reminiscent of the days of Abraham, Turks in balloon-like trousers, Arab merchants lending a brilliant note with their gay turbans and gowns, all rub elbows in that narrow lane of bazaars, shops, and coffee-houses that leads to the Church of the Holy Sepulchre.

Jerusalem is not a melting-pot. It is an uncompromising meeting-place of East and West. Here are accentuated, as if sharply outlined in black and white by the desert sun, the racial peculiarities of Christian, Jewish, and Mohammedan peoples. A stranger must, indeed, have something extraordinary about him to attract attention in the streets of the Holy City. But as this young Bedouin passed by in his magnificent royal robes, the crowds in front of the bazaars turned to look at him.

It was not merely his costume, nor yet the dignity with which he carried his five feet three, marking him every inch a king or perhaps a caliph in disguise who had stepped out of the pages of "The Arabian Nights." The striking fact was that this mysterious prince of Mecca looked no more like a son of Ishmael than an Abyssinian looks like one of Stefansson's red-haired Esquimaux; Bedouin, although of the Caucasin race, have had their skins scorched by the relentless desert sun until their complexions are the colour of lava. But this young man was as blond as a Scandinavian, in whose veins flow Viking blood and the cool traditions of fjords and sagas.

The nomadic sons of Ishmael all wear flowing beards, as their ancestors did in the time of Esau. This youth, with the curved gold sword, was clean shaven. He walked rapidly with his hands folded, his blue eyes oblivious to his surroundings, and he seemed wrapped in some inner contemplation.

My first thought as I glanced at his face was that he might be one of the younger apostles returned to life. His expression was serene, almost saintly, in its selflessness and repose.

"Who is he?" I turned eagerly to the Turk profiteer, who could only manipulate a little tourist English. He merely shrugged his shoulders.

"Who could he be?" I was certain I could obtain some information about him from General Storrs, Governor of the Holy City, and so I strolled over in the direction of his palace beyond the old wall near Solomon's Quarries. General Ronald Storrs, British successor to Pontius Pilate, had been Oriental secretary to the High Commissioner of Egypt before the fall of Jerusalem, and for years had kept in intimate touch with the peoples of Palestine. He spoke Hebrew, Greek, Latin, and Arabic with the same fluency with which he spoke English. I knew he could tell me something about the mysterious blond Bedouin.

"Who is this blue-eyed, fair-haired fellow wandering about the bazaars wearing the curved sword of a prince of ——?"

The general did not even let me finish the question but quietly opened the door of an adjoining room. There, seated at the same table where von Falkenhayn had worked out his unsuccessful plan for defeating Allenby, was the Bedouin prince, deeply absorbed in a ponderous tome on archæology.

In introducing us the governor said: "I want you to meet Colonel Lawrence, the Uncrowned King of Arabia."

He shook hands shyly and with a certain air of aloofness, as if his mind were on buried treasure and not on the affairs of this immediate world of campaigns and warfare. And that was how I first made the acquaintance of one of the most picturesque personalities of modern times, a man who will be blazoned on the romantic pages of history with Raleigh, Drake, Clive and Gordon.

During the period of the World War, years crammed with epic events, among others, two remarkable figures appeared. The dashing adventures and anecdotes of their careers will furnish golden themes to the writers of the future, as the lives of Ulysses, King Arthur, and Richard the Lion-Hearted did to the poets, troubadours, and chroniclers of other days. One is a massive, towering, square-jawed six-footer, that smashing British cavalry leader, Field-Marshal Viscount Allenby, commander of the twentieth-century Crusaders, who gained world fame because of his exploits in driving the Turks from the Holy Land and bringing to realization the dream of centuries. The other is the undersized, beardless youth whom I first saw absorbed in a technical treatise on the cuneiform inscriptions discovered on the bricks of ancient Babylon, and whose chief interests in life were poetry and archæology.

The spectacular achievements of Thomas Edward Lawrence, the young Oxford graduate, were unknown to the public at the end of the World War. Yet, quietly, without any theatrical headlines or fanfare of trumpets, he brought the disunited nomadic tribes of Holy and Forbidden Arabia into a unified campaign against their Turkish oppressors, a difficult and splendid stroke of policy, which caliphs, statesmen, and sultans had been unable to accomplish in centuries of effort! Lawrence placed himself at the head of the Bedouin army of the Shereef of Mecca, who was afterwards proclaimed King of the Hedjaz. He united the wandering tribes of the desert, restored the sacred places of Islam to the descendants of the Prophet, and drove the Turks from Arabia for ever. Allenby liberated Palestine, the Holy Land of the Jews and Christians. Lawrence freed Arabia, the Holy Land of millions of Mohammedans.

I had heard of this mystery man many times during the months I was in Palestine with Allenby. The first rumour about Lawrence reached me when I was on the way from Italy to Egypt. An Australian naval officer confided to me that an Englishman was supposed to be in command of an army of wild Bedouins somewhere in the trackless desert of the far-off land of Omar and Abu-Bekr. When I landed in Egypt I heard fantastic tales of his exploits. His name was always mentioned in hushed tones, because at that time the full facts regarding the War in the Land of the Arabian Nights were being kept secret.

B

Until the day I met him in the palace of the Governor of Jerusalem I was unable to picture him as a real person. He was to me merely a new Oriental legend. Cairo, Jerusalem, Damascus, Bagdad—in fact, all the cities of the Near East— are so full of colour and romance that the mere mention of them is sufficient to stimulate the imagination of matter-of-fact Westerners, who are suddenly spirited away on the magic carpet of memory to childhood scenes familiar through the tales of "The Thousand and One Nights." So I had come to the conclusion that Lawrence was the product of Western imagination overheated by exuberant contact with the East. But the myth turned out to be very much of a reality.

The five-foot-three Englishman standing before me wore a kuffieh of white silk and gold embroidery held in place over his hair by an agal, two black woollen cords wrapped with silver and gold thread. His heavy black camel's-hair robe or abba covered a snow-white undergarment fastened at the waist by a wide, gold-brocaded belt in which he carried the curved sword of a prince of Mecca. This youth had virtually become the ruler of the Holy Land of the Mohammedans, and commander-in-chief of many thousands of Bedouins mounted on racing camels and fleet Arabian horses. He was the terror of the Turks.

Through his discovery that archæology held a fascination for me, we became better acquainted during the following days in Jerusalem before he returned to his Arabian army. We spent many hours together, although I did not suspect that it might possibly be my good fortune to join him later in the desert. When we were in the company of officers whom he had just met he usually sat in one corner, listening intently to everything that was being said but contributing little to the conversation. When we were alone he would get up from his chair and squat on the floor in Bedouin fashion. The first time he did this he blushed in his peculiar way and excused himself, saying that he had been in the desert so long that he found it uncomfortable sitting in a chair.

I made many unsuccessful attempts to induce him to tell me something of his life and adventures in the desert, where few Europeans except Sir Richard Burton and Charles Doughty ever dared venture before him. But he always adroitly changed the subject to archæology, comparative religion, Greek literature, or Near Eastern politics. Even concerning his connection with the Arabian army he would say nothing, except to give the credit for everything that happened in the desert campaign to the Arab leaders, or to

Newcombe, Joyce, Cornwallis, Dawnay, Marshall, Stirling, Hornby, and his other British associates.

Surely Destiny never played a stranger prank than when it selected, as the man to play the major role in the liberation of Arabia, this Oxford graduate, whose life-ambition was to dig in the ruins of antiquity and to uncover and study long-forgotten cities.

CHAPTER II

WHEN we first met in Jerusalem, and later on in the solitude of the desert, I was unable to draw Lawrence out about his early life. So, after the termination of the War, on my way back to America, I visited England in the hope of being able to learn something concerning his career prior to 1914, which might throw a light on the formative period when Destiny was preparing him for his important role. The War had so scattered his family and early associates that I found it difficult to obtain aught but the most meagre information about his boyhood.

County Galway, on the west coast of Ireland, was the original home of the Lawrences. This may partly account for his unusual powers of physical endurance, for the inhabitants of Galway are among the hardiest of a hardy race. But in his veins there also flows Scotch, Welsh, English, and Spanish blood. Among his celebrated ancestors was Sir Robert Lawrence, who accompanied Richard the Lion-Hearted to the Holy Land, seven hundred and thirty years ago and distinguished himself at the siege of Acre, just as the youthful T. E. Lawrence accompanied Allenby to the Holy Land and distinguished himself in its final deliverance. The brothers, Sir Henry and Sir John Lawrence of Mutiny fame, pioneers of Britain's empire in India, were amongst his more recent predecessors.

His father, Thomas Lawrence, was at one time the owner of estates in Ireland and a great sportsman. Losing most of his wordly possessions during the Gladstone period, when the bottom fell out of land values in Ireland, he brought his family across the Irish Sea to Wales, and Thomas Edward Lawrence was born in Carnarvon County, not far from the early home of Mr. Lloyd George, who is to-day one of his warmest friends and admirers, and who once told me that he, too, regards Lawrence as one of the most picturesque figures of modern times.

Five years of his boyhood were spent on the Channel Isle of Jersey. When he was ten years of age his family migrated to the north of Scotland, remaining there for three years. They next moved to France, where young Lawrence attended a Jesuit College, although all the members of the family belong to the orthodox Church of England. From the Continent they went to Oxford, and that centre of English culture, which has been their home ever since, has left its indelible mark on Lawrence. There Ned, as his boyhood companions called him, attended Oxford High School and studied under a tutor preparatory to entering the University. One of his school chums relates that although not a star athlete he had a daring spirit and was filled with the love of adventure.

"Underneath Oxford," this companion tells us, "runs a subterranean stream bricked over, the Trill Mill Stream. Ned Lawrence and another boy, carrying lights and often lying flat to scrape through the narrow culverts, navigated the whole of that underground water passage.

"Oxford is a great boating centre. Every stream that joins the Thames is explored as far up as any slender craft will float. But the River Cherwell above Islip is said by the guide-books to be 'nowhere navigable.' To say that is to challenge boys like Ned Lawrence to prove the statement untrue, and that is what he and a companion did. They trained their canoe to Banbury and came right down the part of the stream that was 'nowhere navigable.'"

He was fond of climbing trees and scrambling over the roofs of buildings where none dared follow. "It was on such an occasion," one of his brothers informed me, "that he fell and broke a leg." His relatives attribute his smallness of stature to that accident. He seems never to have grown since.

All his life he has been as irregular in his ways as the wild tribesmen of the Arabian Desert. Although he completed the required four years' work for his Bachelor's degree in three years, he never attended a single lecture at Oxford, so far as I have been able to discover. He occasionally worked with tutors, but he spent most of his time wandering about England on foot, or reading medieval literature. In order to be alone he frequently slept by day and then read all night.

He was entirely opposed to any set system of education. The aged professor who angrily admonished Samuel Johnson when a student at Oxford, "Young man, ply your book diligently now, and acquire a stock of knowledge," would have been equally displeased with young Lawrence. The idea of obtaining a University education in order to take up a conventional occupation did not please him at all. His unconscious credo from earliest youth, like Robert Louis Stevenson's, seems to have been that "pleasures are more beneficial than duties, because, like the quality of mercy, they are not strained, and they are twice blest."

As a part of his early reading he made an exhaustive study of military writers, from the wars of Sennacherib, Thotmes and Rameses down to Napoleon, Wellington, Stonewall Jackson, and von Moltke. But this he did voluntarily and not as a part of any required work. Among his favourite books was Marshal Foch's *Principe de Guerre*; but he remarked to me on one occasion in Arabia, that his study of Cæsar and Xenophon had been of more value to him in his desert campaign, because in the irregular war which he conducted against the Turks he found it necessary to adopt tactics directly opposed to those advocated by the great French strategist.

As the subject for his Oxford thesis Lawrence chose the military architecture of the Crusades, and so absorbed did he become in this work that he urged his parents to allow him to visit the Near East, so that he might gain first-hand knowledge of the architectural efforts of the early knights of Christendom. In this he was encouraged by the distinguished Oxford scholar and authority on Arabia, Dr. David George Hogarth, curator of the Ashmolean Museum, a man who has had an important influence over his entire life down to the present day, and who even came out to Egypt during the War and acted as his intimate counsellor during the Arabian campaign.

Lawrence's mother was reluctant to have him leave home but, after many weeks of pleading, gave her consent to his visiting Syria as a Cook's tourist and allowed him two hundred pounds for the trip. His family was certain that he would return home after a few weeks, satisfied to settle down for the rest of his days and ready to forget the heat, the smells, and the inconveniences of life in the Orient.

But on reaching the Near East he scorned tourists' comforts and the beaten track. He entered Syria at Beyrouth and, shortly after landing, adopted native costume and set out barefoot for the interior. Instead of travelling as a tourist, he wandered off alone, along the fringe of the Great Arabian Desert, and amused himself studying the manners and customs of the mosaic of peoples who dwell in the ancient corridor between Mesopotamia and the Nile Valley. Two years later, when he finally returned to Oxford to hand in his thesis and receive his degree, he still had one hundred pounds left !

There were five boys in the Lawrence family, of which Thomas Edward was the second youngest. The eldest, Major Montague Lawrence, was a major in the R.A.M.C.; the second, William, a schoolmaster at Delhi, in India; the third, Frank, who finished at Oxford and wandered off to the Near East with Thomas, and the youngest, Arnold, a star track athlete at Oxford, who is also interested in archæology, and for a time took his brother's place in Mesopotamia. Both William and Frank gave their lives to their country on the battlefields of France.

Since the War Major Montague Lawrence has taken up work as a medical missionary in China, far up on the Tibetan frontier; their mother has also gone to this remote corner of Central Asia, while her youngest son is roaming around the museums of the world on a travelling fellowship from Oxford, studying the sculpture of the period of the decadence of Grecian art.

Several years before the War an expedition from Oxford, headed by Lawrence's friend Hogarth, the great antiquarian and archæologist, began excavating in the Euphrates Valley, hoping to uncover traces of that little-known ancient race, the Hittites. Because of his intimate knowledge of their language and his sympathetic understanding of their customs, Lawrence was placed in charge of the digging gangs of unruly Kurds, Turkomans, Armenians, and Arabs. This expedition eventually succeeded in uncovering Carchemish, the ancient capital of the Hittite Empire, and there, amid the ruins of that long-forgotten city, Lawrence amused himself studying inscriptions on pottery and joining up the various stages of Hittite civilization.

He and his associate, C. Leonard Woolley, director of the expedition, actually uncovered ruins which proved to be the missing link between the civilizations of Nineveh and Babylon and the beginnings of Greek culture in the islands of the Mediterranean, which extend back for five thousand years. The Ashmolean Museum at Oxford contains many exhibits "presented by T. E. Lawrence" before he was twenty years of age.

An American traveller and director of missions in the Near East happened to visit the camp of these lonely excavators. He gives us a vivid picture of his visit and an indication of how Lawrence received the training which enabled him to gain such an amazing hold over the desert tribes when the Great War overtook him.

"It was in 1913," says Mr. Luther R. Fowle, "Easter vacation at the American College in Aintab had given us the opportunity to make the three days' trip by wagon to Ourfa, the ancient Edessa. After Ourfa, we had visited Haraun, a

few miles to the south, whither Abraham migrated from Ur
of the Chaldees.

"Our return trip to Aintab was by the road farther to the
south, which brought us to the Euphrates River at Jerablus,
over which the Germans were building their great railway
bridge, an essential link in the Berlin-to-Bagdad dream. On
the western bank, a few hundred yards from the bridge, was
the site of Carchemish, and there we found the quiet British
scholar, who, under the stress of the War, was soon to turn
from his digging among the ancient ruins beside the Euphrates
to become a shereef of Mecca and leader of a vast Bedouin
host in a successful war to throw off the Ottoman yoke.

"Mr. Woolley, the archæologist in charge of the work of
excavation of Carchemish, had just come from the diggings,
clad in business dress of grey flannel shirt and golf trousers.
Lawrence, his youthful associate, also fresh from the works,
was stepping lightly across the mounds of earth clad in what
we Americans would call a running suit, and wearing at his
belt the ornate Arab girdle with its bunch of tassels at the
front, the mark of an unmarried man. But he was out of
sight in a moment, and when we gathered for supper the
freshly-tubbed young man in his Oxford tennis-suit of white
flannel bordered with red ribbon, but still wearing his Arab
girdle, launched into the fascinating story of the excavations;
of relations with the Kurds and Arabs about them; of his
trips alone among their villages in search of rare rugs and
antiquities, that gave opportunity for cultivating that close
touch and sympathy with them that subsequently was the basis
of his great service in the time of his country's need.

"The meal was delicious and was served by a powerful,
swarthy Arab in elegant native dress, with enough daggers
and revolvers in his girdle to supply a museum. Soon he
entered with the coffee, delicious as only Turkish coffee rightly
made can be. And our British friends, who were hardly able
to find interest in the Roman nut-dishes merely a couple of
thousand years old and part of the rubbish to be cleared away
before reaching the Hittite ruins, pointed out with pride that
our little brown earthenware coffee-cups were unquestionably
Hittite, and probably not far from four thousand years old.

"I should not say 'buildings,' or even 'building,' but rather
'room'; for we learned that the British Government, because
of an understanding with the Turkish authorities, had given
permission to build only one room. Accordingly Woolley and
Lawrence had built a room of two parallel walls about ten feet
apart, extending fifty feet south, then thirty-five feet west-

ward, and again fifty feet north. Closed at both ends, this giant letter U was indeed a room; and, although somewhat astonished, the Turkish Government had to concede the fact. Of course, the honourable inspector could not object if little partitions were run across to separate the sleeping portions from the dining-room and office, and in due time convenience demanded that doors be opened from various parts of the structure into the court.

"Thus it was that, when we first saw it, on the right was a series of rooms for the storage of antiquities and for photographic work; on the left were sleeping-rooms of the excavators and their guests; and in the centre was the delightful living-room with open fire-place, built-in bookcases filled with well-worn, leather-bound volumes of the classics with which a British scholar would naturally surround himself, and a long table covered with the current British papers as well as the archæological journals of all the world.

"Around the fire-place we learned much of the good faith and friendship that existed between these two lone Englishmen and the native people around them. They insisted that they were safer on the banks of the Euphrates than if they had been in Piccadilly. The leaders of the two most feared bands of brigands in the region, Kurdish and Arab, were faithful employees of the excavators, one as night-watchman, the other in a similar position of trust.

"Of course, there was no stealing and no danger. Had not these men eaten of the Englishman's salt? Moreover, the even-handed justice of the two Englishmen was so well known and respected that they had come to be the judges of various issues of all sorts between rival villages, or in personal disagreements. Never abusing their prerogatives, their decisions were never questioned. Lawrence had recently been out to a village to settle the difficulties arising out of the kidnapping of a young woman by the man who wished to marry her and who had been unable to overcome her father's objections. Could any training have been better for the part he was to play in the great Arab awakening than these experiences among the native people?

"In the living-room was an ancient wooden chest which may once have held the dowry of a desert bride, but which now served as money-box and safety-deposit vault. Larger than a wardrobe-trunk, there it stood, unlocked and unguarded. It was full of the silver money with which to pay the two hundred men working on the excavations. But such was the unwritten law of the community, such the love of the workers for their leaders, and so sure and summary the punishment which they themselves would mete out to any of their number taking advantage of this trust, that the cash could not have been safer in the vaults of the Bank of England itself.

"All this contrasted sharply with the methods and experiences of the German engineers half a mile away, building the Bagdad railway-bridge across the Euphrates. They and their workers seemed fated to mutual distrust and hatred. The Teuton could not see why the Arab should not and would not accept his regime of discipline and punishment. The Germans were always needing more labourers, while the Englishmen, a few hundred yards away, were overwhelmed with them. Once when the latter were forced to cut down their staff they tried in vain to dismiss fifty men. The Arabs and Kurds just smiled and went on with their work. They were told they would get no pay, but they smiled and worked on. If not for pay, they would work for the love of it and of their masters. And so they did.

"Nor was the excavation without interest to those simple men. They had caught the enthusiasm of their leaders who had taught them to share in the joy of the work; their digging was not meaningless toil for foreign money, but was rather a sharing of the joy of archæology.

"We retired for the night, our minds filled with the stories of the East, in which Christian and pagan, Hittite, Greek, and Roman, the great past and the sordid present of these regions, were mingled with the background of energetic German effort and the calm achievement by two modest and capable representatives of the British breed of men. We slept long and well on the familiar folding cots in our clean, mud-walled room; nor were our slumbers troubled by our bed-covers, Damascus *yorgans* of cloth of gold, upon which a rare arabesque on its background of dull red invited the eye to journeys without end. These ancient covers were some of Lawrence's treasures, brought back from his frequent trips to the Arab villages, when for weeks his whereabouts were unknown.

"It was during these journeys that he, in native garb, joined in the conversation of the village elders on the shady side of a tent, or came to understand and admire the Arab in quiet intercourse before an open fire, where, sitting cross-legged on the floor, when the coffee had been made and silently drunk, one and another spoke. While forty German engineers were building their bridge, which was to enable them to coerce these people in case they would not obey, one broad-minded, kindly Englishman was unconsciously preparing to become the man who in the great crisis was to lead this people, not only to destroy the Teuton dream of conquest, but to break the centuries-old political servitude to the Turk.

"After breakfast we were examining the mosaic floor of the dining-room, a Roman fragment that these men had taken out whole rather than destroy it in their search for the Hittite antiquities hidden below. But just then word came of excitement at the 'works.' We hurried over to find the Arabs and Kurds closely packed around a large excavation. The Greek foreman was removing the age-old earth about a dark stone several feet square, and by the time Mr. Woolley had reached his side he had determined which was the real face of the block. With practised hand Mr. Woolley began to remove the last crust of soil which covered the treasure underneath. There was no one to command those peasants to go back to their work, for the spiritual fruits of discovery belong to all, to the Englishman no more than to the water-boy who left his donkey to find the Euphrates alone, while he joined the breathless group whose eyes were glued on Woolley's jack-knife deftly doing its work.

"A burst of applause greeted the first appearance of something in relief on the hard rock. It was a hand! no, a corner of a building! a lion! a camel! Guess and conjecture flew about, to be greeted by approval or derision, always followed by quick, tense silence, while the jack-knife did its work. Soon Woolley's trained eye revealed to him that it was a large animal standing in a perfect state of preservation, and that he was uncovering its head. His feint to begin at the other end of the figure was greeted by a babble of protest from his workmen, not yet sure what the figure was. Woolley's quick smile acknowledged the reception of his little joke, and back he went to the spot already uncovered.

"Soon head, chest, legs, body, came to light, and exponents of various theories—cow, horse, sheep—were still backing their claims in musical gutturals when Woolley's hand returned to the head of the animal and with a few quick motions lifted off the earth which covered the perfect tracery of a magnificent pair of antlers; alive with the undying art of forty centuries, there stood revealed before us a superb stag. Such a discovery was worth a celebration, and unwritten law had ordained the nature of it. For the excavator nodded in response to the Greek's whispered query, and, as he gave the awaited signal, two hundred boys from fifteen to sixty-five emptied all the chambers of their revolvers in the air.

"I wonder what the Germans thought as they heard the volley from their bridge for, as I found out a few weeks later when I had galloped over for another visit with the Englishman, shots at the German place meant something far different. To-day, perspiring as much because of their intense excitement over the discovery of the Hittite stag as from their labours, the Arabs laughingly sat down to smoke the cigarettes which ended these celebrations, while the water-boy started wildly in search of his donkey, followed by the vigorous epithets of his thirsty friends, who knew that the full flavour of a cigarette comes only with a drink of cold water.

"Noon came all too soon; and it was Thursday, the pay-day. Friday was the Moslem Sabbath, and these Englishmen were too Christian in their relations with their Moslem workers to make them labour on their chosen day. Our drive to Aintab was short, and so we delayed to see the men paid off, on Lawrence's assurance that it would be interesting.

"A table was set in the open court of the room, and Woolley handed out the piastres to the line of workers. That was simple, but the men had learned to bring their discoveries in on pay-days, and they received cash rewards for everything turned in. Of course, the result was exceeding care on their part to lose or break no fragment in their work and in fact rare discoveries were sent in from all the countryside on these pay-days. The excavators would glance at the article offered. One man would receive a ten-piastre bonus for what he brought in, perhaps more to encourage him than because it had any real worth; another would have a fragment of pottery smilingly returned to him by the judge, while his companions laughed at him for trying to pass off on the alert Woolley part of a modern water-jar.

"Never did the Englishman say, 'I can pay you nothing for this, but I will keep it just the same!' It was either paid for or returned to the owner. Occasionally a gold coin, bright as the Arab's eyes, would reward some happy man; but whether he got the gold or a laugh, never was the decision of his master and friend questioned.

"As we tinkled across the plain to the rhythm of the bells on the horses' necks, we had food for thought in what we had seen. If Britain governs much of the world, we wondered if it did not because of the merit, capacity, and good sense of her sons in all lands. Impressions of this chance visit to Carchemish were deepened by residence in Constantinople throughout the World War, where we watched the German play for the big stake, of which the Euphrates bridge was but an incident. And the German lost because of the way he went after it.

"Thomas Lawrence worked another way. His extraordinary achievement was wonderful beyond measure. But it was not a miracle. It was but the outworking of intelligence, imagination, sympathy, character."

Robert Louis Stevenson, in "An Apology for Idlers," deplores that "many who have 'plied their book diligently' and know all about some branch or other of accepted lore, come out of the study with an ancient and owl-like demeanour, and prove dry, stockish and dyspeptic in the better and brighter parts of life." But in Lawrence, Stevenson would have found a kindred spirit. Though scholar and scientist, he is neither bookish nor owlish. During the early days of the Arabian Revolution, a Captain Lloyd, now Sir George Lloyd, recent Governor of Bombay, was in the desert with him for a short while. He once said to me: "It is difficult to describe the delight of intimate association with such a man. I found him both poet and philosopher, but possessor of an unfailing sense of humour."

Mr. Luther Fowle's description of that "U-shaped room" at Carchemish is an illustration of this same sense of humour which makes Lawrence so thoroughly human, and which saved his life on more than one occasion. Major Young, of the Near Eastern Secret Corps, who in pre-war days had known Lawrence in Mesopotamia, relates another incident. Representatives of England, Germany, France, Russia, and Turkey met in 1912 and agreed to an arrangement which gave the Germans control of the important strategic harbour of Alexandretta, and also permission to continue the railway which they long had wanted to extend through from Berlin to Bagdad in order to open up a direct route to the treasure-lands of Hindustan and Far Cathay.

Lawrence, with his intimate knowledge of history, saw in this a bold Prussian threat against British power in Asia. Upon learning of the agreement he immediately hurried down to Cairo, demanded an audience with Lord Kitchener, and asked K. of K. why Germany had been permitted to get control of Alexandretta, the vital port to which Disraeli referred when he said that the peace of the world would one day depend on the control of that point on the coast of Asia Minor toward which the finger of Cyprus pointed. Kitchener replied: "I have warned London repeatedly, but the Foreign Office pays no attention. Within two years there will be a

World War. Unfortunately, young man, you and I can't stop it, so run along and sell your papers."

Although deeply chagrined because Britain, wrapped in slumber, had allowed Germany to extend her sphere of influence all the way from the Baltic to the Persian Gulf, Lawrence decided to amuse himself by "pulling the leg" of the German engineers who were working with feverish haste on the Berlin-to-Bagdad Railway. Loading sections of drain-age-pipe on the backs of mules, he transported them from Carchemish to the hills which looked down on the new railroad right-of-way. There he carefully mounted them on piles of sand. The German engineers observed them through their field-glasses, and, as Lawrence had hoped, they mistook these harmless and innocent pipes for British cannons. Frantically they wired to both Constantinople and Berlin declaring that the British were fortifying all the commanding positions. Meanwhile, Lawrence and Woolley were laughing up their sleeves.

At Jerablus, north-east of Aleppo, the Germans were at work on a great bridge over the Euphrates. In their typically German way they painted numbers on the coats of their native workmen as a means of identifying them. They never even attempted to learn their names. They even committed the folly of allowing blood-enemies to dig together. Of course, instead of digging holes for bridge-piles, they dug holes in each other. This went on for a time, and then the seven hundred Kurd workmen turned on their German masters and attacked them. Three hundred from the digging gang at Carchemish joined their relatives and started a simultaneous attack from the rear. Fortunately for the Kaiser's myrmidons, Lawrence and Woolley arrived on the scene in time to prevent a massacre. As a result of their heroism both archæologists were awarded the Turkish order of the Medjidieh by the Sultan. That was early in 1914, before the Great War found Lawrence.

One of his first expeditions in the Near East was for the Palestine Exploration Fund. Lawrence and Woolley attempted to follow the footsteps of the Israelites through the Wilderness. Along with other discoveries, they found what is believed to be the Kadesh Barnea of the Bible, the historic spot where Moses brought water gushing from the rock. First they located a place in the Sinai Peninsula which the Bedouins called Ain Kadis, where there was one insignifi-cant well, and perhaps it was there that the Israelites began complaining to Moses regarding the shortage of water.

"If that really was the place," remarked Lawrence, "one could hardly blame the Israelites for grousing."

Some five miles distant the two archæologists came upon a number of fine springs in a little valley called Gudurat, and they are of the opinion that this was where Moses succeeded in regaining the confidence of the children of Israel by quenching their thirst with the sparkling waters of these springs. Later on Woolley and Lawrence wrote a small book concerning this expedition entitled, "The Wilderness of Sin." In it they tell of finding traces of a civilization dating back to 2500 B.C., the oldest traces of human habitation ever discovered on the Sinai Peninsula.

Woolley has written a delightful book, published by the Oxford University Press, entitled, "Dead Towns and Living Men," in which he describes the archæological experiences of Lawrence and himself before the World War. One story throws considerable light on the differences between the methods of these two men in dealing with the natives and the tactics of the Germans at work on the Berlin-Bagdad line:

"Our house-boy, Ahmed, was coming back one day from shopping in the village," writes Woolley, "and passed a gang of natives working on the railway whose foreman owed him money. Ahmed demanded payment of the debt, the foreman refused, and a wordy wrangle followed. A German engineer on his rounds saw that work was being hindered by an outsider, but instead of just ordering him off, he called up the two soldiers of his bodyguard, seized the unfortunate Ahmed, and, without any inquiry as to the origin or rights of the dispute, had him soundly flogged. Ahmed returned to the house full of woe, and as I was away Lawrence went up to the German camp to seek redress.

"He found Contzen, and told him that one of his engineers had assaulted our house-servant and must accordingly apologize. Contzen pooh-poohed the whole affair. When Lawrence showed him that he was in earnest, however, he consented to make inquiries and sent for the engineer in question. After talking to him he turned angrily on Lawrence: 'I told you the whole thing was a lie,' he said; 'Herr X—— never assaulted the man at all; he merely had him flogged!'

" 'Well, don't you call that an assault?' asked Lawrence.

" 'Certainly not,' replied the German. 'You can't use these natives without flogging them. We have men thrashed every day; it's the only method.'

" 'We've been here longer than you have,' Lawrence

retorted, 'and have never beaten one of our men yet, and we don't intend to let *you* start on them. That engineer of yours must come down with me to the village and apologize to Ahmed in public.'

"Contzen laughed. 'Nonsense!'" he said, and then, turning his back: 'The incident is closed.'

" 'On the contrary,'' replied Lawrence, 'if you don't do as I ask I shall take the matter into my own hands.'

"Contzen turned round again. 'Which means—?' he asked.

" 'That I shall take your engineer down to the village and there *flog him* !'

" 'You couldn't and you daren't do such a thing !' cried the scandalized German; but Lawrence pointed out that there was good reason for assuming that he both dared and could; and in the end the engineer had to make his apology *coram publico*, to the vast amusement of the villagers."

For seven years Lawrence wandered up and down the desert, often accompanied by Woolley but more frequently alone in native garb. At one time the British Museum sent him on a short expedition to the interior of the island of Sumatra, where he had escapes from head-hunters almost as thrilling as his adventures in Arabia. But of these we could never persuade him to speak. Some day, perhaps, he may tell us of them in his memoirs.

I had often wondered why he had chosen Arabia as the field for his archæological work, instead of Egypt, which is the Mecca and Medina for most men who love to dig among the ruins of antiquity. His reply was typical of him. He said:

"Egypt has never appealed to me. Most of the important work there has been done; and most Egyptologists to-day spend too much of their time trying to discover just when the third whisker was painted on the scarab."

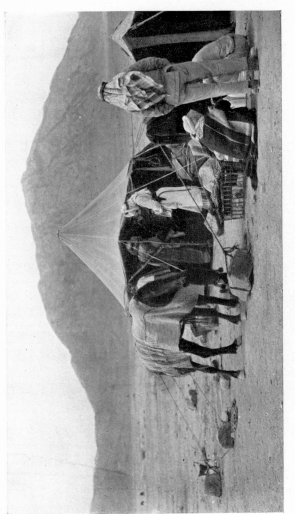

AN ARAB MERCHANT OPENS SHOP IN THE DESERT

THE WILD DESERT TRIBESMEN FROM WHICH LAWRENCE BUILT UP THE ARMY WITH WHICH HE HELPED TO SMASH THE TURKISH EMPIRE

CHAPTER III

AN ARCHÆOLOGIST TURNED SOLDIER

LORD KITCHENER'S advice and his own personal observations led Lawrence to believe that a crash was imminent. When it came he at once attempted to enlist as a private in the ranks of "Kitchener's Mob." But members of the Army Medical Board looked at the frail, five-foot-three, tow-headed youth, winked at one another, and told him to run home to his mother and wait until the next war. Just four years after he had been turned down as physically unfit for the ranks, this young Oxford graduate, small of stature, shy and scholarly as ever, entered Damascus at the head of his victorious Arabian army. Imagine what the members of the medical board would have said if someone had suggested to them in 1914 that three or four years later this same young man would decline knighthood and the rank of general, and would even avoid the coveted Victoria Cross and various other honours!

After his rejection Lawrence returned to his ancient ruins and toiled lovingly over inscriptions that unlocked the secrets of civilizations that flourished and crumbled to dust thousands of years ago. But, with many other scientists, scholars, and a few young men of exceptional ability, such as Mark Sykes, Aubrey Herbert, Cornwallis, Newcombe and others, he was summoned to headquarters in Cairo by Sir Gilbert F. Clayton. Though he was then only twenty-six years old, he was already familiar with Turkey, Syria, Palestine, Arabia, Mesopotamia, and Persia. He had lived with the wild tribesmen of the Interior, as well as with the inhabitants of the principal cities such as Aleppo, Mosul, Bagdad, Beyrouth, Jerusalem, and Damascus; in fact, his knowledge of some parts of the Near East was unique. He not only spoke many of the languages, but he knew the customs of all the different nationalities and their historical development.

To begin with, he was placed in the map department, where generals spent hours poring over inaccurate charts, discussing plans for piercing vulnerable spots in the Turkish armour. After working out a scheme they would turn, not infrequently, and ask the insignificant-looking subaltern if, in view of his personal knowledge of the country, he had any suggestions to offer. Not infrequently his reply would be:
"While there are many excellent points in your plan, it

33

is not feasible except at the expense of great loss of time in building roads for transport of supplies and artillery, and at needless expense of lives in maintaining lines of communication through the territory of hostile native tribes.''

Then, as an alternative, he would point out a safer and shorter route, with which he happened to be familiar because he had tramped every inch of it afoot while hunting for lost traces of the invading armies of Assyrians, Greeks, Romans, and Crusaders. The most staid old army officers on the staff put their confidence in this quiet-voiced junior lieutenant, and in a short time he had established a reputation for himself at G.H.Q.

Later on in Arabia, Lawrence frequently outwitted the Turks because of this same superior knowledge of the topography of the country. He was better acquainted with many distant parts of the Turkish Empire than were the Turks themselves.

From the map department he was transferred to another branch of the Intelligence Service which dealt mainly with affairs inside the enemy lines. It was his duty, as one of the heads of the Secret Corps, to keep the commander-in-chief informed of the movements of various units of the Turkish army. Sir Archibald Murray, then head of the British Forces in the Near East, has told me how highly he valued the knowledge of this youth, under whom were the native secret agents who passed back and forth through the Turkish lines.

It was in the summer of 1915 that the Hedjaz Arabs broke out in revolt against their Turkish masters in that part of the Arabian Peninsula which lies mainly between the Forbidden City of Mecca and the southern end of the Dead Sea, known as Holy Arabia.

In order to understand the reasons for the outbreak of the revolution, and in order to appreciate the delicate and complicated problems which Lawrence was to face upon his arrival in Arabia after the Arabs had won a few initial victories and were confronted with the probability of their revolt collapsing, let us digress for a moment and glance in retrospect through the pages of Arabian history and refresh our memories regarding the romantic story of this historic peninsula and its picturesque peoples.

Legend tells us that Arabia was the home of our common ancestors, Adam and Eve, the land of the Queen of Sheba, home of the heroes of ''The Arabian Nights,'' and a country peopled by a race that lived and hoped and loved before even the prehistoric mound-builders dwelt on the plains of North

America, and before the Druids in woad built their rock temples in Britain. Tradition tells us that it is a land whose peoples founded empires centuries before Moses led the children of Israel out of Egypt, perhaps even before Khufu built the Great Pyramid. Archæologists who have risked their lives to solve Arabia's mysteries tell us that great cities flourished and fell there long before the days of Tut-ankh-Amen, and that in one distant corner of the country the great King Hammurabi formulated his code of justice long before Buddha taught on the banks of the Ganges and before Confucius enunciated the principle of the Golden Rule.

Jazirat-ul-Arab, the Peninsula of the Arabs, is larger than England, Wales, Scotland, Ireland, Holland, Belgium, France, and Spain all combined. The Greeks and Romans traded, fought and studied there, and divided it into three geographical parts: Arabia Petræa to the north; Arabia Deserta to the east; and Arabia Felix (Arabia the blest) to the west.

Although some scholars believe it to have been the birth-place of the human race, we have better maps of the North Pole; in fact we have better maps of Mars than we have of some parts of the interior of Arabia from whence came many of the fighting men of Lawrence's army.

The distance from the city of Aleppo, at the extreme north, to the city of Mecca, half-way down the western coast of Arabia, is as great as the distance from London to Rome. Yet Lawrence and his men trekked all the way from Mecca to Aleppo on the backs of camels, over country as barren as the mountains of the moon.

In order to keep from becoming confused by the strange Arabic names it would be well for the reader to keep in mind that the Arabian campaign opened at Mecca and moved steadily north to Akaba, and then on to Damascus and Aleppo in Syria. Each event described in this account is a little farther north than the last. Although some authorities estimate that there is a total population of twenty million people in the whole of Arabia, for centuries a large portion of them have been held together only by loose travel alliances, like those which existed between the Red Indian tribes of America a hundred years ago.

The peoples of Arabia since time immemorial have been divided into two distinct classes: those who dwell in villages and cities, and those who wander from place to place with all their worldly possessions in their camel-bags. Both classes are called Arabs, but the wandering nomads are referred to as Bedouins whenever it is desired to differentiate between them and their kinsmen of the cultivated areas. The true Bedouin knows nothing about the cultivation of land, and his only animals are his camels and horses. The Bedouins are the more admirable of the two. They are the Arabs who have preserved the love of freedom and the ancient virtues of this virile race.

The foremost of all Arabian travellers was an Englishman, Charles M. Doughty, poet, philosopher, and author of that great classic, "Arabia Deserta," written in quaint Elizabethan style. With the exception of Colonel Lawrence, he was the only European who ever spent any considerable length of time travelling about the interior of Holy Arabia without disguising himself as a Mohammedan. Doughty found, what all who know them have discovered, that the Bedouins are kind hosts if visited in their camps.

But frequently the stranger who falls into their hands in the desert, under circumstances which, according to their unwritten law, do not cause them to regard him as a guest, finds them ruthless. In savage wantonness the Shammar Arabs may even cut his throat. There is a proverb in the desert that a man will slay the son of his mother for old shoe-leather, but, despite this, their hospitality is so sweeping that it has become proverbial throughout the world. "The Bedouins say: 'Be we not all guests of Allah?'" Then, adds Doughty: "After the guests eat 'the bread and the salt' there is a peace established between them for a time (that is counted two nights and a day, in the most whilst their food is in him)."

The word "Arab" comes from "Araba," the name of a small territory in an ancient province south of the Hedjaz, which is said to have been named after Yarab, the son of Kahtan, the son of Abeis, the son of Shalah, the son of Arfakhshad, the son of Shem, the son of Noah, who, they say, was the first to speak Arabic, "the tongue of the angels." They are a Semitic people, of the same race as the Jews.

The world owes much to the Arabs. Not only did they invent many of our boyhood games, such as the humming-top set spinning by pulling a cord, but they made great strides in medicine, and their materia medica was but little different from the modern. Their highly-skilled surgeons were performing difficult major operations with the use of anæsthetics in the days when Europe depended entirely upon the miraculous healing of the clergy. In chemistry we have them to thank for the discovery of alcohol, potassium, nitrate of silver, corrosive sublimate, sulphuric acid, and nitric acid. They even had experimented in scientific farming, and understood irrigation, the use of fertilizers, and such things as the grafting of fruit and flowers. They were world-famous for their tanning of leather, their dyeing of cloth, their manufacture of glass and pottery, of textiles, and of paper, and for their unsurpassed workmanship in gold, silver, copper, bronze, iron and steel.

The richest part of Arabia, excluding Mesopotamia, always has been, and still is, the province of Yemen in the extreme south-western corner, a mountainous region just north of Aden, famous these thousands of years for its wealth, its delightful climate, the fertility of its valleys, and as the home of Mocha coffee. Strabo, the Greek geographer, tells us that Alexander the Great, shortly before his death, planned to return from India and there establish his imperial capital. Many scholars believe this rich region to have been the original habitation of man and the country whence the early Egyptians came. Beginning earlier than 1000 B.C., highly organized monarchies existed here such as the Minæan, the Sabæan and the Himyaritic.

After the destruction of Jerusalem by Titus many Jews fled here, and their quaint descendants still reside in Yemen. But when the Ptolemies introduced the sea route to India, the Yemen became less important, and for centuries the best-known part of Arabia has been the province of Hedjaz on the Red Sea, north of Yemen, bounded on the east by the Central Arabian region known as Nejd, and on the north-east and north by Syria, the Dead Sea, Palestine and the Sinai Peninsula.

The word "Hedjaz," or "Hijaz," means "barrier." The fame of this particular waterless country is due to its two chief cities: Mecca, the birthplace of Mohammed, in olden times called Macoraba; and Medina, the ancient Yathrib, where the Prophet spent the last ten years of his life and where he was interred. It is the duty of all Moslems who can afford it to make a pilgrimage to these sacred cities, just as it was the duty of the people to journey here in idolatrous pre-Islamic times.

About a thousand years before Columbus discovered America, a boy was born in the city of Mecca. This boy was destined to shape very materially the history of the world. As a youth he herded goats and sheep on the hills around Mecca, and then as a young man he hired himself out as a camel-driver to a rich widow in Mecca. He used to drive her camel caravans up to Syria to trade with rich merchants there.

In Syria he became better acquainted with the religions of the Jews and the Christians, and became convinced that his fellow Arabs, who were worshippers of idols, did not possess a true religion. So this camel-driver appropriated some of the tenets of Christianity, some of the principles of Judaism, a few scraps of philosophy from the Persian fire-worshippers, a sprinkling of Arabian tradition, then threw in a number of his own ideas for good measure, and established a new religion. He encouraged his followers to regard Adam, Abraham, Moses and Christ as prophets of Islam. To-day, however, they are looked upon as of infinitely less importance than Mohammed himself, whose teachings are regarded as a later and final revelation of the will of God. Nearly every family in Arabia has at least one child named after the Prophet. There are more men in the world bearing the given name "Mohammed," than there are with such names as "John" and "William."

Is it so strange, after all, that the desert should be the old homestead of three of the world's greatest religions, Judaism, Christianity and Mohammedanism? The Arabs call the desert the Garden of Allah; they say there is no one in the desert but God. Out in the deserts of Arabia, even more than in many parts of the world, "the heavens declare the glory of God; and the firmament sheweth His handiwork. Day after day uttereth speech, and night unto night sheweth knowledge." There is no striving in the desert to amass wealth for wealth's sake; there is no mad rush to get ahead of one's fellow-men. One of the curses of our modern civilization is that we do not have time to think or meditate. The desert is a fitting place for one to ponder over man's destiny and to meditate upon the things that moth and rust do not corrupt and that thieves do not break through and steal.

Mohammed, the camel-boy of Mecca, was the first man to bind together in any sort of unity the peoples of Arabia. He came at the opportune time when a great leader was needed to drive out foreign domination. It was by his amazing evangelization that he succeeded in uniting the Arabs. To an even greater degree than most leaders of men this camel-boy of Mecca had:

> "The Monarch mind, the mystery of commanding,
> The birth-hour gift, the art Napoleon
> Of wielding, moulding, gathering, welding, bending
> The hearts of thousands till they moved as one."

Following the death of Mohammed came that great wave

of fanatical fury when the Arabian peoples, filled with religious fervour, swept out of the desert, over-ran a great part of the world and built up that huge Moslem Empire which was even greater than the empire of the Romans. In those triumphant days of Islam, the Arabs supplied the dominant religious, political, and military leaders for all the countries they conquered. They seemed irresistible.

"When the Arabs, who had fed on locusts and wild honey, once tasted the delicacies of civilization in Syria and revelled in the luxurious palaces of the Khosroes," writes El Tabari, the Moslem historian, "they said, 'By Allah, even if we cared not to fight for the cause of God, yet we could not but wish to contend and enjoy *these*, leaving distress and hunger henceforth to others.'" Within a century after the death of Mohammed the Hedjaz Arabs had built up an empire vaster than either that of Alexander or of Rome; "Islam swept across the world like a whirlwind."

But the vast empire reached its zenith in the seventh century of this era, and its decline dates from the battle of Tours, A.D. 732, when the Arabs were defeated in France by the Christians under Charles Martel.

Many of the Arabs remained in the lands they had conquered. As merchants and missionaries they have carried the crisp, brief creed of Mohammed from Arabia to Gibraltar, Central Africa, Central China, and the islands of the South Seas. Unlike followers of other faiths, they shout their creed from the minarets and housetops of every land where they are to be found: "La-ilahu illa Allah! Allahu akbar!"

And even to-day we find thousands of Arabs occupying positions of affluence in far-off Hong Kong, Singapore, the East Indies, and Spain. The others drifted back to their old life in the Arabian Desert. Once more Arabia stood isolated from the world by the barren mountain-ranges which fringe its coasts and by its trackless belts of shifting sand. In the twelfth century the descendants of Saladin, who was half Kurd, conquered the fringes of Arabia. Then three centuries later a new tribe swept down from the unknown plateaux of Central Asia. They were of the tribe of Othman, forefathers of the modern Turks, and they attempted to govern the Arabs as though they were a people of an inferior race.

The Turks claimed possession of Arabia for four hundred years, simply because they were able to maintain a few garrisons along the coast. A few of these garrisons were successful in holding out to the very end of the Great War, but at last they surrendered, leaving Arabia once again in the undisputed possession of its freedom-loving inhabitants. The Hedjaz tribes have never acknowledged the sovereignty of any foreign ruler. They have preserved their liberty with but little interruption since prehistoric times, and consequently they regard their personal freedom above all else. Great armies have been sent against them, but not even the Assyrians, the Medes, the Persians, the Greeks, or the Romans were able to conquer them.

Ever since the decline of the Arabian Empire, more than a thousand years ago, generals, sultans, and caliphs have attempted to unify the peoples of Arabia, and particularly of the province of Hedjaz, because it contains the two sacred Mohammedan cities. None was successful, but where they failed, Thomas Edward Lawrence, the unknown unbeliever, succeeded. It remained for this youthful British archæologist to go into forbidden Arabia and lead the Arabs through the spectacular and triumphant campaign which helped Allenby break the backbone of the Turkish Empire and destroy the Pan-German dream of world dominion. The way in which he swept the Turks from Holy Arabia and temporarily built this mosaic of peoples into a homogeneous nation, now known as the Kingdom of the Hedjaz, is a story that I should have failed to believe had I not visited Arabia and come into personal contact with Lawrence and his associates during their campaign.

Perhaps no factor played a greater part in simplifying Lawrence's task in Arabia than the existence of an ancient desert fraternity which has been called the "cult of the Blood of Mohammed." We must know something about this cult and its present-day leaders in order to understand the diplomacy and strategy of Colonel Lawrence which we are to follow during the desert war.

CHAPTER IV

THE CULT OF THE BLOOD OF MOHAMMED

DURING all these centuries of uncertain Turkish rule, there had persisted in the sacred cities of the Hedjaz "the cult of the Blood of Mohammed," with its membership limited to descendants of the Prophet. These people were called shereefs or nobles by the other Arabs and they had never lost their hatred for the Turks, whom they regarded as intruders. So powerful was this cult that the Ottoman Government could not destroy it.

However, when shereefs living within reach of the string of fortified Turkish posts along the fringe of the desert protested openly against Ottoman tyranny, her Sultan usually "invited" them to come and reside near him in Constantinople. There they would either remain as virtual prisoners or quietly be put out of the way.

Abdul Hamid, the last great sultan, was an expert in following this private policy of his predecessors, and among the prominent Arabs whom he found it the better part of discretion to have near him at the Sublime Porte was one Shereef Hussein of Mecca. He was the oldest living descendant of Mohammed, and was therefore believed by many to be the man really entitled to the Caliphate, the spiritual and temporal head of Islam. The title of caliph had originally been given only to the lineal descendants of Mohammed, but later had been usurped by the Turks.

No people in the world take more pride in their ancestry than the Arabs. The birth of all the leading princely families are recorded in Mecca at the mosque built around the black stone which millions of people regard as the most sacred spot in the world. Here, on a scroll of parchment, is inscribed the name of Hussein Ibn Ali, direct lineal descendant of Mohammed through his daughter Fatima and her eldest son, Hassan.

When King Hussein was young, he had too much spirit to live tamely with his family in Mecca; instead, he roamed the desert with the Bedouins, and took part in all their raids and tribal wars. His mother was a Circassian and much of his vigour is inherited from her. Abdul Hamid, the Red Sultan, received many disturbing reports regarding the wild life led by this independent shereef. Abdul had two ways of dealing with a man whom he feared or distrusted. He would either tie him in a sack and throw him into the Bosphorus or keep him in Constantinople under close personal observation. Although he was afraid that Hussein might conspire against him, the fact that Hussein was a direct descendant of Mohammed made it difficult for old Abdul to chuck him into the Bosphorus. So he gave him a pension and a little house on the Golden Horn, where the shereef and his family were compelled to live for eighteen years. "Guest" was the word Abdul-the-Damned used, with that deadly smile of his.

During these long years of exile, the wily old sultan, diplomat that he was, used every artifice of which he was capable to keep Hussein contented. Among other gifts, he presented him with a great aluminium-bodied Rolls-Royce saloon. Hussein salaamed even unto the foot of the throne; but let it be known, discreetly, that he preferred his mules.

When the revolution of the Young Turks came in 1912 and Abdul was overthrown, all political prisoners were released from Constantinople, and Hussein and other Arab Nationalist leaders thought they saw the dawn of a new era of freedom and liberty. In fact, they too had assisted the Young Turks in overthrowing the old régime. But their hopes were soon dispelled, for the new Committee of Unity and Progress rashly set out to Ottomanize all the peoples of that complex of races which made up the Turkish Empire. They even went so far as to insist that the Arabs should give up their beautiful language—"the tongue of the angels"—and substitute the corrupt Ottoman dialect.

It was not long before Hussein discovered that the Committee of Unity and Progress, headed by Enver, Talaat, and Djemal, was far more tyrannical than old Abdul in his bloodiest moments. They now looked back on the villainous Abdul as a harmless old gentleman in comparison with his successors. The Young Turks even suggested that in the Koran Turkish heroes should be substituted for the ancient patriarchs. Words of Arabic origin were deleted from the Turkish vocabulary.

In Mecca the exaggerated story was told that the Turks were reverting to the ancient heathenism of Othman, and that soldiers in Constantinople were required to pray to the White Wolf, a deity of the barbaric days before the Ottoman horde left its early home in the wilds of Central Asia.

Although the Arab leaders despaired of seeing a happier day for their country, Shereef Hussein and his sons concealed their hatred for the autocratic triumvirate and the whole

The Arabian revolution commenced at the Holy City of Mecca, and later Emir Feisal and Colonel Lawrence led the Arab army north across the desert to Damascus and Aleppo for a distance of over a thousand miles. Dotted line indicates route followed in this narrative.

Young Turk party. Because of the help he had given the triumvirate before he was disillusioned as to their real aims, they granted him the title of Keeper of the Holy Places of Islam, or the sixty-sixth Emir of Mecca of the Ottoman period.

Miss Gertrude Bell, the only woman staff captain in the British army, and one of the foremost authorities on Near Eastern affairs, in a letter to *The Times* of London declared that the Arab Nationalist movement was given vitality by the Young Turks, who as soon as they came into power changed their whole attitude.

"Liberty and equality are dangerous words to play with in an empire composed of divergent nationalities," wrote Miss Bell. "Of these the Arabs, adaptable and quick-witted, proudly alive to their traditions of past glory as founders of Islam and upholders for 700 years of the authority of the Khalifat, were the first to claim the translation of promise into performance, and in the radiant dawn of the constitutional era the Arab intelligentsia eagerly anticipated that their claim would be recognized. If the Turks had responded with a genuine attempt to allow Arab culture to develop along its own lines under their ægis, the Ottoman Empire might have taken on new life, but their inelastic mentality precluded them from embracing the golden opportunity.

"Moreover, Prussian militarism made to them a peculiarly powerful and, if the political configuration of their Empire be considered, a peculiarly dangerous appeal. The Committee of Union and Progress was determined to hack its way through the sensibilities of subject races, and, not content with this formidable task, by neglecting the cautious diplomatic methods of Abdul Hamid it found itself involved in a disastrous and debilitating struggle with its neighbour States in Europe.

"Before the war of 1914 broke out, not only were the Arab provinces filled with hatred and desire for vengeance . . ."

In the luxurious atmosphere of the Ottoman metropolis Hussein's four sons quite naturally had grown up more like young Turkish bloods than Arab youths. They had spent most of their time rowing on the Bosphorus and attending Court balls. For six years Prince Feisal had acted as private secretary to Abdul Hamid. When the Grand Shereef returned to Mecca he immediately summoned his four sons and informed them that they were altogether too effete and too accustomed to the soft ways of Stamboul to suit him. "Constantinople and its accursed life of luxury are now behind thee. Praise be to Allah! Henceforth thou are to make thy home

under the canopy of heaven with thy brothers of the black
tents in order that the glory of our house may not be disgraced.
Allahu akbar!'' So saying, the aged Emir fitted the deed to
the word and ordered them out to patrol the pilgrim routes.

These routes are mere camel-tracks across the burning
sands connecting the Red Sea coast with Mecca, the Holy City,
and the summer capital of Taif, and between Medina and
Mecca. With each of his sons he sent a company of his best
fighting men. They were not even permitted to use tents, but
were compelled to sleep in their cloaks. They spent their days
chasing robbers. The worst robbers in the desert are the men
of the Harith clan, some one hundred outlaws, nearly all of
them banished members of Shereefian families. These men of
Harith had entrenched themselves in a naturally fortified
village fifty miles north-east of Mecca. Expeditions against
them and other bandits developed Hussein's sons into self-
reliant, capable leaders. That Emir Feisal is such a prominent
figure in the Near East to-day is not entirely because of his
royal blood, but partly because he excels in ways which make
for leadership in the Arabian desert. These are not a knowledge of ''Bridge'' or Browning!

Ali, the eldest son, is a small, thin, well-groomed prince.
He has delightful manners, great personal charm, and is an
accomplished diplomat. He is deeply religious, the essence
of generosity, and a martinet on all questions of morality.
Like the other members of his family he has far-reaching views
and aspirations for his country. But he has not personal
aspirations beyond the Emirate of Mecca, to which he fell heir
upon the abdication of his aged father. Abdullah, the second
son, is ambitious and vigorous, but is not quite such an
idealist. At the termination of the War he became the ruler
of Transjordania with a famous English traveller by the name
of St. John Philby as his adviser.

The youngest member of the family, Prince Zeid, is half
Turk. There is not so much of the Oriental about him, and
when the revolt was at its height he still lacked the seriousness
of his older brothers. This youth left such solid enthusiasms
as Arab nationalism to the rest of his family and devoted himself to fighting and to the lighter joys of life, as one would
expect from a normal prince in his early twenties. He is nevertheless rich in common sense. Zeid loves hunting, riding, and
dancing. After the Arabs and Anzacs took Damascus he
jazzed all over the city, until Feisal convinced him that he
should conduct himself with greater dignity. He also is a man
of considerable charm and, if his ambition to attend Oxford is

realized, may yet prove himself the ablest of an illustrious family.

Feisal, third and best known of Hussein's four sons, is an idealist. Although modest and reserved, he is a man of great personality. Every Arab is a born diplomat, and Feisal is well above the average.

Children of the desert have few games. They do not know how to play as our Western children do. Life is a serious and sober affair from the moment the Arab baby opens his eyes on the woman's side of the black tent. As soon as he is able to crawl, he comes into the tribal council. His only school is the coffee hearth, his only education consists in the handling of men and camels.

Emir Feisal began life as a dirty little shepherd boy. His mother was an Arab girl of Mecca and a cousin of his father. When Feisal was a little baby, Shereef Hussein sent him into the desert to live with a Bedouin tribe, because it is considered more beneficial for a boy to grow up in the open desert country than in a city or village. Later, in Constantinople, Feisal contracted consumption, but since then the desert has cured him. He is still very thin, however, and measures only twenty-one inches around the waist. He smokes cigarettes day and night, and eats sparingly. Among the tribes he is considered an unusually fine shot and good horseman, and an excellent camel rider.

Feisal is enlightened and thoroughly modern in his views, and Colonel Lawrence, who knows him better than anyone else, declares that he is as honest as daylight. His people follow him not through fear, but because they admire him and love him. He is much too kind and liberal-minded to rule as an Oriental despot of the old school. Given the opportunity, he may be depended upon to do his utmost to usher in an entirely new order of things for his people.

Certain statesmen of world prominence choose detective stories for their moments of relaxation; Prince Feisal, in the lull between campaigns, refreshes himself for renewed battle and the cares of state with classical Arabic poetry. His favourite poet is Imr el Kais, the most renowned of all Arab bards, who lived just before Mohammed, and who wrote about camels, the desert, and love. Among Feisal's other favourites are Ibn Isham, Ibn el Ali, Zuhair, Zarafa, Al Harith, and Mutanabbi, great writers of the Middle Ages, when Arabian learning and culture penetrated to the most remote corners of Europe. Mutanabbi's couplet must have struck a responsive chord in Feisal's heart:

"Night and my steed and the desert know me——
And the lance-thrust and battle, and parchment and pen."

I also saw him frequently reading the works of Antara, the famous poet who wrote a huge epic of his own life filled with tales of raids and love lyrics. The recent war of liberation inspired many new poets to arouse the people by means of patriotic songs. Even the humblest camel-driver improvised songs built around Lawrence, Feisal, and that celebrated warrior, Auda Abu Tayi.

Poetry, song and proverb all exalt the virtue of hospitality among the Arabs. An Arab, from Hussein down to the humblest of his subjects, will risk his own life rather than allow any harm to befall a guest, even if the latter happens to be his worst enemy. For many months prior to the outbreak of the Arabian revolution, Shereef Hussein and his sons were secretly preparing for it, while leading the Turks to believe that they were mobilizing against the Allies.

Emir Feisal happened to be in Damascus during this period as the guest of Djemal Pasha, the Turkish viceroy of Syria and Palestine. His father sent word to him that he had succeeded in gathering together a number of tribes for an attack on the Turkish garrison at Medina, so Feisal excused himself on some pretext and said he must return south. Djemal urged him to delay his departure for a few days, saying that he and Enver Pasha would like to accompany him to Medina. When Feisal arrived at Medina with Djemal and Enver, they attended a review of over five thousand Arab tribesmen who whirled by on camels and horses, firing their rifles into the air. The two members of the Turkish triumvirate were delighted with the warlike display, and told Feisal that his men would be of great assistance to the Sultan and his illustrious fellow-Mohammedan ruler, Kaiser William Pasha, in their war against the Unbeliever.

That night, during the usual banquet, Ali Ibn Hussein, of the robber Harith clan, and a number of other shereefs and sheiks stole up to Feisal and whispered:

"We have the palace surrounded and are going to kill these Turkish dogs."

Realizing that his followers were in dead earnest, Feisal waved them aside for the moment and, turning to Djemal and Enver, said:

"Now, gentlemen, according to our custom, after a banquet of this kind, you must spend the night in my house."

Feisal then established his guests in his own room and slept outside the door all night. Without leaving them for a single moment, he took them to the train the next morning and accompanied them on their three-day journey to Damascus. This required no little nerve, for if Djemal and Enver had suspected that anything was wrong in Medina, and that the Arabs did not intend to co-operate with Turkey and Germany in the War, they would either have killed Feisal or held him as a hostage to guarantee the good behaviour of his father.

An Arabian banquet, such as Feisal gave for Enver and Djemal, is an occasion to be remembered. After the War King Hussein entertained at the *Belediyah*, the town hall of Jeddah, in honour of Prince Georges Lotfallah of Egypt. Rows and rows of small tables were placed end to end and then piled high with food until they groaned under the weight. Eighty guests were served at one sitting, and the waiters walked up and down on top of the tables, looking down at you. If your plate was not full they would slice off a slab of sheep or goat and then step over the cake and attend to your neighbour. After the first eighty had dined the next sitting was served in like manner.

EMIR FEISAL, DIRECT DESCENDANT OF THE PROPHET
MOHAMMED, WHO WAS THE ARAB COMMANDER-
IN-CHIEF IN THE FIELD

THE SACRED MOSQUE IN MECCA

The square black building in the centre is the holy Kaaba, covered over with the famous pilgrimage
carpet. Imbedded in one corner of the Kaaba is the sacred stone which millions of Mohammedans
come from all parts of the world to kiss.

CHAPTER V

THE FALL OF JEDDA AND MECCA

WHEN the World War pulled Turkey into the maelstrom, with Great Britain, France, Russia, and Italy pitted against her, it was the hour of opportunity for Arabia. Unable to obtain sufficient funds and ammunition, Shereef Hussein was compelled to let many months pass by without declaring himself. Then came the news of the surrender of Kut el Amara by General Townsend. This was a serious reverse for the Allies and an important victory for the Turks. Hussein could no longer hold his followers. He sent word to the British Government that he could not stand by and permit his people to remain subject to the Turks. He asked for assistance, but before receiving a reply, with all the pent-up fury and hatred of five hundred years of oppression and dishonour, the Arabs of the Hedjaz leaped at the throats of the Turks. From all parts of the desert came the swarthy, lean, picturesque sons of Ishmael to avenge and free themselves at last.

Hussein and his four sons had worked out all the details of their plan for the revolution, but kept them secret until a few weeks before they touched off the fuse. They did not even dare to trust their close associates, because in Turkish territory plots were usually discovered before they matured, and no man knew whom he could trust. Not only were there spies but innumerable spies on spies.

Early in 1916, when Lieutenant Lawrence was making a reputation for himself with the Secret Corps in Cairo, Grand Shereef Hussein sent word to all the tribes of Holy Arabia to be ready at a moment's notice. Then, on June 9th, he gave the signal. At the same instant he himself publicly denounced Enver, Talaat, Djemal, and their infamous Committee of Unity and Progress. Simultaneous attacks were launched against Mecca, Jeddah, the seaport to the holy city, and Medina, three of the least known and most interesting cities in the world. And before we continue on to the point in the Arab revolt where Lawrence made his entrance, let us stop and see these centres of life in the Hedjaz whence came so many of Lawrence's associates.

49

D

When you land at Jeddah you blink your eyes and pinch yourself to see if you are awake. The Koran forbids the use of intoxicating liquors, but either the architects who designed this city were not faithful Mussulmans or most of the buildings were constructed before Mohammed introduced prohibition into Arabia. The streets of Jeddah are a bewildering maze of narrow zigzag cañons between tall tottering houses, which look as though they had been joggled about by incessant earthquakes. Many of the houses are of five and six stories and are used only for the accommodation of pilgrims who pass through on their way to Mecca during Ramadam, a time when the population of the city increases from twenty thousand to perhaps one hundred thousand. The most fitting way I can think of describing this weird Arabian seaport is to say that it looks like any ordinary Oriental city might look to a man suffering from delirium tremens. The Leaning Tower of Pisa would be in an appropriate setting if it were transferred to Jeddah.

Symmetry seems to be an unknown quantity in this part of the Near East. It is said that an Arab carpenter cannot draw a right angle, and an Arab waiter never puts a tablecloth on square. The sacred shrine of the Mohammedans in Mecca, known as the Kaaba, meaning "cube," has none of its sides or angles equal. Arab streets are seldom parallel, and even "the street that is called straight" in Damascus is not straight! Jeddah, with its inebriated buildings, its crazy, fragile balconies, its leaning minarets, its lazy Arab merchants squatting cross-legged on top of tables in front of chaotic shops, its fantastic arcaded bazaars covered in with patchwork roofs pieced together like the sails of a Chinese junk, is the nearest approach to a futurist paradise of any city in the world.

Arabia is indeed a topsy-turvy land. Where we measure most of our liquids and weigh most of our solids, they weigh their liquids and measure their solids. Where we use knives and forks and spoons, they use their hands. Where we use tables and chairs they recline on the floor. Where we mount from the left, they mount their camels and horses from the right. We read from left to right, while they read from right to left. The desert dweller keeps his head covered in the summer and winter alike, and his feet usually unprotected. Where we take off our hats in entering a friend's house, they take off their shoes.

In addition to its Arab population, Jeddah is inhabited by the remnants of a thousand pilgrimages, descendants of pilgrims who had sufficient money to enable them to reach

Mecca but not enough to enable them to leave Arabia after fulfilling their religious vows. Many of them are poverty stricken and barely able to eke out a living at the odd jobs which they get during the short pilgrimage season each year. Among them are Javanese, Philippinos, Malays, representatives of a dozen different Indian races, Kurds, Turks, Egyptians, Sudanese, Abyssinians, Senegalese, tribesmen from the Sahara, Zanzibaris, Yemenites, Somalis, and numerous others.

One afternoon, accompanied by Major Goldie, an officer attached to the British mission which had its headquarters there during the campaign, I rode out through the Mecca gate to the Abyssinian quarters. The dwellings of these primitive people are round huts with conical thatched roofs, surrounded by high kraal fences made of rusty petrol and preserved meat tins. We pulled up our ponies in front of a hut where a negro woman was busy tanning a hide. The moment she saw us she began screaming: "Oh, why have you come to destroy my home? Oh, why are you going to carry away my child? Oh! Oh! Oh! What have I done that you should want to shoot me?" Although Goldie did his best to reassure her, she continued this wail until we rode out of hearing.

On either side of Jeddah, a few miles distant, are small ports which foreigners scrupulously avoid visiting. Tourists have never been welcome because these villages for many years have been slave-trading centres. Here negroes, smuggled across from the African coast, were sold to wealthy Arabs. The Turkish Government winked at this vicious commerce, but Hussein and his sons have tried to stamp it out. As a result of their stand on the slavery question, the price of a well-built young negro has advanced from the pre-War quotation of £50 to £300 or even as high as £500. Although the trade may continue surreptitiously for a short time, the new King, Amir Ali, is bitterly opposed to it and doing his best to drive it out.

Beyond the north gate of the Jeddah wall Major Goldie took me to see what thousands of Mohammedans believe to be the tomb of the common ancestor of us all. There is a century-old tradition to the effect that it was here near Jeddah that the ark grounded after the Great Flood. According to one version of the story, on his six hundred and first birthday, not long after the waters had abated, Noah and his three sons, Shem, Ham, and Japheth, were walking along the beach when they came to a depression in the sand. This depression seemed to resemble a human form. It was about three hundred feet long. Ham asked his father what he thought it could be, and the venerable patriarch replied: "Ham, my lad, that is the last resting-place of Mother Eve."

Of course there are many educated Mohammedans who laugh at this legend, but, nevertheless, a wall three hundred feet long has been built around the supposed depression, and within this enclosure is a white mosque where thousands of women worship every year. They believe Mother Eve was three hundred feet in height. Just think how the rest of us must have degenerated! But the city takes its name from this tomb, for the word "Jeddah" means grandmother or ancestress.

Since the time of Mohammed, no Jews, Christians, followers of Zoroaster, or other unbelievers, have been welcome anywhere in the Hedjaz except along the coast. None but the faithful are even allowed to go beyond the Jeddah wall through the east gate, which leads in the direction of Mecca. The British officers who were stationed in Jeddah from the outbreak of the revolution until the end of the War scrupulously observed this unwritten law. During the campaign no Allied representatives ever visited the forbidden capital of the king of the Hedjaz—at any rate not officially or for publication. King Hussein even went so far as to request the British authorities to instruct all officers piloting seaplanes attached to warships cruising in the Red Sea under no circumstances to profane the air by flying over either Mecca or Medina.

This very day millions of Moslems are turning their faces five times toward Mecca and declaring over and over again:

"La ilaha Allah wa Muhammad-ar-rasul Allah! There is but one God, Allah, and Mohammed is His Prophet."

Mecca and Medina, its sister metropolis of the desert, are the two most mysterious cities in the world. Any man in the vicinity of either who declared that Christ was the Son of God would be torn to pieces.

Since the time of Mohammed, Mecca and Medina have been forbidden to all but Moslems. In fact, the fanatical followers of the founder of Islam would destroy any intruder whom they even suspected of being an unbeliever. For this reason all conferences between King Hussein and the representatives of the British and French Governments were held in Jeddah.

We have a record of only a dozen or so Christians who have visited Mecca during the past one thousand years—and lived to tell the tale. The most celebrated of these, of course, was Sir Richard Burton. Fewer still have visited Medina. At the end of the eighteenth century a puritanical and fanatical sect from Central Arabia called the Wahabis overran the Hedjaz and captured Mecca. They were driven out by an Egyptian army under Mohammed Ali, and for a time an adventurer and ex-sergeant in the Black Watch had the unique honour of acting as governor of Medina and guardian of the Tomb of the Prophet.

Not only do all Mohammedans turn toward Mecca to pray, because it was the birthplace of their Prophet, but many of them build their houses, and even their outhouses, facing Mecca; and when they die, they are buried facing Mecca.

Mohammed enjoined his followers to make pilgrimages to Mecca. He advocated this in order to satisfy the pagans of Arabia, who had been doing it for centuries. The city has no economic importance, but the pilgrims who go there each year during the month of Zu el Hajz are a source of income to its one hundred and fifty thousand inhabitants.

Tens of thousands of pilgrims visit Mecca annually, although for many who come from far-off lands two years are required to make the trip.

Some journey overland across Central Africa from the valley of the Senegal and the mouth of the Congo; others cross overland through the heart of Asia; and I have been in Singapore when pilgrim ships passed through the Straits of Malacca with thousands of pilgrims packed on their open decks. After performing the religious rites at Mecca the pilgrims return home, paint their beards, and are for ever afterwards known as *haj* or holy men. While in Mecca they are given a ticket which guarantees their entrance into paradise.

Those who approach Holy Arabia by sea are required to take off their usual garments before leaving the ship and garb themselves in the *ihram*, a costume consisting of two white strips of cloth, one to go round the waist and the other to be thrown over the shoulders. Frequently two ordinary Turkish towels are used for this purpose. When those who make the pilgrimage by land arrive within thirty-five miles of Mecca they are treading on holy ground. They remove their head-dress and their shoes, and the remainder of the journey is made with uncovered head and bare feet. They bathe and shave and trim their nails and wear nothing but the *ihram*. Nor are they allowed to shave or bathe or trim their nails again until after they have performed their religious rites in Mecca, and until they have visited Mount Ararat near Mecca and completed a ceremony known as throwing stones at the three devils.

What a spectacle for the cinema when that vast stream of humanity, many riding on camels, many of them trudging barefoot and bareheaded, starts up the desert road from Jeddah to Mecca garbed in nothing but Turkish towels! Of course the women who make the pilgrimage wear a different garment. Their costume consists of a long strip of linen which not only completely covers the body but envelops the head as well. Over their faces they place straw masks with thin slits through which they see. Many of the women and old men ride in *shukdufs*, weird wooden shelters on the backs of camels.

The region about Mecca is all holy. Pilgrims are not permitted to disturb the wild animals nor even to cut the thorns or desert herbs. The holy city of Islam is located in a narrow pocket between the hills where two valleys join. Three forts frown down upon Mecca from the heights and were occupied by Turkish troops until King Hussein's followers drove them out.

In the centre of Mecca is the Great Mosque, which was built as a place of pagan worship many centuries before the birth of Mohammed. It is known as the Mosque of the Kaaba or Masjid Al Haram, which means "the sacred temple." Within the courtyard is a small cube-shaped building, the famous Kaaba. It is covered over with a gorgeous holy carpet of black silk with a wide border of gold lettering, texts from the Koran. The roof is supported by pillars of aloe wood. Around the edge is a spout of gold, which carries off rain-water.

Embedded in one of the walls is the most sacred object in the world to more than two hundred millions of people. It is the black stone of meteoric origin which the Mohammedans believe was tossed down from heaven by the Angel Gabriel to Father Abraham. They say it was once whiter than milk but that it has been turned black by the sins of the people who have kissed it. Others say that it derived its colour from Adam's tears. It has been broken in seven pieces, and its parts are now held together by a background of cement surrounded by a silver band studded with silver nails.

The followers of the Prophet believe that this cube-shaped building rests directly underneath the throne of God. They say it was lowered down from heaven at the request of Adam and that it is an exact duplicate of one that he had seen in Paradise before his expulsion, called Beit al Mamur, and frequented by angels. Very few people ever enter the Kaaba, but those who do keep their eyes down in an attitude of reverence and humble submission to divine power. If a pilgrim from Syria enters it, for the rest of his life he never goes barefoot, because he believes that his skin has touched holy ground and therefore must never be placed on profane earth again.

The holy carpet which covers the Kaaba is replaced each year by a new one. Formerly there were two sent each year, one of which came down from Damascus from the Sultan of Turkey, while the other was made in Cairo and presented to the mosque by the Sultan of Egypt. When a new one is put up, the old one is cut into bits by the pilgrims, who take the pieces home for souvenirs.

According to tradition, from the dawn of creation to judgment day at least one pilgrim is always supposed to be engaged in walking seven times around the Kaaba. But about every twenty years great floods come and fill all the streets of Mecca, including the mosque, and when these floods occur men are hired to swim around it day and night in order that the ceremony may never be interrupted.

The pilgrims kiss the black stone, run around the building seven times, take a drink from a holy well called Zem Zem and kiss the stone again. Sir Richard Burton said that when he tried to kiss the black stone he found himself in a milling throng of religious devotees, each of whom was trying to force his way through the crowd in order that he might press his lips against the most sacred object in the world. He said that these religious enthusiasts were all calling out their prayers in loud voices, and between sentences of their prayers they would stop and curse the man who was elbowing them away from the black stone.

The most important well in Mecca is this well of Zem Zem in the courtyard of the mosque. The water in it is slightly brackish but is said to be delightful when one becomes accustomed to using it. The well is eight feet wide and quite deep. According to Moslem tradition one of the direct routes to heaven is through the bottom of this well. The pilgrims from India, who take such superstitions literally, frequently threw themselves into the well, making the water undrinkable for days. In fact, so many people tried this short cut to paradise that it became necessary to stretch a net over the bottom to break their fall.

There is an ancient tradition among Mohammedans that the approach of the day of resurrection will be indicated by the sun rising in the West, and by the appearance of a monster which will rise out of the earth in the courtyard of the Masjid

Al Haram. This beast is to be sixty cubits in height, just twice as high as the Lord commanded Noah to make the ark. It is to be a complex combination of eleven different animals, having the head of a bull, the eyes of a hog, the ears of an elephant, the horns of a stag, the neck of a giraffe, the breast of a lion, the colour of a tiger, the back of a cat, the tail of a ram, the legs of a camel, and the voice of an ass. She is to bring with her the rod of Moses and the seal of Solomon. So swift will be this monster that none will escape. With the rod of Moses she will smite all true believers on the cheek, branding them with a mark which will indicate that they are of the faithful. Unbelievers will be stamped with the seal of King Solomon.

It is also believed that this strange beast will speak Arabic. After the appearance of this mammoth creature all mortals who have inhabited the earth since the dawn of Creation will be required to cross a valley on a hair, from which the iniquitous will tumble off into the fires of hell, while the pure in heart will cross safely into Paradise. There are many different versions of this tradition which were believed in by the adherents of other religions long before the time of Mohammed.

Among other signs believed by some to be indications of the approach of the day of resurrection are a war with the Turks; the advancement of the meanest to positions of dignity and power; the coming of Antichrist from Khorasan, mounted on an ass and followed by seventy thousand Jews; the return of Jesus, who certain Mohammedans believe will embrace the Mohammedan religion, marry a wife, slay Antichrist, and rule the earth in peace and security; and the bestowal of the power of speech on all animals, birds, fishes, reptiles, and inanimate things.

Until recently Mecca was, perhaps, the most evil and licentious city in the world: "The holier the city, the wickeder its people," runs the Arab proverb. A block away from the Holy Kaaba stands the slave market, which was closed not long ago by Hussein. There were in the city of Mecca until recently, and perhaps still are, many women who are legally married and divorced almost monthly, and sometimes bi-monthly. A pilgrim arriving at Mecca, before King Hussein's puritanical regime, could be legally married during the time he was a resident and performing his religious rites. He could then have his marriage legally dissolved when he left the city.

The people of Mecca do not share those fine primitive

virtues and simplicity of tastes which have made the Bedouin famous. Since olden times those born there have been distinguished from other Arabians by three scars on the cheek— a trade-mark of viciousness, say visitors to Mecca. The language of the Meccans is the most salacious to be found anywhere in the dissolute East. The city is filled with unspeakable diseases and practices. Travellers have described scenes occurring in the Great Mosque as licentious as any reported to have occurred in the most dissolute days of ancient times.

But now to return to the story of the capture of these holy cities.

Hussein supervised the attack on Mecca, while Feisal and Ali were in command of the force directed against Medina. The Grand Shereef was successful at Mecca. The forts on the three hills overlooking that forbidden and sacred city were garrisoned by the Sultan's most faithful Circassian mercenaries and by picked Turkish troops. On the day of the attack the Arabs swept through the gates and captured the main bazaar, the residential section, the administration buildings, and the sacred mosque of the Holy Kaaba. For a fortnight the battle raged around the two smaller forts, which were finally taken. During all this fighting the aged Shereef remained in his palace directing operations in spite of scores of Turkish three-inch shells that riddled his residence.

The Turks might have been able to hang on for many months had it not been for their own folly. The Ottoman seems to be a Mohammedan in theory only, occasionally adhering to the ritual, and even less frequently adhering to the spirit of the Koran. Heedless of the deep-set religious feelings of their enemies and co-religionists, they suddenly began to bombard the mosque of the Kaaba, the most sacred shrine of all Islam. One shell actually struck the black stone, burning a hole in the holy carpet and killing nine Arabs who were kneeling in prayer. Hussein's followers were so enraged by this impious act that they swarmed over the walls of the great fort and captured it after desperate hand-to-hand fighting with knives and daggers.

Both Mecca and the near-by seaport of Jeddah were captured during the first month's fighting. Jeddah was taken in five days as a result of the co-operation of five small British merchantmen under Captain Boyle, a daring red-headed Irishman, who was second in command to Sir Rosslyn Wemyss, then admiral of the Near Eastern Fleet.

More than a thousand Turkish and German prisoners were taken at Jeddah. The bombardment of this port of entry to the holy city of Mecca nearly started a revolution in India. The eighty million Mohammedans living in India are the most fanatical of all Islam in many respects. They erroneously charged the British with having bombarded one of their holy places. As a matter of fact Jeddah, being merely the port to Mecca, has never been regarded as a holy city by the Arabs themselves, and is the one city in the Hedjaz to which unbelievers have always been admitted.

At Medina the Bedouin, under Shereefs Feisal and Ali, were less successful. The tribesmen in northern Hedjaz who had rallied round the Shereefian flag, swept out of the desert mists early on the same morning in June on which the attack was launched against Mecca. Occupying all the palm-groves which extend for miles around the outskirts, they drove the Turkish outposts from the gardens of the Medina palaces, fabled for their sparkling fountains, apricot, banana and pomegranate orchards. The troops of the garrison withdrew inside the city walls. There they knew they had the additional protection afforded by the Tomb of Mohammed, the tomb which causes Medina to be regarded as the second holiest city of Islam. Although Feisal and Ali could have brought up cannon from Jeddah and perhaps taken the city by storm after a bombardment, Hussein refused to permit this for fear of causing the destruction of the Prophet's tomb, a catastrophe which would have incurred the anger of every one of the two hundred and fifty million Mohammedans in the world.

Medina is the city to which Mohammed made his hegira or flight from Mecca in July, 622 A.D., to save himself from the daggers of assassins hired by his religious enemies. All Mohammedans count time not from the birth of Christ, but from the date of that flight. Mohammed was buried in Medina, and on one side of him rests his favourite daughter, Fatima, and on the other side the second of the great Arabian rulers, Caliph Omar. But between the graves of Mohammed and Omar a space was left, so the Moslem say, that Christ upon His second coming and death may be buried by the side of the Prophet. So Medina, in addition to being a city of considerable commercial importance, is a great pilgrimage centre.

Shortly after the War commenced, the Turks, in order to facilitate the movement of troops to quell uprisings in Arabia, but ostensibly to make it easier for pilgrims to reach Medina from the north, built a single-track railway-line all the way down from Damascus. One of the first acts that the attacking

Bedouin hordes committed when they approached Medina was to tear up several miles of rails with their bare hands, in order to isolate the garrison. After surrounding the town the Arabs sat down to await its surrender; but the Turks, encouraged by their inactivity, slipped out of the gates at dawn, surprised some of the Arabs who were camping in the suburb of Awali, and set fire to all the houses. Large numbers of women and children were shot down by machine-guns, and scores of others were burned alive in their homes.

This so enraged the Bedouins, and the thousands of Arab townsmen who came out of Medina to join Feisal and Ali, that they immediately assaulted the great Turkish fort just outside the walls of the city. But the Turks opened fire with their heavy artillery and mowed great gaps in the tightly-packed whirling mass of frenzied Arabians. Never having encountered artillery fire before in their lives, the frenzy soon turned to panic, and the mob fled to the shelter of a near-by hill. Seeing this, the Turkish commander sent out a force of picked men to cut them to pieces.

Shereef Feisal saw the plight of his men and dashed up on his horse, utterly regardless of the bursting shrapnel and machine-gun fire from the fort which raked the intervening open ground. The Bedouins whom he had brought up to help him rescue the broken and panic-stricken forces that had made the original attack on the fort, held back, reluctant to face the enemy fire that formed such a deadly barrage between them and their comrades. But Feisal laughed and rode on alone. To give his followers confidence he even made his horse walk across the open space.

Unwilling to be put to shame by their fearless commander, the relieving force gave a wild desert cry and charged, the name of Allah on the lips of every warrior. The two forces then combined and made a second attempt to storm the fort. Their ammunition was nearly exhausted. Night, which comes in Arabia with a suddenness suggestive of an electrician switching off the sun's light, dropped down like a black curtain just in time to save them from annihilation.

On the morrow, Feisal and Ali called all the tribal chieftains to a conference at their pavilion, and it was agreed that for the present it was futile to continue the attack; so they retired into the hills fifty miles to the south and camped astride the pilgrim road to prevent any Turkish forces from attempting to retake Mecca. The Turks at once repaired the railway line connecting them with Damascus, drove the thirty thousand civilian Arabs living in Medina out into the desert, brought down reinforcements from Syria, and fortified the city to resist all future attacks. After the war refugees from Medina were found all over the Turkish Empire, in Jerusalem, Konia, Damascus, Aleppo, and Constantinople.

The Arabs, however, were still in undisputed possession of Mecca, and with the possible exception of the capture of Jerusalem and, later on, the combined capture of Damascus, Beyrouth and Aleppo by Allenby's army and the Arabs, the fall of Mecca is sure to rank in history as one of the greatest disasters ever suffered by the descendants of Othman. To her control of the holy city of Mecca Turkey largely owed her leadership of the Mohammedan peoples of the world. .

Then came a long pause. The Arabs were unable to go on with their revolution because they had expended all their ammunition. Shereef Hussein again appealed to the Allies, and the British responded. At that critical moment young Lawrence appeared on the Arabian stage.

CHAPTER VI

THE GATHERING OF THE DESERT TRIBES

CHAFING under the red tape of army regulations, certain slight differences had arisen between the chiefs at G.H.Q. and independent young Lawrence. In the Arab uprising Lawrence saw an avenue of escape from his Cairo straitjacket. Ronald Storrs, then Oriental secretary to the high commissioner of Egypt, was ordered to make a trip down the Red Sea to Jeddah, with messages to Emir Hussein, instigator of the Mecca revolt. Although he had played no part in starting the Hedjaz revolution, Lawrence had long realized the possibility of the Arabs helping prick the Kaiser's imperialistic bubble, so he asked permission to take a fortnight's vacation, and he has been on that leave of absence ever since!

Some of his superiors at the Savoy Hotel in Cairo were delighted at the prospect of getting rid of this altogether too obstreperous, upstart, "shavetail" lieutenant, and his request was granted with alacrity. But Lawrence, contrary to the custom of war-worn veterans on leave, did not go sailing down the Nile to the races at Alexandria, or up stream to Luxor to while away his holiday at the Winter Palace. Instead, he accompanied Ronald Storrs down the Red Sea.

On arrival at Jeddah, Lawrence succeeded in getting permission from Grand Shereef Hussein to make a short camel journey inland to the camp of Emir Feisal, third son of the Grand Shereef, who was attempting to keep the fires of revolution alive. The Arab cause looked hopeless. There were not enough bullets left to keep the army in gazelle meat, and the troops were reduced to John the Baptist's melancholy desert fare of locusts and wild honey.

After exchanging the usual Oriental compliments over many sweetened cups of Arabian coffee, the first question Lawrence asked Feisal was: "When will your army reach Damascus?"

The question evidently nonplussed the Emir, who gazed gloomily through the tent-flap at the bedraggled remnants of his father's army. "In sh'Allah," replied Feisal, stroking his beard. "There is neither power nor might save in Allah, the high, the tremendous! May He look with favour upon our cause. But I fear the gates of Damascus are farther beyond

61

our reach at present than the gates of Paradise. Allah willing, our next step will be an attack on the Turkish garrison at Medina, where we hope to deliver the tomb of the Prophet from our enemies."

A few days with Emir Feisal convinced Lawrence that it might be possible to reorganize this rabble into an irregular force which might be of assistance to the British army in Egypt and Sinai. So absorbed did he become in working out this idea that when his two-weeks' furlough came to an end he stayed on in Arabia without even sending apologies to Cairo. From then onward Lawrence was the moving spirit in the Arabian revolution.

When Lieutenant Lawrence arrived at Jeddah, the situation was critical. The Turks had rushed an army corps down from Syria to strengthen Medina, and they had sent down mule and camel transport, armoured cars, aeroplanes, cavalry, and more artillery with which to stamp out the revolution. An expeditionary force from Medina was already on its way south to recover Mecca and hang the rebel leaders higher than Haman. To be sure, this advancing army had two hundred and fifty miles of desert to cross, but they would have crossed it had not strange events occurred causing them hurriedly to revise their plans. As the Arab chroniclers recount: "The hosts of Othman, the minions of the usurper caliphs, advanced defiantly. But God was not with them! Praise be to Allah, the protector of all those who trust in him!"

Lawrence had no definite plan, but the thought was in his mind to devise a way of harassing the Turk and attracting the attention of a portion of the Ottoman forces opposing the British to the north in Sinai. He had startled Feisal with the remark that he believed his troops would be in Damascus within two years. "If Allah wills," had replied the Emir with a dubious smile as he stroked his beard and gazed at his riff-raff army lolling in the shade of the date palms. But something in Lawrence's quiet manner impressed him with confidence, and he accepted the offer of co-operation.

To the young archæologist turned soldier the thought of participating in a desert war appealed greatly. Here he saw an opportunity not only of beating the Germans but of testing the theories of the great military experts whose books had so fascinated him.

Once he had made up his mind to help the Arabs, Lawrence was immediately transformed from a scholarly student of the metaphysical and philosophical side of war to a student of the stern realities of war. To reach Mecca he

thought the Turkish expedition would first attempt to drive
Feisal's force out of the hills in order to capture Rabegh, the
tiny but strategically important Red Sea port one hundred
miles north of Jeddah.   Here, behind coral reefs, under a
picturesque grove of palm trees, were excellent wells.

Lawrence's first plan was to supply the Bedouin irregulars
in the hills between Medina and Rabegh with modern rifles
and plenty of ammunition, in the hope that they would be
able to hold up the advancing Turks in the narrow defiles until
a regular army of Arab townsmen, more amenable to
discipline, could be whipped into shape.   Next, he planned to
entrench them outside Rabegh, where they could co-operate
with the British fleet, and give battle to the enemy when the
latter finally broke through the hills.

The Turks, however, upset this scheme with alarming
speed.   Much sooner than anticipated, and without warning,
they pushed straight through the hills as though the Bedouin
irregulars were not there.   The situation now was even more
precarious than when Lawrence first arrived.   It seemed to
the Arabs as though "the Maker of the Sun and Moon and
Stars were guiding the destiny of the enemy."

It was at this stage in the campaign that Lawrence decided
to disregard Foch's dictum that the object of modern war is
to locate the enemy army and annihilate it.   He came to the
conclusion that to win a war against the Turks, or any other
well-trained troops in the desert, it would be better to imitate
the tactics of Hannibal and other military leaders of pre-
Napoleonic wars.   He realized that in a stand-up fight against
the better-disciplined Turks the Arabs would be doomed.   On
the other hand, he figured that if Hussein's followers confined
themselves exclusively to the hit-and-run type of guerilla
warfare, to which they were so thoroughly accustomed, the
Turks would be helpless to retaliate.   The failure of his first
plan opened Lawrence's eyes, and the situation as he now saw
it resolved itself into this:

Shereef Hussein's followers had captured Mecca, the most
important city of the Hedjaz.   They had also taken Taif and
Jeddah, and had swept the hated Turk from the whole of their
country, with the exception of the city of Medina and the
fortified posts protecting the Hedjaz Railway, connecting
Medina with Damascus.   In other words, the Arabs were
already in possession of all of their country with the exception
of a very small part.

Furthermore, the Turkish garrisons at Medina and along
the Hedjaz Railway could not move easily from their base

without the consent of the Arabs, for they were surrounded by that mysterious element to which they were not accustomed, the unknown and unfathomable desert. An army corps of Turkish infantry would be as helpless in the desert as they would be at sea.

On the other hand, the Arabs were at home among the shifting dunes. When a Bedouin tribe starts off on a raid, each man and his camel are a separate unit, each desert warrior as independent as a warship at sea; there are no lines of communication. Mounted on his racing camel, a Bedouin can cruise across the desert sands for weeks without returning to his base of supplies. The dictum of a Bedouin strategist is quite contradictory to the dictum of Marshal Foch. His theory is not to hunt out his enemy and fight it out to the finish, but to stalk his prey as a hunter stalks his game. At an unguarded moment he sweeps down upon him, accomplishes his mission, and then, before his opponent has time to collect his wits, he vanishes, swallowed up by the trackless sands. This was the game Lawrence decided to play for all it might be worth.

When he came to this decision, he was lying in his tent stricken with a fever, and the Turkish expeditionary force was bearing rapidly down upon Rabegh. Instead of strengthening the system of trenches around the port and awaiting them, Lawrence and Feisal started north, leaving Shereef Hussein's youngest son Zeid with a small band of Bedouin to harass the enemy. This left Jeddah and Mecca practically unprotected and gave the Turkish army a clear right of way.

What was Lawrence's scheme?

To the north were two small ports, Yembo and El Wejh. These were still held by the Turks as a protection for the Hedjaz Railway, the life-cord both of the Medina garrison and of the Turkish army marching south on Mecca. His plan was to capture both of these important posts, threaten the railway, and compel the enemy expeditionary force to return to Medina or run the risk of being cut off in the desert without supplies.

The more Lawrence thought about this the more he became convinced that if the Turkish expedition could be drawn back to Medina the Arab war would be won; at any rate, won so far as the liberation of the Hedjaz was concerned. He estimated that there were about one hundred and fifty thousand square miles of territory in the country, and that if the Turks wanted completely to subjugate it and to stamp out all revolution they would need at least half a million soldiers. Since they had a maximum of only one hundred thousand troops for the purpose, Lawrence concluded that if he could

MOHAMMED EL DEIHLAN, "FATHER OF ELOQUENCE," WITH
HIS SLAVE SQUATTING AT HIS FEET

AN ARAB SENTINEL IN THE MOUNTAINS OF EDOM

succeed in welding the scattered inhabitants of the desert into an army he might be able not only to drive the Turks from Holy Arabia but to invade Syria as well.

To do this he must convince them that they should give up cutting each other's throats over century-old tribal disputes. He must convince them that, instead, they must risk their lives for the freedom of their country, and that they should die willingly for the liberation of the whole Arab world from Ottoman oppression.

The General Staff at headquarters in Cairo raised no objection to Lawrence's remaining in Arabia when he failed to return at the end of his furlough. General Sir Gilbert Clayton, head of the Intelligence Corps, knew that he could speak the language, that he understood the people, and, indeed, that he was something of a Bedouin at heart himself. G.H.Q. merely hoped that he might encourage the Arabs a little and help keep the rebellion alive. They gave him complete freedom of action in order that he might make the most of any opportunities that might arise. That was in October, 1916, and by October, 1918, this youngster, not yet out of his twenties, had raised a formidable, vaporous irregular army and had led it through the gates of Damascus.

It was by the process of accretion that Lawrence and Feisal built up their army. With only two companions the former started out across the desert. He stopped at every nomad encampment, and, calling the headmen together, in faultless classic Arabic he explained his mission. The fact that Lawrence was visiting them in the name of Sidi Feisal, the most beloved of Shereef Hussein's sons, insured him against personal harm, in spite of the fact that he was a Christian trespassing on sacred ground.

At nightfall, after prayers, he would sit by the camp fires before the black tents, discussing with his Bedouin hosts the past greatness of Arabia and her present condition of servitude, until he had every member of the tribe worked up to a high pitch of frenzy. Over roasted goat killed in his honour and cups of sweetened tea, in phrases more eloquent than the words of the tribal wise men, he would discuss with them the possibility of driving out the Turks. He convinced them that they would be flying in the face of Allah if they hesitated longer, since their ancient enemy was at the moment too busy fighting the British, French, Italians, and Russians to offer serious resistance to an Arab uprising.

That he succeeded in persuading the Bedouin to renounce their blood-feuds and unite against their common enemy was

E

demonstrated by the fact that within six months he had united
nearly all of the tribes of the Hedjaz into a loose alliance.

The first three tribes won over were the Harb, who inhabit
the desert between Medina and Mecca; the Juheina, who dwell
in the region between the Red Sea coast and Medina; and the
people of the Billi tribe, who roam the country east of El
Wejh. The first of these includes over two hundred thousand
people and is one of the largest tribes in all Arabia.

Throughout the entire first phase of the desert campaign
the Arabs were given invaluable assistance by the British
Navy. While Lawrence trekked north through the interior,
encouraging and supervising the gathering of the clans, Feisal
left the Mecca road undefended and started up the coast
accompanied by every man available, except the few snipers
who remained with Shereef Zeid. By the time Feisal had
advanced within striking distance of Yenbo, the first port
north of Rabegh, Lawrence had sent several thousand more
tribesmen to his support. The Turkish garrison evacuated
before the Arabs arrived, the guns of the British warships
causing them to take to their heels.

The entry into Yenbo was splendid and barbaric. Emir
Feisal, as commander-in-chief of the Arabian army, rode in
front, dressed in robes as white as the snows of Lebanon. On
his right rode another shereef, garbed in dark red, his head-
cloth, tunic and cloak dyed with henna. On Feisal's left rode
"Shereef" Lawrence, in pure white robes, looking like the
reincarnation of a prophet of old. Behind them were Bedouin
carrying three large banners of purple silk, topped with gold
spikes, and followed by a minstrel twanging a lute and three
drummers playing a weird march. After them came a bounc-
ing, billowy mass of thousands of wild sons of Ishmael, on
camels, all members of Feisal's and Lawrence's bodyguard.
They were packed together in a dense throng as they passed
down the corridor of palm trees, under the minarets of the
mosque. The riders were wearing robes of every colour, and
from their saddles hung gay trappings and rich brocades. It
was indeed a resplendent cavalcade. All were singing at the
tops of their nasal voices, improvising verses descriptive of the
virtues of Emir Feisal and his fair-haired "grand vizier."

From Yenbo they at once pushed on north along the coast,
for another two hundred miles toward El Wejh, which was
held by a thousand Turkish troops. The name of this port
recalls to mind another expedition. About 24 B.C. Augustus
Cæsar sent Allius Gallus to Arabia with eleven thousand of
the picked soldiers of Rome. After wandering for six months

through the thirst-stricken land they finally gave up their attempt to reach the frankincense country, and when they sailed back to Egypt from this same port of El Wejh there was but a sorry remnant left. They had learned to their grief what Lawrence already knew, that an army in Arabia must be able to endure much and live on little.

By now Lawrence and Feisal had collected ten thousand men, and this force was divided into nine sections. They converged at the village of Um Lejj, about half-way. There they received fresh supplies from the British warships, with whom perfect liaison was maintained throughout the entire coastal operations. From Um Lejj on the north, one hundred and twenty miles of waterless desert lay before the Arab army. So barren was this region that there were not even thorns on which the camels might subsist.

But an armed merchantman of the Indian merchant marine followed up the coast, ran the risk of ripping wide her hull on hidden coral reefs, and put into an uncharted bay with a small quantity of water for the mules but none for the camels. Hundreds of the latter were lost, but the army reached the hills overlooking El Wejh on January 25, 1917, without the loss of a single man from hunger or thirst.

El Wejh stands at the south-western corner of a small coraline plateau, bounded on the west by the sea, on the south by a dry wadi, and on the east by an inland plain. The British warships bombarded the Turks out of their main fortress by firing from fourteen thousand yards, which enabled them to keep far outside the range of the Turkish guns. After shelling them for a few hours, a landing-party of Arabs, who had been carried up by sea for the purpose, went ashore and attacked the demoralized garrison. At the same time Lawrence and his men swept in from the desert and took a hand both in the street-fighting and the looting. True to tradition, Lawrence's Bedouins made off with every movable object in El Wejh.

Admiral Sir Rosslyn Wemyss directed the sea attack in person. To use the Arab phrase, Admiral Wemyss was the "father and mother" of the Arabian revolution during its early stages. Much of the credit for the early successes of the Arabs should go to him. Whenever Lawrence wanted to stage a cinema show, as he described demonstrations made to impress the rather restive Arabs, who were too much inclined to revert to their old habit of fighting among themselves, he would simply notify the admiral who would steam down from Suez in his huge flagship, the *Euryalus*, and engage in target-practice with his nine-inch guns along the coast within sight of the Shereefian Army.

On two occasions the admiral anchored the *Euryalus* in Jeddah harbour at critical moments, obstensibly to present his compliments to the Grand Shereef.   There is no doubt that the mammoth size of the admiral's flagship was largely responsible for the impression which the aged monarch gained of Britain's Power.

"She is the great sea in which I, the fish, swim," he remarked on one occasion.   "And the larger the sea the fatter the fish!"

CHAPTER VII

THE BATTLE AT THE WELLS OF ABU EL LISSAL

SIMULTANEOUSLY with Feisal's attack on the small Red Sea ports of Yenbo and El Wejh, his brother Abdulla appeared out of the desert several miles to the east, near Medina. He was accompanied by a riding party mounted on she-racing camels. These raiders wiped out a few enemy patrols, blew up several sections of track and left a formal letter tacked, in full view, on one of the sleepers, and addressed to the Turkish commander-in-chief, describing in redundant and lurid detail what his fate would be if he lingered longer in Arabia.

The Turkish forces advancing on Mecca received news of the fall of Yenbo and El Wejh, more than a hundred miles to the north-west of them, and of Shereef Abdulla's raids a hundred miles to the north-east, at almost the same moment. They were amazed and bewildered, for a few days previously the Arab army had been sitting in front of them at Rabegh.

Thanks to the sniping of Emir Zeid's handful of followers by day and to small raids by night, the Turks had been tricked into thinking the main Hedjaz army still there, but now there appeared to be Arab armies on all sides of them. The relentless rays of the sun, beating down with blistering ferocity on the parched region where they encamped, not only increased their thirst but stimulated their imagination as well. To their feverish, sunken eyes, every mirage now seemed to be a cloud of Bedouin horsemen.

Each hour brought camel couriers with news of raids on El Ula, Medain Saleh, and other stations north of Medina, and of the capture of two more of their Red Sea garrisons at Dhaba and Moweilah. Thoroughly frightened by the news of these unexpected reverses, as well as by the rumours of fictitious Arab victories circulated purposely among them by Lawrence's secret agents, the Turks, panic-stricken, fled back to defend their base at Medina and to defend the railway, which was their sole line of communication with Syria and Turkey.

In the north of Holy Arabia, near the head of the Gulf of Akaba, the Turks had another garrison far more important than any as yet taken in the campaign, except the garrisons at Mecca and Jeddah. Before Feisal's followers could hope to sweep their ancient enemy out of all the Hedjaz, excepting

Medina, this important strong-hold at the head of the gulf must be accounted for. This accomplished, Lawrence had in mind a far bolder and vaster plan which he hoped to execute.

Of all the strategic places along the west coast of Arabia north of Aden, the most important from a military stand-point is the ancient seaport of Akaba, once the chief naval base of King Solomon's fleet, and also one of the first places where the Prophet Mohammed preached and made his head-quarters. For any army attempting to invade Egypt or strike at the Suez Canal from the east, Akaba must be the left flank, as it must be the right flank for any army setting out from Egypt to invade Palestine and Syria. From the begin-ning of the war the Turks had maintained a large garrison there, both because they intended to wrest Egypt from the British, and because it was essential to the security of the Hedjaz Railway.

It was Lawrence's intention to capture Akaba and make it the base for an Arab invasion of Syria! This was a truly ambitious and portentous plan.

On June 18, 1917, with only eight hundred Bedouins of the Toweiha tribe, two hundred of the Sherart, and ninety of the Kawachiba, he set out from El Wejh for the head of the Gulf of Akaba, three hundred miles farther north. This force was headed by Shereef Nasir, a remote descendant of Mohammed, and one of Feisal's ablest lieutenants. As usual, Lawrence went along to advise the Arab commander; he always made it a point to act through one of the native leaders, and much of his success may be attributed to his tact in making the Arabs believe that they were conducting the campaign themselves.

The advance on Akaba is an illustration of how ably Lawrence handled Feisal's army, in spite of his complete lack of military training and experience. In order to outwit the Turkish commander at Medina he led a flying column nearly one thousand miles to the north of El Wejh; but instead of going right up the coast toward Akaba, he led them far into the interior, across the Hedjaz Railway not far from Medina, where they blew up several miles of track on the way, then through the Wadi Sirhan, famous for its venomous reptiles, where some of his men died of snake-bite, then across the territory of the Howeitat tribe east of the Dead Sea, and still on, north into the land of Moab.

He even led a party of picked men through the Turkish lines by night, dynamited a train near Amman (the ancient Greek city of Philadelphia), blew up a bridge near Deraa, the most important railway junction just south of Damascus, and mined another several hundred miles behind the Turkish front-line trenches near the Syrian industrial city of Homs.

It was possible for Lawrence to conduct raids on such a grand scale only because of the extraordinary mobility of his forces. With his camel corps he could cruise across the desert for six weeks without returning to his supply base. As long as the members of his party kept to the desert and out of sight of the Turkish fortified posts along the frontiers of Palestine and Syria, they were as safe as though they were on another planet. When they saw an opportunity to dash in and make a surprise attack, they would do so, and then dash back into the desert where the Turks dared not follow because they neither had the camels, the intimate knowledge of the desert, nor the phenomenal powers of endurance which the Bedouins possessed. During a six weeks' expedition, Lawrence's followers would live on nothing but unleavened bread, each man carried a half-sack of flour weighing forty-five pounds, enough to enable him to trek two thousand miles without obtaining fresh supplies. They could get along comfortably on a mouthful of water a day when on the march; but wells were rarely more than two or three days' march apart, so that they seldom suffered from thirst.

For these expeditions, far to the north and within territory occupied by the Turks, Lawrence divided his men into several different raiding-parties, in order to confuse and bewilder the enemy. After annoying them in the hills of Moab, to the east of Jericho, and then a day or two later away up around Damascus, he swept south again. It is sixty miles from Akaba to the Hedjaz Railway, and in order to prevent the Turks from guessing that Akaba was his real objective, he made a feint against Maan, the most important fortified town on the railway between Medina and the Dead Sea. At the same time, seventeen miles south-west of Maan, he swooped down upon Fuweilah station and wiped out its garrison. When news of this reached the Turks at Maan they despatched one of their crack mounted regiments in pursuit, but when the regiment reached the station only the vultures were found in possession; Lawrence and his raiders had disappeared into the blue again, and so far as the Turks knew, had been swallowed up by the desert. But, lest they should be forgotten, on the evening of the following day they reappeared out of the mist many miles distant. There they merrily planted more mines, demolished a mile of track, and destroyed a relief train. The heat during these July days was intense. In describing it, Lawrence remarked that the burning ground seared the skin from the forearms of the snipers, and the camels went as lame as the men did, with agony from the sunburned flints.

By this time Lawrence and Shereef Nasir had been joined by the Beni Atiyeh tribe, who supplied them with four thousand fresh fighting men, and also by the Abu Tayi section of the Howeitat tribe, made up of some of the finest warriors in Arabia, under the leadership of Auda, a veritable human tiger who was Lawrence's intimate companion from then onward.

The pursuing Turkish column decided to spend the night in the bottom of a valley near some wells at Abu el Lissal, fourteen miles from Maan, where I camped with Lawrence and Feisal some months later. Lawrence, in the meantime, left his column and galloped off across the desert, to see if he could locate the Turkish battalion. As soon as he found it he hurried back for his men, brought them on to the heights around Abu el Lissal, and by dawn had the Turks completely surrounded.

For twelve hours the Arabs sniped at the Turks from their positions on the hills around the wells, picking off many of them. The Sultan's forces were indeed in a tight corner, but Lawrence knew full well that if they were under capable and daring leaders they could easily fight their way out through his thin line of Bedouins. The Turk commander, however, lacked the necessary courage. So at sunset Auda Abu Tayi, with fifty of his fellow tribesmen, crept up to within three hundred yards of the Turks and after a moment's rest boldly pushed out from under cover and galloped straight into the enemy camp. So surprised were the Turks by this audacity that when the old Bedouin chieftain crashed into their midst their ranks broke, but not before bullets had smashed Auda Abu Tayi's field-glasses, pierced his revolver-holster, nicked the sword he was holding in his hand, and killed two horses under him. In spite of these incidents that old Arab was delighted and maintained afterward that it was the best scrap he had had since Ramadan.

Lawrence, who was watching from the hill on the opposite side of the basin, dashed down the slope as fast as his dromedary could carry him and charged into the midst of the now demoralized Turks, followed by four hundred other Bedouins on camels. For twenty minutes a thousand Turks and Arabs were mixed together in a wild, frenzied mass, all shooting madly. In the charge Lawrence accidentally shot his own camel through the head with his automatic; it dropped dead, and he was hurled from his saddle and lay stunned in front of it, while his followers charged right over him. Had

he not been thrown directly in front of his mount he would
have been trampled to death by the onrushing camels.

The Turks made their fatal error in scattering, just as
Lawrence had surmised they would do, and the battle ended
in massacre. Although many escaped in the darkness, the
Arabs killed and captured more than the total number of their
own force. The next morning more than three hundred dead
were counted around the water-hole. Most of the prisoners
taken were rounded up by Shereef Nasir and Lawrence,
because the rest of the Bedouin dashed off to the Turkish
tents, as usual thinking of nothing but loot. The desire to
loot is an all-consuming passion with the Bedouin and is not
considered a form of stealing by them, but is listed among
the cardinal virtues.

So bitter were the Arabs that they wanted to kill their
prisoners in retaliation for the atrocities the Turks had been
committing against their women and children. They were also
aching to avenge the death of Sheik Belgawiya of Kerak, one
of their leaders, whom the Turks had harnessed between four
mules and torn apart limb from limb. The sheik's tragic
death had been the climax of a series of executions by torture
which had so enraged the Arabs that they swore never to give
quarter to another Turk. But Lawrence had other ideas. He
wanted the rumour spread far and wide through the Turkish
army that the Arabs were not only accepting prisoners but
were treating them well, and so he finally prevailed upon his
revengeful followers to treat these captives with special consideration. Just as he had hoped, this propaganda brought
immediate results, and in the days following the battle of
Abu el Lissal groups were contantly coming in holding their
weapons above their heads and crying: "Moslem! Moslem!"
in imitation of the German cry of "Kamerad."

CHAPTER VIII

THE CAPTURE OF THE ANCIENT SEAPORT OF KING SOLOMON

LAWRENCE had left El Wejh, hundreds of miles to the south, with but two months' rations. After giving a part of his supplies to the captured Turks, the food situation became critical. Nevertheless the half-starved Arab army, led by this youngster, continued its march through the jagged, barren mountains that bite the North Arabian sky. The news of their victories travelled ahead of them, and when Lawrence arrived at Gueirra, a Turkish post in King Solomon's Mountains, twenty-five miles from Akaba, at the entrance to an extremely narrow pass known as the Wadi Ithm, the Gueirra garrison came out and laid down their arms without firing a shot. He then proceeded to march his Bedouins on, down the Wadi Ithm to Kethura, another outpost guarding the only land approach to Akaba. There Lawrence charged another garrison and captured several hundred more men. Trekking through the gorge they came to an ancient well at Khadra where two thousand years before the Romans had constructed a stone dam across the valley, the remains of which can still be seen. The Turks had massed their heavy artillery behind that ruined wall. It constituted the outermost defence of Akaba. By the time the Shereefian army arrived in front of this final barricade the Bedouin of the Amran Darausha and Neiwat tribes, who lived in the desert near Akaba, had heard of the great victories at Fuweilah and Abu el Lissal, and were scampering across the lava mountains by the hundreds, to join the advancing Arab forces.

The overwhelming defeat of the Turkish battalion at Abu el Lissal was really the first phase of the battle of Akaba. The second consisted in the spectacular manœuvre when Lawrence accomplished what the Turks thought impossible and succeeded in leading his scraggly, undisciplined horde of Bedouin through the precipitous King Solomon Mountains, over the old Roman wall, right past the bewildered Turkish artillerymen, and down into Akaba on the morning of July 6, 1917. But to save the Akaba garrison from massacre Lawrence and Nasir had to labour with their fierce followers from sunset to dawn. They would not have succeeded then, had not Nasir walked down the valley into No-Man's-Land and sat on a rock to make his men quit firing.

Akaba is picturesquely located at the southern end of the wide Wadi Araba, perhaps the driest and most desolate valley in the world, which runs down from the Dead Sea to the Gulf of Akaba. Up this same wadi Moses and the Israelites are believed to have made their way toward the Promised Land, and down this valley rode Mohammed, Ali, Abu Bekr, and Omar. It was here that Mohammed preached many of his first sermons. Beyond a narrow semi-circle of date-palms which fringe the shore, lie the blue waters of the now deserted gulf where Solomon's fleets, Phœnician galleys, and Roman triremes rode at anchor. Behind Akaba loom jagged, volcanic, arid mountains. Like most of the smaller towns of the Near East the place itself is a chaotic jumble of mud huts. Awnings cover the narrow streets, and the stalls in the bazaar are filled with brocades, shabby prayer rugs, cones of cane sugar swarming with flies, piles of dates, and dishes of glistening brass and hammered copper.

The Turks and Germans were so paralysed and bewildered by the unexpected achievement of the Arabs in getting across the mountains and through the passes that they surrendered without further ado. Immediately after the entrance into Akaba a German officer stepped up and saluted Lawrence. He spoke neither Turkish nor Arabic and evidently did not even know there was a revolution in progress.

"What is all this about? What is all this about? Who are these men?" he shouted excitedly.

"They belong to the army of King Hussein"—the Grand Shereef had by this time proclaimed himself king—"who is in revolt against the Turks," replied Lawrence.

"Who is King Hussein?" asked the German.

"Emir of Mecca and ruler of this part of Arabia," was the reply.

"Ach Himmel! And what am I?" added the German officer in English.

"You are a prisoner."

"Will they take me to Mecca?"

"No, to Egypt."

"Is sugar very high over there?"

"Very cheap."

"Good." And he marched off, happy to be out of the War, and happier still to be heading for a place where he could have plenty of sugar.

This time the plans of Emir Feisal's youthful British adviser went through true to form. From now on the Turks were kept on the defensive. They were obliged to weaken their army by splitting it into two parts, one half remained in Medina, and the other defended the pilgrimage railway. If he had wanted to do so Lawrence could have dynamited the railway in so many places that the Turks would have been completely cut off at Medina; then, by bringing up a few long-range naval guns from the Gulf of Akaba, he could have blown Medina off the map and compelled the garrison to surrender. But he had an excellent reason for not attempting this, as we shall soon see. In his mind he had worked out a far finer and more ambitious scheme, the successful carrying out of which demanded that the Turks should be inveigled into sending down more reinforcements to Medina, and as many guns, camels, mules, armoured cars, aeroplanes, and other war materials as they could be compelled to spare from their other fronts. He hoped they would keep a huge garrison there until the end of the War, which would mean so many less Turks opposing the British armies in Palestine and Mesopotamia; and the supply-trains which would necessarily have to be sent down from Syria might be made a constant source of supply for the Arabs. If Medina were captured and the Turks all driven north, it would deprive Lawrence of this magnificent opportunity of maintaining his army on Turkish supplies. That was far more to his advantage than occupying Medina.

After the capture of Akaba, Lawrence and his men lived for ten days on unripe dates and on the meat of camels which had been killed in the battle of Abu el Lissal. They were compelled to kill their own riding camels at the rate of two a day to save themselves and their hundreds of prisoners. Then in order to keep his army from starving, Lawrence jumped on his racing camel and rode her continuously for twenty-two hours across the uninhabited mountains and desert valley of the Sinai Peninsula. Completely worn out after this record ride, which came at the end of two months' continuous fighting and a thousand miles of trekking across one of the most barren parts of the earth and living on soggy unleavened bread and dates and without having a bath for more than a month, he turned his camel over to an M.P. at one of the street corners in Port Tewfik, Suez, walked a little unsteadily into the Sinai Hotel, and ordered a bath. For three hours he remained in the tub with a procession of Berberine boys serving him cool drinks. That day, he declares, was the nearest approach to the Mohammedan idea of paradise that he ever expects to experience. From Suez he went on to Ismailia, the midway station on the canal.

Lawrence's arrival in Arabia had been unheralded, even

G.H.Q. in Cairo were ignorant as to his movements. His exploits first became known when he met General Allenby at Ismailia on the arrival of this new leader who had just been assigned to take over command of the Egyptian Expeditionary Forces.

The incident was dramatic in its simplicity. Allenby had been sent out from London to succeed Sir Archibald Murray as commander-in-chief. He had just landed and was at the railway station in Ismailia walking up and down the platform with Admiral Wemyss. Lawrence standing near by in Arab garb, saw the important-looking general with the admiral.

"Who's that?" he asked of Wemyss's flag-lieutenant.

"Allenby," was the reply.

"What's he doing here?" queried Lawrence.

"He has come out to take Murray's place."

A few minutes later Lawrence had an opportunity to report to Admiral Wemyss, who had been the godfather of the Arab "show." He told him that Akaba had been taken but that his men were badly in need of food. The admiral immediately promised to send ships, and a moment later he told Allenby what Lawrence had said. The general sent for him at once. The station was crowded with staff officers and a throng of vociferous natives who were welcoming Allenby, when out of the mob stepped this barefooted, fair-faced boy in Bedouin garb.

"What news have you brought?" asked Allenby.

In even, low tones, without any more expression on his face than if he were conveying compliments from the Grand Shereef, Lawrence reported that the Arabs had captured the ancient seaport at the head of the Gulf of Akaba. He gave all the credit for the victory to the Arabs, making no reference to the part he himself had played in the affair. He conveyed the impression that he was acting as a courier, although, as a matter of fact, the capture of that important point was due entirely to his own leadership and strategical genius.

The general was immensely pleased, because Akaba was the most important point on his right flank and the principal Turkish base on the western coast of the Arabian Peninsula.

Then, when Lawrence explained in more detail the plight of the Arab troops, Admiral Wemyss promised to send a vessel filled with food to Akaba. But Sir Rosslyn went even beyond that and acted in a way that will immortalize him in Arabian history. The Arabs were afraid lest the Turks should return with reinforcements and capture Akaba; so the admiral moved his office, all his personal effects, and his staff ashore to a hotel in Ismailia, and sent his flagship round Sinai to Akaba for a whole month to bolster up the morale of the Arabs. The presence of this huge floating fortress encouraged the Bedouins and convinced them that they were not going to be obliged to play a lone hand against the Turkish Empire. The British flagship was more tangible evidence of the strength of Britain than these desert nomads had ever seen before.

Admiral Wemyss also lent Lawrence and his Arabs twenty machine-guns from his ships and several naval guns. The latter are still "somewhere" in Arabia, probably mounted on the roof of Auda Abu Tayi's mud palace. Several months after the termination of the War Lawrence received a letter from the Admiralty asking him kindly to return one of their long-range guns which had been taken ashore for the Arab show. He replied that he was very sorry but that he had "mislaid it."

As a result of Lawrence's victory at Akaba and his visit to Egypt, the British decided to back the Arabs to the limit in their campaign to win complete independence. The young archæologist was sent back to Akaba with unlimited resources, and within a few months he had conducted the campaign in such a brilliant manner that he was raised in rank from lieutenant to lieutenant-colonel, despite the fact that he hardly knew the difference between "right incline" and "present arms."

The Germans and Turks were not long in finding out that there was a mysterious power giving inspiration to the Arabs. Through their spies they discovered that Lawrence was the guiding spirit of the whole Arabian revolution. They offered rewards up to fifty thousand pounds for his capture dead or alive. But the Bedouins would not have betrayed their leader for all the gold in the fabled mines of Solomon.

The fall of Akaba, next to the capture of the holy city of Mecca, was the most significant event of the Arabian revolution, because it unified the Arabs whom Lawrence had already won over to the cause of the revolution, and gave them confidence in themselves.

After winning his victory, Lawrence was shrewd enough to take full advantage of it. Although his own strategy and personal bravery had played an all-important part in the success of these operations, he was astute enough to give all the credit to the principal Arab leaders under him, such as Auda Abu Tayi and Shereef Nasir. Like children, these doughty old warriors were not at all reticent about accepting it, and, of course, from then on they were Lawrence's sworn friends.

Anxious to make the most of this initial success, Lawrence sent couriers to all the tribes of the desert although news of the battle of Abu el Lissal and the advance on Akaba seemed to travel as though flashed about Arabia by radio. He realized the tremendous importance of propaganda and sent some of his cleverest Arab lieutenants through the enemy lines to spread the news of the fall of Akaba far and wide to the remote corners of the Turkish Empire.

So it was that this young Briton, just down from Oxford, away in a long-forgotten corner of the earth, captured the ancient seaport of Solomon where a battle had probably not been fought for a thousand years and more, thereby winning the second important victory of the War in the Land of the Arabian Nights and paving the way for an invasion of Syria. From a mere local squabble, Lawrence's victory at Akaba transformed the Hedjaz revolt into a campaign of far-reaching importance directed against the heart of the Turkish Empire; and from that day his undisciplined rabble of swarthy desert brigands became the right wing of Allenby's army, and from then on this second lieutenant played the role of a lieutenant-general.

CHAPTER IX

ACROSS THE RED SEA TO JOIN LAWRENCE AND FEISAL

EMIR FEISAL and Colonel Lawrence had got as far as Akaba with their campaign when we arrived from Palestine with our battery of cameras. It was by no means an easy matter to even get to the Arab base camp, and our adventures in doing so may even justify another digression from the story of Lawrence and his associates, in order to better illustrate how remote this campaign really was from the rest of the World War.

Shortly after I had met Lawrence in Jerusalem, while lunching with General Allenby and the Duke of Connaught, the name of the archæologist turned soldier came up during the conversation. Out of curiosity I asked the commander-in-chief why the Arabian campaign and Lawrence's exploits had been kept such a secret. He replied that it had been considered advisable to say as little as possible, because they hoped that large numbers of the conscript Arabs fighting in the Turkish army might desert and join Shereef Hussein in his fight for Arabian independence. They were afraid lest the Arabs of Syria, Palestine, and Mesopotamia whom the Turks had conscripted should get the mistaken idea that the Allies were inspiring the Hedjaz revolt and hence erroneously conclude that it was not a patriotic rebellion. For this reason the Allies were anxious that the campaign should appear in its true light as an independent Arabian movement. But so successful had been Lawrence's efforts that Allenby said it was no longer quite so necessary to maintain such strict secrecy, adding that if I happened to be interested in what was going on in Arabia he would be glad to have me join King Hussein's army, and afterward tell the world a little of what the Arabs had done toward helping to win the Great War.

This was exactly what I had often thought of asking permission to do; but I had been warned that because of the secrecy with which the campaign was being conducted there was not the slightest chance of receiving the commander-in-chief's consent. I of course lost no time in accepting, and jumped at this opportunity of going on what I was sure would be an adventure of a lifetime.

We were told that it would be practically impossible to

OLD AUDA ABU TAYI, THE FIGHTING SHEIK WHO LED
THE CHARGE AT THE WELLS OF ABU EL LISSAN

ONE OF LAWRENCE'S SCALLAWAGS WEARING THE BOOTS THAT HE HAS TAKEN FROM A
DEAD TURKISH OFFICER

make the journey overland from Palestine to Arabia, or at any rate that it could only be done by going through the Turkish lines in disguise. We had neither the time nor the inclination nor the necessary knowledge of the country and the language to attempt this; so, accompanied by Mr. Chase, my artist colleague, I returned to Egypt to consult the heads of the Arab Bureau in Cairo. There we were told:

"You can get as far as Akaba in a cargo-boat, but next to Timbuctoo it is the most out-of-the-way place in the world. You will find no hotel porters at the dock to receive you, and you will have to be content with a block of coral for your pillow and a date-palm for your shelter."

In pre-War days a tramp wind-jammer returning from Borneo or the Solomon Islands with a cargo of copra would occasionally lose its way in a storm and drive up the Gulf of Akaba, but apart from rare occasions like that almost no one had visited the place for a thousand years.

"You will get nothing to eat but unleavened bread, dates, and perhaps a few dried locusts," remarked one general, on whose advise we bought many little luxuries, including fifty bars of milk chocolate. A colonel cheerfully warned me, "If you value your lives take plenty of cigarettes for the Bedos." So we filled every crevice of our outfit with "gaspers," which proved worth their weight in sovereigns. On the day we landed in Arabia the thermometer happened to register above the melting point of chocolate, and when I opened my kit-bag I found a semi-fluid mass of bullets, matches, cigarettes, pencils, note-books and chocolate.

On our way to Arabia we followed a roundabout route, sailing fifteen hundred miles up the Nile into the heart of Africa to Khartoum, and then across the Nubian Desert for five hundred miles to Port Sudan on the Red Sea, where we hoped to get accommodation on a tramp vessel of some sort.

Our first stop up the Nile was at Luxor, where we were given a welcome that had not been equalled since "Teddy" Roosevelt stopped there on his way back from hunting big game in East Africa. A swarm of haggard guides, who had been waiting four long years in vain for American tourists, mobbed us from sheer joy. Our welcome resembled a battle royal, and the runners from the Luxor Hotel eventually succeeded in dragging us into their ramshackle gharry, and off we careened through streets lined with deserted tourists' shops, with the rest of the crowd howling and gyrating behind us like dancing dervishes.

Our visit to Hundred-gated Thebes, the Temple of Karnak,

F

and the Tombs of the Kings the following day was rather
spoiled by a pitiful tale that our guide poured into our ears.
"American tourist he no come no more. All we guides
starve. Oh, woe! Oh, woe!" wailed this melancholy old
Arab. "Me guide here thirty-five years, and so help me Allah,
the only real tourist in the world is you Americans. The
Inglisse [English], German, and French spend all their time
counting their centimes. If American see something he want
he say, 'How much?' You tell him and, praise be to Allah,
no matter what price is, he say, 'All right, wrap 'er up!' All
us best guides specialize on Americans. Before the War me
no more bother guiding anybody but Americans than you
bother to shoot baby elephant if you see big one. Why
President Wilson no stop the War, and why," he added in
a pleading voice, "you Americans send money and food to
Armenians and nothing to us poor starving guides of Egypt?"

On the first evening after our arrival in Khartoum we were
dining with the chief of the Central African Intelligence
Department at the House of the Hippopotamus Head when
suddenly I noticed his face turn pale. Glancing at the sky
to the east I saw the reason. Coming straight toward Khartoum
was a great black wall that looked like a range of mountains
moving down upon us. It was the dread *huboob*, a terrific
African sand-storm. The dinner-party broke off abruptly, and
the other guests raced for their homes. Jumping on a donkey
which was awaiting me in the outer court, I made a dash for
the Charles Gordon Hotel, half a mile away.

It was a glorious moonlight night with stars twinkling
radiantly all around to the north, west and south, but straight
ahead to the east I could see that mountain wall of sand
churning toward me. It looked as though the crack o' doom
were approaching. Soon it was only a few hundred yards
away, and then it broke over us.

Flying sand stung my face like needles and blinded me.
Leaning forward over the neck of my diminutive mount I
tried to offer as little resistance to the storm as possible, but
it was all we could do to fight our way against that whirling
mass of sand and reach the hotel.

The heat indoors was so unbearable that everyone tried
sleeping with their windows open, and the sand threatened to
bury us, beds and all. When I closed the windows the
atmosphere was stifling, and the sand still swept in sheets
through the crevices. The storm raged for hours. There was
not a house in Khartoum that the sand did not penetrate. I
have been through cyclones, cloud-bursts, arctic blizzards,

fierce gales in the Southern Ocean, monsoons, typhoons, and
Sumatras, but none of them could hold a candle to that
huboob. In Alaska when a newcomer, or *cheechacko*,
remains in the Far North through the long dark winter he
becomes a "sourdough" and is admitted to the fraternity of
Arctic Pioneers. In the Sudan there is a similar saying that
he who survives a *huboob* forthwith becomes a *pucko* African.
But seventy below in the Yukon is preferable to one hundred
above in a Sudan *huboob*!

One afternoon a representative from the British Intelligence
Office took me a few miles distant from Khartoum to call on
"the holiest man in the Sudan." So rich had the natives grown
from the War that they were refusing to sell their grain
supplies, which were badly needed by the armies in Palestine
and Arabia. I had expressed a desire to meet this holy man,
and it occurred to the authorities that a visit from a foreigner
might flatter him, and put him in a sufficiently pleasant frame
of mind to enable them to wheedle him into selling his store
of grain, which would cause the other natives to follow suit.

We set out in the governor's gharry, a picturesque victoria
drawn by high-spirited white horses. Our driver was a wild-
eyed fuzzy-wuzzy with a mop of crinkly hair full of mutton
fat, with long wooden skewers sticking out at all angles. Off
we galloped across the desert to the village of Berri, where we
found Shereef Yusef el Hindi, the holy man, awaiting us at
the gate of his mud-brick palace. The shereef, a tall, thin-
faced, distinguished-looking Arab with hypnotic eyes, garbed
in sandals, a robe of green and white silk, and green turban,
ushered us into his garden, where we were invited to review
the most bewildering array of drinks that I had ever seen.
There were concoctions of everything from pomegranate juice
to sloe-gin, and from rose-water to a horse's neck. They were
of every shade from mauve to taupe. They were served in
every sort of container from cut-glass tumblers to silver goblets.
Fortunately custom only required us to take a sip of each,
otherwise the result would have been catastrophic, for many
were of subtle potency.

I remember that afternoon call as a series of surprises, of
which the first was the beauty of the garden inside the ugly
adobe outer walls of the Shereef's palace. The second was
the variety of fluid refreshment placed before us. Surely
Shereef Yusef el Hindi must have one of the genii from "The
Arabian Nights" mixing drinks in his palace. Even in pre-
prohibition days, when assigned to cover a national college
fraternity convention, never was I invited to pass through such

an ordeal by drink as I faced at Shereef Yusef el Hindi's oasis. The third surprise came when I saw the attractive interior of his palace as we passed through on our way to a Moorish balcony near the roof, where we were confronted with another relay of drinks. But the climax came when I discovered that my host instead of being an African witch-doctor was a savant of wide learning. His library even contained Arabic translations of the speeches of Mr. Lloyd George, Lord Balfour, Theodore Roosevelt and Woodrow Wilson. In fact I found that this Sudanese holy man knew more about the history of my own country than I did!

. . . .

We discussed religion, and I was impressed by his spirit of tolerance. "I believe, as do all Moslems who deserve to be called educated," said he, "that the fundamental principles underlying the world's greatest religions: Judaism, Christianity, Buddhism and Mohammedanism are the same; that there is but one God and that He is supreme; that we should be tolerant of the opinions of others; that all men should live together as brothers and do unto others as we would have others do unto us."

It was not difficult to understand why Shereef Yusef el Hindi was looked upon as a holy man by his ignorant, half-civilized fellow countrymen. His princely manners, his dignity and poise, his musical, bell-like voice, his large lustrous, hypnotic brown eyes, and his wisdom would have won him distinction in any country. He is not an Ethiopian, but is a descendant of the Arabian tribe of Koreish to which Mohammed belonged.

Being a holy man in the Sudan is a lucrative profession. Shereef Yusef el Hindi spends most of his time naming babies. When a child is born the father comes running to him, prostrates himself at the Shereef's feet, and says: "O Noble one, what name shall I bestow upon my child?"

Whereupon the holy man replies: "O faithful one, arise! Go thy way and return again upon the morrow."

Then, when the father returns the next day, the Shereef intones: "Allah be praised. In a vision last night the Prophet appeared and revealed to me that your faith should be rewarded and your child blessed with the name of his own daughter, Fatima. A guinea, please!"

From Khartoum we crossed the Nubian Desert to Port Sudan on the Red Sea. Here, as we had hoped, we found a tramp steamer bound for the Arabian coast. She was a much-torpedoed cargo-boat which had been transferred from the British Indian coastal service to the Mediterranean, where during the first years of the war she had survived several harrowing years, serving as a target for the Kaiser's U-boats. On board with us were 226 Sudanese sheep, 150 horses and mules from America and Australia, sixty-seven donkeys from Abyssinia, ninety-eight deserters from the Turkish army, eighty-two Egyptian fellaheen labourers, thirty-four Gordon Highlanders, six British officers, and two obsolete aeroplanes. Our crew consisted of Hindus, Javanese, Somalis, Berberines and Fuzzy-Wuzzies. The skipper of this modern ark was a rotund, jovial Scotsman by the name of Rose. I doubt whether Captain Kidd in the palmiest days of Caribbean piracy ever put to sea with such a motley cargo and crew.

The different nationalities on board segregated themselves into little racial colonies and did their own cooking in various parts of the main deck. It would be impossible to imagine what the good ship *Ozarda* looked like after we had been at sea for a few days—and what she smelled like ! Some of the Sudanese were from the Nubian Desert, where it is difficult enough to get water for drinking purposes, to say nothing of water for bathing; some of them had never had a real bath in their lives. But there was one of them whom the Highlanders nicknamed Bathing Bert. This man insisted on having his tub out of a bucket five times each day.

The Egyptian labourers entertained us incessantly with their fantastic ceremonial dances. There was not room enough for all of them to dance at a time, and so they went at it in relays. Some of them danced until they collapsed on the deck from exhaustion. Fainting, to them, was merely a sign that their spirits had been transported to heaven for a few minutes' sojourn with the Almighty.

There was no passenger accommodation, so that we had to sleep out on the deck with the donkeys and mules. I bunked beside a mouse-coloured mule from Hannibal, Missouri, the home of Mark Twain. She was very pessimistic. She seemed to be worrying about something back home and did not sleep well. Neither did I? Mark Twain would have lost his sense of humour if he had been in my place.

We had a British officer on board who was bound for the Persian Gulf. He was labouring under the erroneous impression that he had fallen heir to the mantle of George Robey or Harry Lauder. He used to tell a story until we were almost bored to extinction. I am going to repeat one of his tales, not because I think it is funny but because I know it is not funny! I want to show you the sort of thing we had to endure. He said that he was out hunting lions once in Central Africa; none of us doubted that, for he had knocked about all over the world from Kamschatka to the Kameroons. He said that one day a lion jumped at him out of the bush but that he ducked, just in time, causing the lion to go right over his head. Some minutes passed, and as the lion failed to return he crawled along on his stomach to reconnoitre. Coming to an open space he peered cautiously through the tall grass and there he saw that same lion—practising low jumps! One day we hit upon the idea of giving cigarettes to the Turkish deserters, who could understand only a few words of English, in order to get them to listen to his stories. They would laugh when he laughed and it satisfied him and certainly relieved the rest of us.

When we finally arrived at the ancient and long-deserted seaport of King Solomon at the head of the Gulf of Akaba, our ark anchored a half-a-mile offshore. We eventually pushed off, bound for the distant fringe of palm-trees at the base of King Solomon's Mountains on board a lighter loaded down with donkeys and mules. One unlucky donkey was kicked overboard by a nervous mule. Immediately two sharks appeared and attacked him fore and aft. One seized a front leg and the other the poor donkey's rump, and literally they pulled him in two. We were told by the skipper of our ark that there are more sharks in the Red Sea than in any other waters of the globe.

When we grounded on the coral beach we were greeted by several thousand Bedouins, who welcomed us by blazing into the air with their rifles and pistols. This firing had begun when we were still afar off, and Mr. Chase and I thought we were arriving in the midst of a battle. So fantastic and full of colour was that palm-fringed coral shore, and so picturesque were the Bedouins with their flowing beards, their gorgeous robes, their strange head-dress, and their array of ancient and modern weapons of every sort, that it all seemed like some bizarre Oriental pageant. So indeed it was, and these were some of Colonel Lawrence's modern Arabian knights.

King Solomon's long-forgotten port had been turned into a great base-camp, and enormous piles of supplies lay stacked on the sand and under the palms. Several of the British officers who were in charge of the receiving of supplies at Akaba took us to a nearby tent and slaked our growing thirst, and a few hours later Lawrence himself came down the Wadi

Ithm, returning from one of his mysterious expeditions into the blue.

With Lawrence, no two days in the desert were ever the same, so that it would be impossible to describe a typical one. But the camp routine at the headquarters of the Arabian army, when no *ghazu* (raid) was in progress, followed some such programme as this: At 5 A.M., as the first rays of dawn fell on the jagged peaks of Sinai, the army imam would climb the highest sand-dune and give the morning call to prayer. He was a chap with such astonishing vocal powers that his nasal chant woke every man and animal in Akaba. Immediately after he had finished calling the Arabian proletariat, Emir Feisal's private imam would softly intone the morning call at the door of his tent: "Praise be to Allah who makes day succeed the night!"

Miss Gertrude Bell, the famous Syrian traveller, who, although a woman, served on the Intelligence Staff in the Near East during the war, has written a vivid description of the glorious intoxication of a desert morning: "To wake in the desert dawn is like waking in the heart of an opal. To my mind the saying about the Bay of Naples should run differently. See the desert on a fine morning and die if you can." Surely a fascinating book of adventure and romance could be written about the war-time experience of Miss Bell in the Mesopotamian Desert. As a staff officer she did everything required of any man but wear a spine-pad and shorts.

A few minutes after the call to prayer had aroused the camp, a cup of sweetened coffee would turn up, brought in by one of Feisal's slaves. The Emir had five young Abyssinian blacks; slaves who were the acme of fidelity, because the Emir did not treat them as slaves, nor regard them as such. Whenever one of them desired money Feisal ordered him to help himself to whatever he needed from his bag of gold. No matter what was taken he never complained, and as a result, the thought of robbing never seemed to occur to them.

At 6 A.M. Lawrence was in the habit of breakfasting with Feisal in the Emir's tent, squatting Bedouin fashion on an old Baluchi prayer-rug. Breakfast on lucky days included a many-layered pastry of richly-spiced puffed bread called "Mecca" cakes, and cooked *durra*, a small round white seed —rather nasty stuff. Then, of course, there were the inevitable dates. After breakfast little glasses of sweetened tea were produced. From then until 8 A.M. Lawrence would discuss the possible events of the day either with the British officers or with some of the more prominent Arab leaders. At that time Feisal worked with his secretary or talked over private affairs in his tent with Lawrence. At 8 A.M. Feisal would hold court and grant audiences in the Diwan tent. According to the regular procedure, it was customary for the Emir to sit at the end of a great rug on a daïs. Callers or petitioners sat in front of the tent in a half-circle until they were called up. All questions were settled summarily and nothing was left over.

One morning I was in the tent with Lawrence when a young Bedouin was hauled in, charged with having the evil eye. Feisal was not present. Lawrence ordered the offender to sit at the opposite side of the tent and look at him. Then for ten minutes he regarded him with steady gaze, his steel-blue eyes seeming to bore a hole into the culprit's very soul. At the end of the ten minutes Lawrence dismissed the Bedouin. The evil spell had been driven off! By the Grace of Allah.

Another day a member of Lawrence's bodyguard came to him with the complaint that one of his companions possessed the evil eye. Said he, "O, sea of justice, yonder fellow looked at my camel, and straightway it went lame." Lawrence settled this difficulty by putting the man charged with the evil eye on the lame camel and giving the defendant's camel to the man who brought up the charge.

Blue eyes terrify the average Arab. Lawrence possesses two that are bluer than the waters of the Mediterranean, and so the Bedouin decided there was something superhuman about him. They themselves nearly all have eyes like black velvet.

Whenever Feisal was present, Lawrence would step aside and decline to decide disputes. He had no ambition to become the ruler of Arabia himself and he knew that it would be far better for the future of the Arabs and for Emir Feisal if their differences were handled in the usual way by one of their own people. In fact Lawrence never did anything himself that he could delegate to an Arab who was capable of handling it successfully.

Usually at 11.30 A.M. Feisal arose and walked back to his living tent, where a little lunch would be served. Lawrence in the meantime, would spend half-an-hour or so reading the inevitable Aristophanes, or a favourite English poet. He carried three books all through the campaign: "The Oxford Book of English Verse," Mallory's "Morte d'Arthur," and Aristophanes, which shows his catholic taste.

Lunch usually consisted of dishes such as stewed thorn-buds, lentils, unleavened bread cooked in the sand, and rice or honey cakes. I ate with a spoon, although the Arabs used their fingers, as did Lawrence. After lunch there followed a short delay of general talk, rounding off the conversation of the luncheon hour, and, in the meantime, black bitter coffee and sweetened tea would be served. In drinking tea and coffee the tribesmen would make as much noise as possible. It is the polite way of indicating that you are enjoying your drink. The Emir would then dictate letters to an Arab scribe, or enjoy a siesta, while Lawrence, absorbed in Wordsworth or Shelley, squatted on a prayer-rug in his own tent. If there were afternoon cases to be disposed of, Shereef Lawrence or Shereef Feisal would again hold court in the reception tent. From 5 until 6 P.M. Feisal would usually grant private audiences, and at such times Lawrence sat with him, since the discussion nearly always would have to do with the night's reconnaissance and future military operations.

Meanwhile, behind the servants' tent a fire would be started with a pile of thorns. Another sheep's throat would be cut, in the name of Allah the Merciful and Compassionate, and put on to roast. At 6 P.M. would come the evening meal, much like lunch, but with large fragments of mutton crowning the rice-heap, after which would follow intermittent cups of tea until bedtime, which for Lawrence was never any fixed hour. At night Lawrence would have many of his most important consultations with the Arab leaders, but occasionally Feisal would entertain his intimate associates with stories of his adventures in Syria and Turkey during the eighteen years when his family lived at the Sublime Porte under the wary eye of the Red Sultan.

The rest of us would often read well into the night. Before leaving Egypt I had picked up secondhand copies of the records of a few great Arabian travellers, such as Burkhardt, Burton, and Doughty. With the exception of Doughty's monumental masterpiece I found none of the books in my haphazard collection more fascinating than Miss Bell's "The Desert and the Sown." My interest in it was stimulated by the stories which Colonel Lawrence related to me of the wartime adventures of the brilliant authoress. This extraordinary Englishwoman had been wandering about remote corners of the Near East for a number of years prior to the war. She was a scholar and a scientist, not an idle traveller in quest of notoriety. With a lone Arab companion or two she had trekked for hundreds of miles along the fringe of the Great Arabian Desert, visiting the wild tribes and studying their language and customs. So vast was her knowledge that the heads of the British Intelligence Department in Mesopotamia asked her to accept a staff appointment and she played no small part in winning the friendship of some of the most blood-thirsty tribesmen residing in the Tigris and Euphrates Valleys. In her book, "The Desert and the Sown," Miss Bell throws much interesting light on the life of the desert-dwellers.

"The fortunes of the Arab are as varied as those of a gambler on the Stock Exchange. One day he is the richest man in the desert, and the next morning he may not have a single camel foal to his name. He lives in a state of war, and even if the surest pledges have been exchanged with the neighbouring tribes there is no certainty that a band of raiders from hundreds of miles away will not descend on his camp in the night, as a tribe unknown to Syria, the Beni Awajeh, fell, two years ago, on the lands south-east of Aleppo, crossing three hundred miles of desert, marduf (two on a camel) from their seat above Bagdad, carrying off all the cattle and killing scores of people. How many thousand years this state of things has lasted, those who shall read the earliest records of the inner desert will tell us, for it goes back to the first of them, but in all the centuries the Arab has bought no wisdom from experi-ence. He is never safe, and yet he behaves as though security were his daily bread. He pitches his feeble little camps, ten or fifteen tents together, over a wide stretch of undefended and indefensible country.

"He is too far from his fellows to call in their aid, too far as a rule to gather the horsemen together and follow after the raiders, whose retreat must be sufficiently slow, burdened with the captured flocks, to guarantee success to a swift pursuit. Having lost all his worldly goods, he goes about the desert and makes his plaint, and one man gives him a strip or two of goats' hair cloth, and another a coffee-pot, a third presents him with a camel, and a fourth with a few sheep, till he has a roof to cover him and enough animals to keep his family from hunger. There are good customs among the Arabs, as Namrud said. So he bides his time for months, perhaps for years, until at length opportunity ripens, and the horsemen of his tribe with their allies ride forth and recapture all the flocks that had been carried off and more besides, and the feud enters another phase. The truth is, that the *ghazu* (raid) is the only industry the desert knows and the only game.

"As an industry it seems to the commercial mind to be based on a false conception of the laws of supply and demand, but as a game there is much to be said for it. The spirit of adventure finds full scope in it—you can picture the excite-ment of the night ride across the plain, the rush of the mares in the attack, the glorious popping of rifles and the exhilaration of knowing yourself a fine fellow as you turn homewards with the spoil.   It is the best sort of fantasia, as they say in the desert, with a spice of danger behind it.   Not that the danger is alarmingly great: a considerable amount of amusement can be got without much bloodshed, and the raiding Arab is seldom bent on killing.   He never lifts his hand against women and children, and if here and there a man falls it is almost by accident, since who can be sure of the ultimate destination of a rifle-bullet once it is embarked on its lawless course?   This is the Arab view of the *ghazu*."

CHAPTER X

THE BATTLE OF SEIL EL HASA

As they pushed northward from the head of the Gulf of Akaba, the Hedjaz forces were joined by the Ibn Jazi Howeitat and the Beni Sakhr, two of the best fighting tribes of the whole Arabian Desert. About the same date the Juheinah, the Ateibah, and the Anazeh came riding in on their camels to join Feisal and Lawrence.

After the fall of Akaba, Lawrence had made several trips to Palestine to confer with Allenby. From that time the British in Palestine and King Hussein's army were in close co-operation.

The Arab army had been divided into two distinct parts, one known as regulars and the other as irregulars. The regulars were all infantrymen, there were not more than twenty thousand of them. They were either deserters from the Turkish army or men of Arab blood who had been fighting under the Sultan's flag and who had volunteered to join the forces of King Hussein after being taken prisoner by the British in Mesopotamia or in Palestine. At first they were used mainly for garrisoning old Turkish posts captured by the advancing Shereefian horde. Later on, after they had been thoroughly trained, they were used as storm troops in attacking fortified positions. The Arab regulars were under an Irishman, Colonel P. C. Joyce, who, next to Lawrence, perhaps played a more important part in the Arabian campaign than any other non-Moslem. The irregulars, who were by far the most numerous, were Bedouin, mounted on camels and horses. In all, Lawrence had now over two hundred thousand fighting men available.

The battle of Seil el Haha illustrates the manner in which he handled King Hussein's forces. A Turkish regiment, under the command of Hamid Fahkri Bey, composed of infantry, cavalry, mountain artillery, and machine-gun squads, was sent over the Hedjaz Railway from Kerak, south-east of the Dead Sea, to recapture the town of Tafileh, which had fallen into the hands of the Arabian army. The Turkish regiment had been hurriedly formed in the Hauran and Amman and was short of supplies.

When the Turks came in contact with the Bedouin patrols at Seil el Hasa, they drove them back into the town of Tafileh.

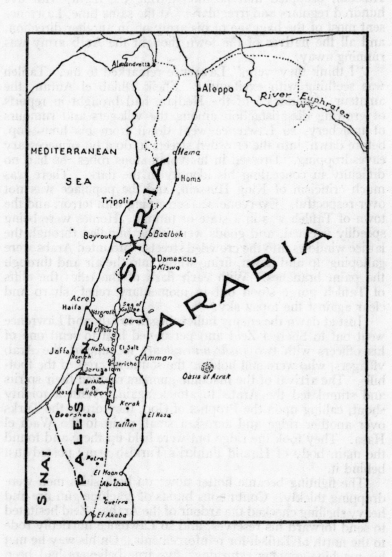

Lawrence and his Shereefian staff had laid out a defensive position on the south bank of the great valley in which Tafileh stands, and Shereef Zeid, youngest of the four sons of King Hussein, occupied that position during the night, with five hundred regulars and irregulars. At the same time, Lawrence sent most of the baggage of his army off in another direction, and all the natives of the town thought the Arab army was running away.

"I think they were," Lawrence remarked to me. Tafileh was seething with excitement. Sheik Dhiab el Auran, the amateur "Sherlock" of the Hedjaz, had brought in reports of growing dissatisfaction among the villagers and rumours of treachery, so Lawrence went down from his house-top, before dawn, into the crowded streets to do a bit of necessary eavesdropping. Dressed in his voluminous robes, he had no difficulty in concealing his identity in the dark. There was much criticism of King Hussein, and the populace was not over-respectful. Everyone was screaming with terror, and the town of Tafileh was in a state of tumult. Homes were being speedily vacated, and goods were being bundled through the lattice windows into the crowded streets. Mounted Arabs were galloping up and down, firing wildly into the air and through the palm branches. With each flash of the rifles the cliffs of Tafileh gorge stood out in momentary relief, sharp and clear against the topaz sky.

Just at dawn the enemy bullets began to fall, and Lawrence went out to Shereef Zeid and persuaded him to send one of his officers with two *fusils-mitrailleurs* to support the Arab villagers, who were still holding the southern crest of the foot-hills. The arrival of the machine-gunners revived their spirits and stimulated the Arabs to attack again. With a mighty shout, calling upon the Prophet of God, they drove the Turks over another ridge and across a small plain to the Wadi el Hasa. They took the ridge but were held up there and found the main body of Hamid Fahkri's Turkish army posted just behind it.

The fighting became hotter now; on both sides men were dropping thickly. Continuous bursts of machine-gun fire and heavy shelling checked the ardour of the Arabs. Zeid hesitated to send forward his reserves, and so Lawrence hurriedly rode to the north of Tafileh for reinforcements. On his way he met his machine-gunners returning; five true believers had been sent to Paradise, one gun had exploded, and they were out of ammunition. Lawrence sent back urgent messages to Zeid to rush forward a mountain-gun, more ammunition, and all other available machine-guns to one of his reserve positions at the southern end of the little plain between El Hasa and Tafileh Valley.

Then Lawrence galloped back to his front line on the ridge, where he found things in a precarious state. The ridge was being held by just thirty Ibn Jazi Howeitat mounted men and a handful of villagers. He could see the enemy working through the pass and along the eastern boundary to the ridge of the plain, where twenty Turkish machine-guns were concentrating their fire. An attempt was being made to flank the ridge which the Arabs were holding. The German officers directing the Turks were also correcting the fusing of the shrapnel, which had been grazing the top of the hill and bursting harmlessly over the desert plain. As Lawrence sat there, they began to spray the sides and top of the hill with steel splinters and with startling results, and he knew that the loss of the position was but a matter of minutes. A squadron of Albatross scouts came up and helped to minimize the chances of the Shereefian forces by bombing them from the air.

Lawrence gave his Motalga horsemen all the cartridges that he could collect, and the Arabs on foot ran back over the plain. He was among them. Since he had come straight up the cliffs from Tafileh, his animals had not caught up with him, the mounted men held out for fifteen minutes more and then galloped back unhurt. Lawrence collected his men in the reserve position on a ridge about sixty feet high, commanding an excellent view of the plain. It was now about noon. He had lost fifteen men and had only eighty left. But, a few minutes later, several hundred Ageyl and some of his other men, with a Hotchkiss automatic machine-gun, came up. Letfi el Assli, a Syrian, arrived with two more machine-guns, and Lawrence held his own until three o'clock, when Shereef Zeid came up with mountain artillery and more machine-guns and with fifty cavalrymen and two hundred Arabs on foot.

Meanwhile, the Turks had occupied his old front lines. Fortunately, Lawrence had their exact range. He had coolly paced it off while his followers were retreating pell-mell to their reserve position. He then rushed all his artillery to the top of the ridge and dispatched the cavalry to the right, to work up beyond the eastern boundary ridge. These mounted men were fortunate enough to get forward without being seen, until they had turned the Turkish flank at two thousand yards. There they made a dismounted attack, dancing forward with white puffs of smoke rippling from their rifles.

Meanwhile more than a hundred Arabs of the Aimi tribe, who had refused to fight the previous day because they were not satisfied with the amount of loot they were receiving, came up and joined Lawrence. There are few Bedouin who can resist the temptation to participate in a good fight when they see one coming on. He sent them to his left flank, and they crept down behind the western ridge of the plain to within two hundred yards of the Turkish Maxims. The ridge which the Turks occupied at that time was of a flint-like rock, so that entrenchment was impossible. The ricochets of the shells and shrapnel as they struck the flint boulders and glanced off were horrible, causing heavy losses among the enemy. Lawrence ordered the men on his left flank to fire an unusually heavy burst from their Hotchkiss and Vickers machine-guns at the Turks manning the Maxims. These were so accurate that they completely wiped the latter out. Then he ordered his cavalry to charge the retreating Turks from the right flank, while he also moved forward from the centre with his infantry and banners waving defiantly. Horse and man, the Turks collapsed and their attack crumpled. At the sun's decline Lawrence occupied the Turkish lines and chased the enemy back past their guns into the Hasa Valley. It was dark before his followers gave up the pursuit, exhausted from lack of sleep and food. "Allahu Akbar," cried the weary men as they fell upon their knees with their faces toward Mecca, giving praise to Allah for their victory. Lawrence had put to flight a whole Turkish regiment. Among the slain lay Hamid Fahkri.

IT WAS DOWN THE BARREN WADY ITHM THAT LAWRENCE AND HIS ARMY ADVANCED ON AKABA.

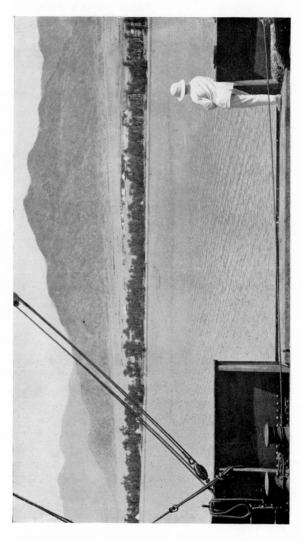

AT THE HEAD OF THE FAR-OFF GULF OF ALSABA

A coraline shore and a fringe of waving palms, with King Solomon's Mountains in the background.

CHAPTER XI

LAWRENCE THE TRAIN-WRECKER

FATE never played a stranger prank than when she transformed this shy young Oxford graduate from a studious archæologist into the leader of a hundred thrilling raids, creator of kings, commander of an army, and world's champion train-wrecker.

One day Lawrence's column was trekking along the Wadi Ithm. Behind him rode a thousand Bedouins mounted on the fleetest racing camels ever brought down the Negb. The Bedouins were improvising strange war-songs describing the deeds of the blond shereef whom General Storrs had introduced to me as "the uncrowned king of Arabia." Lawrence headed the column. He paid no attention to the song lauding him as a modern Abu Bekr. We were discussing the possibility of ancient Hittite civilization forming the connecting link between the civilizations of Babylon and Nineveh and ancient Crete. But his mind was on other things, and suddenly he broke off to remark:

"Do you know, one of the most thrilling sights I have ever seen is a train-load of Turkish soldiers ascending skyward after the explosion of a tulip!"

Three days later the column started off at night in the direction of the Pilgrim Railway. In support of Lawrence were two hundred Howeitat. After two days' hard riding across a country more barren than the mountains of the moon, and through valleys reminiscent of Death Valley, California, the raiding column reached a ridge of hills near the important Turkish railway centre and garrisoned town of Maan. At a signal from Lawrence all dismounted, left the camels, walked up to the summit of the nearest hill, and from between sandstone cliffs looked down across the railway track.

This was the same railway that had been built some years before to enable the Turkish Government to keep a closer hand on Arabia through transport of troops. It also simplified the problem of transportation for pilgrims to Medina and Mecca. Medina was garrisoned by an army of over twenty thousand Turks and was strongly fortified. Lawrence and his Arabs could have severed this line completely at any time, but they chose a shrewder policy. Train-load after train-load of supplies and ammunition must be sent down to Medina over that railway. So whenever Lawrence and his followers ran

G

out of food or ammunition they had a quaint little habit of slipping over, blowing up a train or two, looting it, and disappearing into the blue with everything that had been so thoughtfully sent down from Constantinople.

As a result of the experience he gained on these raids Lawrence's knowledge of the handling of high explosives was as extensive as his knowledge of archæology, and he took great pride in his unique ability as a devastator of railways. The Bedouins, on the other hand, were entirely ignorant of the use of dynamite; so Lawrence nearly always planted all of his own mines and took the Bedouins along merely for company and to help carry off the loot.

He had blown up so many trains that he was as familiar with the Turkish system of transportation and patrols as were the Turks themselves. In fact he had dynamited Turkish trains passing along the Hedjaz Railway with such regularity that in Damascus seats in the rear carriages sold for five and six times their normal value. Invariably there was a wild scramble for seats at the rear of a train; because Lawrence nearly always touched off his tulips, as he playfully called his mines, under the engine, with the result that the only carriages damaged were those in front.

There were two important reasons why Lawrence preferred not to instruct the Arabs in the use of high explosives. First of all, he was afraid that the Bedouins would keep on playfully blowing up trains even after the termination of the war. They looked upon it merely as an ideal form of sport, one that was both amusing and lucrative. Secondly, it was extremely dangerous to leave footmarks along the railway line, and he preferred not to delegate tulip planting to men who might be careless.

The column crouched behind great chunks of sand-stone for eight hours until a number of patrols had passed by. Lawrence satisfied himself that they were going at intervals of two hours. At midday, while the Turks were having their siesta, Lawrence slipped down to the railway line, and, walking a short distance on the sleepers with bare feet in order not to leave impressions on the ground which might be seen by the Turks, he picked out what he considered a proper spot for planting a charge. Whenever he merely wanted to derail the engine of a train he would use only a pound of blasting gelatin; when he wanted to blow it up he would use from forty to fifty pounds. On this occasion, in order that no one might be disappointed, he used slightly more than fifty pounds. It took him a little more than an hour to dig a hole between the sleepers, bury the explosive, and run a fine wire underneath the rail, over the embankment, and up the hillside.

Laying a mine is rather a long and tedious task. Lawrence first took off a top layer of railway ballast, which he placed in a bag that he carried under his cloak for that purpose. He next took out enough earth and rock to fill two five-gallon petrol tins. This he carried off to a distance of some fifty yards from the track and scattered along so that it would not be noticed by the Turkish patrols. After filling the cavity with his fifty-pound tulip-seed of dynamite, he put the surface layer of ballast back in place and levelled it off with his hand. As a last precaution he took a camel's-hair brush, swept the ground smooth, and then, in order not to leave a footprint, walked backward down the bank for twenty yards and with the brush carefully removed all trace of his tracks. He buried the wire for a distance of two hundred yards up the side of the hill and then calmly sat down under a bush, right out in the open, and waited as nonchalantly as though tending a flock of sheep. When the first trains came along the guards stationed on top of the cars and in front of the engine, with their rifles loaded, saw nothing more extraordinary than a lone Bedouin sitting on the hillside with the shepherd's staff in his hand.

Lawrence allowed the front wheels of the engine to pass over the mine, and then, as his column lay there half paralysed behind the boulders, he sent the current into the gelatine. It exploded with a roar like the falling of a six-story building. An enormous black cloud of smoke and dust went up. With a clanking and clattering of iron the engine rose from the track. It broke squarely in two. The boiler exploded, and chunks of iron and steel showered the country for a radius of three hundred yards. Numerous bits of boiler-plate missed Lawrence by inches.

Instead of provisions, this train carried some four hundred Turkish soldiers on their way to the relief of Medina. They swarmed out of the coaches and started in a menacing manner toward Lawrence. All this time the Bedouins, lining the tops of the hills, were popping at the Turks. Evidently one Turkish officer suspected that the lone Arab was the mysterious Englishman for whom rewards up to fifty thousand pounds had been offered. He shouted something, and the men, instead of shooting, ran toward Lawrence with the evident intention of taking him prisoner; but before they had advanced six paces Lawrence whipped out his long-barrelled Colt from the folds of his abba, and used it so effectively that they turned and fled.

He always carried a heavy American-frontier model weapon. Although very few persons ever actually saw him, it was well known among the British officers that he had spent many hours at target-practice, with the result that he had made himself an expert shot.

Many of the Turks dodged behind the embankment and began shooting through the carriage-wheels; but Lawrence, in anticipation of this, had posted two Lewis machine-guns just around a curve in the track, where they covered the opposite side of the railway embankment behind which the Turks had taken refuge. The gun crews opened fire, and before the Turks knew what had happened their line was raked from end to end and every man behind the embankment either killed or wounded. The rest of the Turks who had remained on the train fled panic-stricken in all directions.

The Arabs, who were crouching behind the rocks popping away with their rifles, charged down, tore open the carriages, and tossed out everything on board that was not nailed down. The loot consisted of sacks of Turkish silver coin and paper currency, and many beautiful Oriental draperies. The Bedouin raiders piled all the loot along the embankment, and with shouts of glee commenced dividing it among themselves, while Lawrence signed the duplicate way-bills and playfully returned one copy to a wounded Turkish guard whom he intended to leave behind. They were just like children around a Christmas tree. Occasionally two men would want the same silk Kermani rug and begin fighting over it. When that happened, Lawrence would step between them and turn the rug over to some third man.

Early in September, accompanied by two sheiks of the Ageilat Beni Atiyah from Mudowarrah, Lawrence left Akaba and trekked up to the multi-coloured sand-stone cliff country which the tribesmen called "Rum." In less than a week he had been joined by a force of 116 Toweiha, Zuwida, Darausha, Dhumaniyah, Togatga, Zelebani and Howeitat.

The appointed rendezvous was a small railway bridge near Kilo 587 south of Damascus. Here Lawrence buried his usual bit of tulip seed between the rails, and stationed Stokes and Lewis guns at vantage-points three hundred yards or so distant. The following afternoon a Turk patrol spotted them. An hour later a party of forty mounted Turks put out from the fort at Haret Ammar to attack the mine-laying party from the south. Another party of over a hundred set forth to out-flank Lawrence from the north, but he decided to take a chance and hold his ground.

A little later a train with two engines and two box-cars moved slowly up from Haret Ammar, machine-guns and rifles spitting lead from the roofs and from loopholes in the cars as the train advanced. As it passed, Lawrence touched his electric switch and exploded a mine directly under the second engine. The jar was sufficient to derail the first, demolish the boiler, as well as smash the cab and tender of the second, up-end the first box-car, and derail the second. While the Arabs swarmed around looting the wrecked train, Lawrence fired a box of gun-cotton under the front engine, completing its destruction. The box-cars were full of valuable baggage, and the Arabs went wild with joy. In all, seventy Turks were killed, ninety taken prisoner, and an Austrian lieutenant and thirteen Austrian and German sergeants blown up.

Every fourth or fifth man of the famous fighting Howeitat tribe is a sheik. Naturally the head sheik has but little power. Frequently these men would accompany Lawrence on a raid. On one such expedition to the railway near Biresh-Shediyah he had to adjudicate for them in twelve cases of assault with weapons, four camel thefts, one marriage settlement, fourteen feuds, a bewitchment, and two cases of evil eye. He settled the bewitchment affair by counter-bewitching the hapless defendant. The evil eye cases he cleverly adjusted by sending the culprits away.

On still another occasion, during the first week of the following October, Lawrence was sitting out in the open near Kilo 500. His Bedouin followers were concealed behind him in the broom-brush. Along came a heavy train with twelve coaches. The explosion following the turning on of the electric current shattered the fire-box of the locomotive, burst many of the tubes, hurled the cylinders into the air, completely cleaned out the cab, including the engineer and fireman, warped the frame of the engine, bent the two rear driving-wheels, and broke their axles. When Lawrence put in his official report on this raid he humorously added a postscript to the effect that the locomotive was "beyond repair." The tender and first coach were also demolished. Mazmi Bey, a general of the Turkish General Staff, who happened to be on board, fired two shots out of the window of his private car with his Mauser pistol, which then evidently jammed. Although it appeared advisable for him to take to the camels and the distant hills, Lawrence and his band swooped down on the train, captured eight coaches, killed twenty Turks, and carried off seventy tons of foodstuffs without suffering any losses.

His only European companion on some of his wildest train-blowing parties was a daring Australian machine-gunner, Sergeant Yells by name. He was a glutton for excitement and a tiger in a fight. On one occasion, when out with a raiding-party of Abu Tayi, Yells accounted for between thirty and forty Turks with his Lewis gun. When the loot was divided among the Bedouins, Yells, in true Australian fashion, insisted on having his share. So Lawrence handed him a Persian carpet and a fancy Turkish cavalry sword.

Shereefs Ali and Abdullah also played an important part in the raids on the Hedjaz Railway and in the capture of great convoys of Turkish camels near Medina. In 1917 Lawrence and his associates, in co-operation with Feisal, Ali, Abdullah and Zeid, blew up twenty-five Turkish trains, tore up fifteen thousand rails and destroyed fifty-seven bridges and culverts. During the eighteen months that he led the Arabs, they dynamited seventy-nine trains and bridges! It is a remarkable fact that he participated in only one such expedition that turned out unsatisfactorily. General Allenby, in one of his reports, said that Colonel Lawrence had made train-wrecking the national sport of Arabia!

Later in the campaign, near Deraa, the most important railway junction south of Damascus, Lawrence touched off one of his tulips under the driving-wheels of a particularly long and heavily-armed train. It turned out that Djemal Pasha, the commander-in-chief of the Turkish armies, was on board with nearly a thousand troops. Djemal hopped out of his saloon and, followed by all his staff, jumped into a ditch.

Lawrence had less than sixty Bedouins with him, but all were members of his personal bodyguard and famous fighters. In spite of the overwhelming odds, the young Englishman and his Arabs fought a pitched battle in which 125 Turks were killed and Lawrence lost a third of his own force. The remainder of the Turks finally rallied around their commander-in-chief, and Lawrence and his Arabs had to show their heels.

At every station along the Hedjaz-Pilgrim Railway were one or two bells which the Turkish officials rang as a warning to passengers when the train was ready to start. Nearly all of them now decorate the homes of Lawrence's friends. Along with them are a dozen or more Turkish mile-posts and the number-plates from half the engines which formerly hauled trains over the line from Damascus to Medina. Lawrence and his associates collected these in order to confirm their victories. While in Arabia, I often heard the half-jocular, half-serious remark that Lawrence would capture a Turkish post merely for the sake of adding another bell to his collection; and it was no uncommon thing to see Lawrence, or one of his officers, walking stealthily along the railway embankment, between patrols, searching for the iron post marking Kilo 1,000 south of Damascus. Once found, they would cut it off with a tulip-bud, a stick of dynamite. When not engaged in a major movement against the Turks or in mobilizing the Bedouins, Lawrence usually spent his time blowing up trains and demolishing tracks.

So famous did this young archæologist become throughout the Near East as a dynamiter of bridges and trains that after the final defeat of the Turkish armies, when word reached Cairo that Lawrence would soon be passing through Egypt en route to Paris, General Watson, G.O.C. of troops, jocularly announced that he was going to detail a special detachment to guard Kasr el Nil, the Brooklyn Bridge of Egypt, which crosses the Nile from Cairo to the residential suburb of Gazireh.

It had been rumoured that Lawrence was dissatisfied at having finished up the campaign with the odd number of seventy-nine mine-laying parties to his credit. So the story spread up and down along the route of The Milk-and-Honey Railway between Egypt and Palestine that he proposed to make it an even eighty, and wind up his career as a dynamiter in an appropriate manner by planting a few farewell tulips under the Kasr el Nil, just outside the door of the British military headquarters.

CHAPTER XII

DRINKERS OF THE MILK OF WAR

WHILE Lawrence was travelling from sheik to sheik and from shereef to shereef, urging them, with the eloquence of all the desert dialects at his command, to join in the campaign against the Turks, squadrons of German aeroplanes were swarming down from Constantinople in a winged attempt to frighten the Arabian army with their strange devil-birds. But the Arabs refused to be intimidated. Instead, they insisted that their resourceful British leader should get them some "fighting swallows" too.

Not long after a particularly obnoxious German air-raid over Akaba a royal courier galloped up to Lawrence's tent on his racing dromedary. Without even waiting for his mount to kneel, he slid off the camel's hump and delivered a scroll on which was inscribed the following:

"O faithful one! Thy Government hath aeroplanes as the locusts. By the Grace of Allah I implore thee to ask thy King to despatch us a dozen or so.

"(*Signed*) HUSSEIN."

The people of Arabia are exceedingly ornate and poetical in expressing themselves. They swear by the splendour of light and the silence of night, and love to talk in imagery as rich as the colours in their Turkoman prayer-rugs.

An American typewriting concern startled some people by advertising that more people use the Arabic alphabet than use either Roman or Chinese characters. They are very proud of their language, and call it the language of the angels; they believe it is spoken in heaven. It is one of the most difficult languages in the world to master. According to our way of thinking the Arabs begin at the end of a sentence and write backwards. They have 450 words meaning "line," 822 words meaning "camel," and 1,037 words meaning "sword." Their language is full of colour. They call a hobo "a son of the road," and a jackal "a son of howling." Arab despatch writers penned their accounts in picturesque vein. "The fighting was worth seeing," wrote Emir Abdullah to Colonel Lawrence. "The armed locomotives were escaping with the coaches of the train like a serpent beaten on the head."

Inspired by a squadron of antiquated bombing and reconnaissance planes which Lawrence had brought down from Egypt, the Arabs won an important victory over the Turks in the desert just south of the Dead Sea. Thereupon the commander of the Arabian army sent this message to King George:

"To His Majesty the King of England. Our victorious troops have captured one of the enemy's divisions near Tafileh. The truth follows by post.—FEISAL."

Another Arab chieftain in writing an account of an engagement said:

"I sallied forth with my people, drinkers of the milk of war. The enemy advanced to meet us, but Allah was not with them."

During the war the British Government ran telephone and telegraph wires from Jeddah on the Red Sea to the king's palace in the Forbidden City. The lines were strung by Mohammedans from Egypt, not by Christians. In spite of his abhorrence of all modern inventions, the king permitted the installation merely because he realized the urgent importance of being able to keep in touch with his Allies. As he insisted on living in the Forbidden City, the telephone and telegraph were a military necessity. There are about twenty branch 'phones on this official telephone system. One day a British general telephoned to His Majesty from Jeddah to discuss some urgent military and political question with him. In the middle of the conversation the king overheard other voices on the line and shouted angrily down the wire to the exchange: "I command thee to cut off every telephone in the Hedjaz for one hour! It is I, the king, who speaks." And so it came to pass that the entire Arabian telephone system was tied up by a royal command. If you ever happen to be in Arabia and want to telephone to the King of the Hedjaz, just call up "Mecca Number One."

Shortly after the capture of Jeddah, Lawrence, in company with Colonel C. E. Wilson, the governor of Port Sudan, Mr. Ronald Storrs and Emir Abdullah, for their amusement, made the Turkish band, which they had captured a few days before, play: "Deutschland, Deutschland Über Alles," "The Hymn of Hate," and other German songs. The king happened to ring up in the middle of the concert. Hearing the medley of discord, he requested that the receiver be left down, and for half-an-hour he sat in his palace in Mecca chuckling with glee while the band did its worst.

The British aviators who came down to Arabia not only had to wear Arab head-dress, but they had to fly at a considerable height to avoid being shot at by the Bedouins, who have an irresistible desire to shoot anything that is moving fast. They peppered an armoured car on one occasion and then sent around profuse apologies. They admitted they knew it was a friendly machine, but said it was going so fast they simply could not resist the temptation to see if they could hit it.

Colonel Lawrence and his associates introduced the first motor-cars into Holy Arabia, and Emir Feisal used a one-ton truck as his royal limousine. I went with him on one of his journeys from Akaba to the front line outposts at Waheida in the desert, north of the Turkish stronghold at Maan on the Hedjaz railway. We camped for the day on the summit of a high hill amid the ruins of an old Turkish fortress. That noon Feisal gave a dinner in our honour. We sat around on empty boxes instead of squatting on the ground Arab fashion, and a table was improvised for our special benefit. The others present were General Nuri Pasha, Malud Bey, and old Auda Abu Tayi. Before the meal they served us with cups of sweetened tea. Then for dinner a great plate of rice crowned with chunks of lamb and goat was placed in the centre of the table. Besides this there was another dish of rice mixed with pieces of meat. Beans with tomato sauce, lentils and peas, pomegranates, dried dates and figs, and a sort of candy made from sesame seed and sugar, resembling raw asbestos, heaped the groaning banquet board. For dessert we were to have had a tin of California pears; they had been sent down from Egypt as a gift for the Emir.

Old Auda Abu Tayi had never seen such delicious-looking pears in his life, and the temptation to sample them so sorely tried his patience that he was unable to await the end of the meal. Disregarding the food before him, and throwing formality to the winds, he attacked them at once and devoured all of them before the rest of us were through with the first course ! At the end of the meal small cups of coffee flavoured with cardamom, an Indian seed with a minty taste, were served to us, and a bowl of water was solemnly passed around in order that we might remove remnants of gravy still lingering in our beards. Then the Emir's Abyssinian slaves brought cigarettes, and we strolled out with our field-glasses to watch the battle in progress a few miles distant in the hollow of the land around Maan.

Both before and after lunch scores of Arabs filed into the

tent to kiss Feisal's hand. He never allowed them to touch it with their lips, but pulled it away just before they had an opportunity to kiss it, to show them how reluctant he was to be treated with special deference.

Both Feisal and Lawrence owed much of their authoritative leadership to their recognition of the traditional independence of the tribes. The gallant old brigands who had roamed freely all their lives over the vast stretches of Arabia, making little private wars of the own, were not to be commanded or conscripted; they had to be gently cajoled into the bigger war and made to feel the sense of their own importance.

CHAPTER XIII

AUDA ABU TAYI, THE BEDOUIN ROBIN HOOD

"BY the grace of Allah, I, Auda Abu Tayi, warn you to quit Arabia before the end of Ramadan. We Arabs want this country for ourselves. Unless this is done, by the beard of the Prophet, I declare you proscribed, outlawed, and fair game for anyone to kill."

This was the official and personal declaration of war issued by Auda Abu Tayi, the Howeitat chieftain, the greatest popular hero of modern Arabian history, the most celebrated fighting-man the desert has produced in four generations. The proclamation was addressed to the Sultan of Turkey, to Djemal Pasha, the viceroy of Syria, Palestine, and Arabia, and to the Mutesarif of Kerak, who was the Ottoman governor of the important district on the edge of the desert near the southern end of the Dead Sea where Auda lived. The Arabian revolution appealed to the Bedouin Robin Hood, largely because it furnished him with an ideal excuse to declare personal war against the Turkish Government.

When Auda heard that Shereef Hussein had started a revolt against the Turks, he and his fearless Howeitat followers jumped into their saddles, galloped across the desert sands to Feisal's headquarters and swore on the Koran that they would make the Shereef's enemies their enemies. Then they all sat down to a banquet in honour of the occasion. Suddenly old Auda uttered a potent Moslem oath and reminded himself and his friends that he was wearing a set of Turkish false teeth. Cursing the Turkish dentist who had made them, he dashed out of the tent and smashed them on a rock. For two months he was in agony and could eat only milk and boiled rice. When Lawrence came down from Egypt, Auda's mouth was giving him so much trouble that he had to send to Cairo for a British dentist to make the old brigand a special set of Allied teeth!

His undying loyalty and friendship proved a most valuable asset to Hussein and the Allies in the Arabian campaign. Besides, he offered his rich and rare experience in the kind of warfare suitable to his country. With the exception of Lawrence, he has been the greatest raider of modern Arabia. During the last seventeen years he has killed seventy-five men in hand-to hand combat; all of them Arabs, for he does not include Turks in his game-book. I do not think that his claim is far wrong, for he has been wounded twenty-two times, and in his battles has seen all his tribesmen hurt and most of his relatives killed. His right arm is so stiff that he can't scratch himself, and has to use a camel-stick. Although the Howeitat territory is situated inland near the Gulf of Akaba, Auda has led expeditions six hundred miles south to Mecca, north as far as Aleppo, and a thousand miles east to Bagdad and Basra. Occasionally the tables are turned on him. One year, while he was leading an expedition against Ibn Saud, the ruler of Central Arabia, the Druses came down from Jebel Hauran, in the hills south of Damascus, and spirited away all his camels. Auda took his loss calmly and philosophically, but word of his misfortune reached the ears of his friend, Nuri Shalaan, Emir of Jauf and ruler of North Central Arabia. In accordance with one of the unwritten laws of the desert, Nuri Shalaan immediately sent Auda half of all his possessions.

Old Auda prides himself on being the quintessence of Arabian tradition. A hundred successful raids have taken him from his home near the Dead Sea to all parts of the Arabian world. His loot he dispenses in staggering hospitality. He talks long, loud, and abundantly in a voice like a mountain-torrent.

Although Auda has probably captured more loot on his raids than any other Bedouin chieftain, he is a comparatively poor man, as the result of his lavish hospitality. The profits of a hundred successful raids have provided entertainment for his friends. One of his few remaining evidences of transitory wealth is an enormous copper kettle around which twenty-five people can gather at a meal. His hospitality is sometimes very inconvenient except to guests in the last stages of starvation. One day, when he was helping me to a heaped portion of rice and mutton from the copper kettle, I was discussing the subject of camels with him, and mentioned the fact that we had none in my country except in the Zoos. The old Bedouin couldn't understand this and insisted on presenting me with twenty of his prize dromedaries to take back to America to start a camel industry. It required all Lawrence's persuasive eloquence to convince him that it was impossible for me to accept the regal gift owing to the difficulty of transporting his camels half-way round the world.

In May, 1918, the Turks sent a large number of camels down from Syria. They put them into an impromptu corral at Maan railway station. Auda heard of this, and at the head of a small party of twelve of his tribesmen he dashed boldly into Maan. There were thousands of Turkish soldiers all around, but before they realized what had occurred Auda had rounded up twenty-five of the camels and had driven them off at a twenty-five-mile-an-hour gallop. He was full of such pranks as this and recounted his adventures afterward with great gusto.

One of the most amazing bits of brigandage in Auda's long and lurid career was when he held up his intimate friend and prince. Feisal was on his way across the desert on an expedition and had four thousand pounds in gold coin. Unluckily his route lay through Auda's country, and somehow the latter got to know about the treasure. So he insisted that Feisal and retinue remain as his guests until they had given the old pirate three thousand out of the four thousand sovereigns. Auda, of course, did not use force; he merely intimated that he was entitled to the gold !

Auda Abu Tayi is a handsome old chieftain, a pure desert type. He is tall, straight and powerful, and, although sixty years of age, as active and sinewy as a cougar. His lined and haggard face is pure Bedouin. He has a broad, low forehead, high, sharp, hooked nose, greenish-brown eyes inclined to slant outward, black pointed beard, and moustache tinged with grey. The name "Auda" means "Father of Flying," which recalls the day on which he made his first aeroplane flight. Instead of showing any fear he urged the pilot, Captain Furness-Williams, to take him higher and higher.

The old hero is as hard-headed as he is hot-headed. He receives advice, criticism, or abuse with a smile as constant as it is charming, but nothing on earth would make him change his mind or obey an order or follow a course of which he disapproves. He is modest, simple as a child, honest, kind-hearted and affectionate, and warmly loved even by those to whom he is most trying—his friends. His hobby is to concoct fantastic tales about himself and to relate fictitious but humorously horrible stories concerning the private life of his host or guests. He takes wild delight in making his friends uncomfortable. One time he strolled into the tent of his cousin, Mohammed, and roared out for the benefit of all present how villainously his kinsman had behaved at El Wejh. He told how Mohammed had bought a beautiful necklace for one of his wives. But, alas, Mohammed met a strange woman, a very beautiful strange woman, in El Wejh who was as fascinating as starlight, and, succumbing to her charms, he presented her with the necklace. It was a wonderful necklace with gems that sparkled as the stars, with blues that recalled the seas, and reds of desert sunsets. Most eloquently Auda embroidered on the lady's charms. On the other side of the partition the women of Mohammed's household heard of their lord and master's perfidy. Although the tale was mischievously fabricated, there was a great commotion in the household of Mohammed and his life was made unbearable for several weeks.

Auda's home is on a mud-flat eighty miles east of Akaba. During his association with Lawrence in the Arabian campaign, he picked up many interesting details of life in Europe. His eyes sparkled at tales of hotels and cabarets and palaces, and he was suddenly fired with the determination to abandon his tent for a house as splendid as any Sidi Lawrence had known in London.

The first problem that confronted him was the question of labour. This was solved by raiding a Turkish garrison and taking fifty prisoners, whom he put to work digging wells. After they had finished that job, he promised them their liberty if they would build him a beautiful house. They constructed one with forty rooms and four towers, but on account of the scarcity of timber in the desert no one could figure out how to roof such an enormous building. Auda, keen as a steel trap, immediately worked out a plan. Summoning his warriors, he started out across the sands to the Pilgrim's railway, overpowered the passing Turkish patrol, and carried off thirty telegraph-poles, which now form the framework of his desert palace.

Even a forty-room palace is none too large for Auda, who has not been strictly abstemious in his nuptial aspirations. In fact he is noted throughout Arabia for his reckless polygamy. Every Mohammedan is permitted to have four wives at one time—if he can support them. Old Auda has been married twenty-eight times, and is ambitious to raise that record to fifty before he dies. But in spite of his numerous marriages he has only one son living. All the others have been killed in raids and feuds. Young Mohammed Abu Tayi was eleven years old when I saw him, but so undersized that his father could pick him up by the scruff of the neck and swing him into the saddle on his camel with one hand. When the caravan was on the march at night, his father, afraid that Mohammed when asleep would fall off the camel, often picked him up and stuffed him into one of his own saddle-bags, where the boy would spend the night. The youngster fought beside his father and Colonel Lawrence through the whole Arabian campaign.

Auda's enthusiasm in making the Turks his enemies to the Nth power, pouring into the cause all the hatred he had reserved for personal feuds, brought many of the tribes to Lawrence's personal standard. Lawrence once remarked that Auda was somewhat like Cæsar in his ability to keep around him a free country of faithful friends, and around that a great ring of enemies. Even the renowned Nuri Shalaan, as well as many other powerful chiefs friendly to Auda, were in constant terror lest they should offend him.

The Howeitat tribe was formerly under the control of Ibn Rashid and his tribe, which long roamed the North Arabian Desert. Later, under the leadership of Ibn Jazi, the tribe broke up into discordant sections. The Abu Tayi subsection is the joint work of Auda, the fighting man, and Mohammed el Dheilan, the thinker. Ibn Jazi mistreated a Sherari guest of Auda's, and the proud and hospitable chief was infuriated. In the fifteen-year feud that followed, Annad, Auda's eldest son and the pride of his heart, was killed. This feud between the two sections of the Howeitat was one of Feisal's greatest difficulties in the operations around Akaba and Maan. It drove Hamed el Arar, the Ibn Jazi leader of to-day, into the arms of the Turks, while Saheiman Abu Tayi and the rest of the subtribe went to El Wejh to join Lawrence and Feisal. Auda made peace with his sworn enemies at the request of Feisal, and it was the hardest thing the old man ever had to do in his life. The death of Annad had killed his hopes and ambitions for the Abu Tayi and had made his life seem a bitter failure. But Feisal ruled that his followers were to have no more blood-feuds and no Arab enemies except the adherents of Ibn Rashid in North Arabia, who have carried on perpetual and bitter warfare with all the other tribes of the desert. Feisal's success in burying the innumerable hatchets of the Hedjaz is pregnant with promise. In all Arab minds a shereef now stands above tribes, men, sheiks and tribal jealousies. A shereef now exercises the prestige of peacemaker and independent authority.

THE NARROW GORGE WHICH IS THE ONLY ENTRANCE TO THE
LOST CITY

FIELD-MARSHAL VISCOUNT ALLENBY,
UNDER WHOSE ORDERS LAWRENCE
WAGED HIS DESERT WAR

CHAPTER XIV

KNIGHTS OF THE BLACK TENTS

AFTER Auda, Mohammed el Dheilan is the chief figure of the
Abu Tayi. He is taller than his cousin and massively built; a
square-headed, thoughtful man of forty-five, with a melancholy humour and a kind heart carefully concealed beneath
it. He acts as master of ceremonies for the Abu Tayi, is
Auda's right hand man, and frequently appears as his spokes-
man. Mohammed is greedy, richer than Auda, deeper and
more calculating. Allah has endowed him with the eloquence
of an Arabian Demosthenes; his tribesmen address him as
"Father of Eloquence." In a tribal council he can always
be relied upon to persuade his audience to accept his views.
He can wield a sword right lustily too, and is "a drinker of the
milk of war" second only in prowess to the mighty Auda.

Zaal Ibn Motlog is Auda's nephew. He is twenty-five,
something of a dandy, with polished teeth, carefully curled
moustache, and a trimmed and pointed beard. He, too, is
greedy and sharp-witted, but without Mohammed's mentality.
Auda has been training him for years as chief scout to the
tribe, so that he is a most daring and acceptable commander in
a *ghazu*.

Nuri Shalaan, Emir of Jauf, is not such a picturesque
character as his friend and kinsman, Auda Abu Tayi, but as
ruler of the Rualla Anazeh tribes, two hundred thousand
strong, the largest single tribe in the desert, occupying nearly
all the territory between Damascus and Bagdad, he is one of
the great men of Arabia. His friendship was most vital to
Hussein and Lawrence in the taking of Deraa and Damascus,
and might have been of tremendous weight to Feisal now that
he has been placed on the throne of Mesopotamia had he not
sold himself to the French in Syria in 1919, after the War.
Lawrence would not let Nuri declare war on the Turks until
the last minute, because Nuri's allegiance would have meant
too many mouths to feed. Nuri Shalaan was the deadly
enemy of Ibn Rashid, who co-operated with the Turks, but
who since the Great War has lost his portion of Arabia to
Sultan Ibn Saud of Nejd.

At one time Nuri Shalaan wanted an armourer. He
captured Ibn Bani of Hail, Ibn Rashid's armourer, the most
skilled man of his craft in Arabia, and put him in prison with

H

his own smith, Ibn Zarih. He gave them both forges and tools and declared that they should languish in prison until Ibn Zarih could make swords and daggers that could not be distinguished from those of Ibn Bani. They sweated and worked and the forges were kept burning until late every night, and finally, after many weeks, Ibn Zarih produced a wonderful dagger with an edge that could almost cut the wind. Nuri was satisfied, he released his two prisoners, and sent Ibn Bani back to his country with rich presents.

Nuri Shalaan was an old man of seventy when the Arab revolution broke out. He was always ambitious, and determined to be a leader. Thirty years ago he killed his two brothers and made himself chief of the tribe. He ruled his people with a rod of iron, and they were practically the only Bedouins who obeyed orders. If they failed him he had their heads cut off; but in spite of his cruelty his followers all admire and are proud of him. Most Arab sheiks talk like magpies, but Nuri remains silent in the tribal council and settles everything with a few final clean-cut words of decision. Until the end of the war he had preferred tent life to that of all the palaces from Bagdad to the Bosphorus, and kept great state in the largest black goat's-hair tent in the desert, where sheep were slaughtered every few minutes for the endless stream of guests. He owned the best wheat land in Syria and the finest camels and horses. He is so rich he does not know how to measure his wealth.

Motlog Ibn Jemiaan, sheik of the Beni Atiyeh, south of Maan, added four thousand fighting men to King Hussein's forces. He is hard-working and brave as a lion. He helped Lawrence blow up trains near Maan, and was in the thick of the fray whenever there were railway stations to be captured or any other little jobs of a particularly dangerous nature. During the scouting around Maan, two of Lawrence's officers were trying to find an ancient Roman road in the desert. Motlog, always eager for adventure, went with them. In the deep sand their Ford careered madly from left to right, and then at one point swerved so sharply that Motlog was thrown on his head. The officers jumped out of the car and ran back to pick him up and apologize to him, thinking he would be very angry. But the old sheik brushed off the sand and said ruefully: "Please don't be offended with me, I have not learnt to ride one of these things yet." He regarded riding in a motorcar as an art that had to be mastered just like riding a camel.

The Robber Harith Clan may not have been in the good graces of Hussein before the War, but their shereef, Ali Ibn

Hussein, a youth of nineteen, was responsible for converting nearly the whole of the Hauran to the revolt. He was the most reckless, most impertinent, and jolliest fellow in the Arabian army. The fastest runner in the desert, he could catch up with a camel with bare feet and swing into the saddle with one hand while holding his rifle with the other. When Ali went into battle he took off all his clothing except his drawers. He said it was the cleanest way to get wounded. He had a wild sense of humour, and made jokes about the king in his presence. He was one of the two shereefs in the Hedjaz who did not stand in terror of King Hussein. The other was Shereef Shakr, a cousin of Feisal, and the richest man in the Hedjaz. He was the only big shereef who plaited his hair, and, in addition, he encouraged lice in it, to show his respect for the old Bedouin proverb: "A well-populated head is a sign of a generous mind." His home was in Mecca, but he spent most of his time in the saddle with the Bedouin tribesmen.

These are a few of the leading chieftains, in some of whom enthusiasm for Arabian nationalism had to be kindled, others cajoled by appeals to their vanity, and almost all inflamed with the zest for war on a big scale—the game they had known and played at from childhood. When they had once sworn allegiance they were as true as steel. Without their loyalty and dauntless courage and epic love of blood-curdling adventure the Arabian campaign would have been a dream on paper fabricated by an impractical young archæologist.

In his dealings with Auda and other Arab chiefs, Lawrence found their rich sense of humour an important asset. Make an Arab laugh and you can persuade him to do most things. Arabic is a solemn language, full of ceremony and stateliness; and the young British archæologist, who had an unusual knowledge of the various dialects spoken in Arabia, made the discovery that the direct translation into Arabic of ordinary colloquial English spiced with wit delighted his hearers. Another highly-useful weapon in Colonel Lawrence's mental armoury was the faculty of mastering the unexpected with some inspired improvisation. Time and again he happened upon a desperate situation from which there was no obvious means of escape. In the space of a few seconds his alert brain would work out some seemingly fantastic but really brilliant method of dealing with the emergency.

Such an instance was one of his many adventures in the Syrian desert. He was at the town of Azrak, among the shifting sand-dunes south-east of Damascus, when a courier brought news that some Turkish spies were in a caravan of Syrian merchants which was on its way to the Arabian army supply base at Akaba, 300 miles to the south. He immediately decided that in order to draw the teeth of the spies he must reach Akaba either in company with the caravan or soon after its arrival. Normally the journey from Azrak to Akaba is twelve days by camel, and already the Syrian caravan had a start of nine days.

Realizing that his followers could not stand the forced pace at which he meant to travel, Lawrence took with him but one man—a half-breed Haurani—who was famous in the North Arabian desert for his endurance. The pair were racing over the ridges between Azrak and Bair, eighty miles south of the camp from which they started, when suddenly a dozen Arabs appeared over the edge of a sand-dune and galloped their camels down the slope to cut off the strangers. As they approached the Arabs shouted a request that Lawrence and his companion should dismount and at the same time announced themselves as friends and members of the Jazi Howeitat tribe. When only thirty yards away they themselves dismounted by way of encouraging the lone couple to do likewise. But Lawrence had recognized the Arabs as of the Beni-Sakr, allies of the Turks and blood enemies of most of the Bedouin tribes that were fighting for King Hussein and Emir Feisal. It was known to the Beni-Sakr that gold passed up and down the caravan route and they were out looking for loot.

This particular sector was the only war-time trade route between Syria and Arabia along which the merchants of Syria had for many months journeyed to Akaba for the purchase of Manchester cotton. Lawrence used cotton both as an aid to propaganda and as a means of getting as much gold as possible from Syria and Turkey. The Ottoman Empire needed cotton urgently, and for this reason the military authorities allowed traders to pass back and forth through the lines. When they reached Akaba, Lawrence and the Arab leaders would make converts among them by preaching Arab nationalistic doctrines. At the same time they would collect much valuable information regarding conditions in Turkey. The merchants were also useful in smuggling down to Akaba German field-glasses which Lawrence needed for the equipment of his desert troops.

Meanwhile, the dismounted marauders of the Beni-Sakr stood on the sand and fingered their rifles expectantly, while still passing friendly greetings. Of a sudden Lawrence grinned so genially that they became mystified.

"Come near, I want to whisper something to you," he said to their leader. Then bending down from the saddle of his camel he asked: "Do you know what your name is?"

The sheik looked speechless and rather amazed. Lawrence continued: "I think it must be 'Terrace!'" (Procurer).

This is the most terrible insult that one can offer a Bedouin. The Beni-Sakr leader was dumbfounded and rather nervous. He could not understand how an ordinary traveller would dare to say such a thing to him in the open desert when numbers and arms were on his side. Before the sheik had time to recover himself, Lawrence remarked pleasantly:

"May Allah give you peace!"

Quietly telling the Haurani to come along, he swung off across the sand. The men of Beni-Sakr remained half-bewildered until the pair had ridden about a hundred yards. Then they recovered their senses and started shooting; but the blonde Prince of Mecca galloped over the nearest ridge and escaped. Bullets, by the way, have but little immediate effect on a camel that is travelling at twenty miles an hour.

Both Lawrence and his Haurani nearly killed their camels during the journey. They rode on an average of twenty-two hours a day. From dawn to setting sun they crossed the burning sands, only stopping then for a moment's rest for their camels. When they reached Auda Abu Tayi's country, east of the southern end of the Dead Sea, they exchanged their mounts for fresh beasts. They covered the whole distance of 300 miles in just three days—a record for fast camel trekking that may stand for some years.

This weird adventure was but one of a hundred that befell Lawrence. I heard of another which explains why he always carried a Colt revolver of an early frontier model.

Some years ago, while wandering in Asia Minor, near Marash, a fever came upon him and he made for Birgik, the nearest village. He happened to meet a Turkoman. They are a semi-nomadic crowd of Mongol descent—men with crooked eyes and faces that look as though they had been modelled in butter and then left out in the sun. He wasn't quite sure of his directions, and asked the Turkoman to point out the way. He replied: "Right across those low hills to the left." As Lawrence turned away from him the Mongol sprang on his back, and they had a bit of a dog fight on the ground for a few minutes. But Lawrence had walked over a thousand miles and, apart from the fever, was nearly done up. Soon he found himself underneath.

"He sat on my stomach, pulled out my Colt," said

Lawrence, "pressed it to my temple and pulled the trigger many times. But the safety-catch was on. The Turkoman was a primitive fellow and knew very little about revolver mechanism. He threw the weapon away in disgust, and proceeded to pound my head with a rock until I was no longer interested. After taking everything I had, he made off. I went to the village and got the inhabitants to help me chase the scoundrel. We caught him and made him disgorge the things he'd relieved me of. Since then I've always had a profound respect for a Colt, and have never been without one."

CHAPTER XV

MY LORD THE CAMEL

No knowledge that could increase his influence over the peoples of Arabia was neglected by Lawrence. He even made a minute study of that beast of mystery, the camel, the character and quality of which few Arabs are altogether familiar with, although it plays such an all-important part in their lives. Lawrence is the only European I have ever met who possesses "camel instinct"—a quality that implies intimate acquaintance with the beast's habits, powers, and innumerable idiosyncrasies. Auda Abu Tayi, the Bedouin Robin Hood, had this instinct developed to an unusually high degree.

There are six different species of camels found in Central Arabia, from whence come the finest breeds. The Bedouins call their country the Mother of the Camel. Arabian camels have but one hump; in fact, most of the Arabs have never even heard of the two-humped variety, which is found only in Central Asia, to the north-west of Persia, chiefly in the Gobi Desert. The two-humped breed is slow and of little use except as a beast of burden. The one-humped camel is the dromedary, which is the Greek word for a camel that runs.

The chief unit of wealth in Arabia is the camel. A man is not spoken of as owning so many service flats or quick-lunch restaurants, but as owning so many camels. From biblical down to modern times wars have been waged in the desert for the possession of camels. One tribe will swoop down upon another and steal all its camels; then that tribe will mount its horses, dash across the desert, and drive off all the camels of another tribe. So, in the course of twelve months, one camel may become the stolen property of half a dozen different tribes. The very existence of human life in the desert depends upon the camel. The Arabs use it not only as a beast of burden; they drink its milk, and use its hair for making cloth, and when it becomes old they kill it and use its flesh for food. Camel steak in Arabia is regarded much as blubber is among the Esquimaux, but the most of us would prefer to worry along on *chicken à la king*.

The camel is practically the only animal that can exist on the scant vegetation of the desert. Its teeth are so long that it can chew cactus without the thorns pricking either its lips or the roof of its mouth. Although camels can go for long periods without water, when they *do* drink they more than make up for lost time. It takes half an hour to water them, but each camel can accommodate a nice little swallow of twenty gallons. It is very irritating when suffering from thirst in the desert to hear your camel drawing on the copious reserve of water inside its body. At such times the Arabs, when in dire straits, will kill a camel and drink the water in its stomach. The water is of a greenish colour and has a greenish taste, but one can't be too fastidious when perishing from thirst.

In judging a camel, some of the many things to be considered are the length of the dromedary's belly, the way the beast lifts its feet, the way it carries its head, the depth of the neck, the length of the front legs, the length of the front and back shoulders, and the girth and shape of the hump. A very long leg is particularly desirable, as is a small circumference around the waist. A camel should be neither too fat nor too thin. The hump, which should be of hard, fatless muscle, is of paramount importance. The dromedary actually seems to live on its hump, and if it be worked too hard the hump gradually disappears. If it has no hump, or a low one or a thin one or a fat one, the animal is of little value and will break down in a short time. Age is judged by the teeth, as with the horse. Camels usually live for about twenty-five years, being in their prime between the ages of four and fourteen. Over good ground first-class Arabian dromedaries can trot up to twenty-one miles an hour, canter up to twenty-eight miles an hour, and gallop up to thirty-two with their legs going like huge pistons.

For a whole day's travel, however, the most desirable pace is a jog-trot of seven miles an hour. The ordinary speed for a long journey of many days across the desert is only about four-and-a-half miles an hour; and if the journey extends over hundreds of miles, it is advisable always to keep the camel at a walk. Lawrence's feat in making a forced trek of three hundred miles in three days was therefore looked upon by his followers as almost a miracle. A good camel makes absolutely no sound when it walks; a trait which is of great assistance both to the Bedouins during their night-raids and to desert traders who fear assault. The Arab teaches his mount not to whine, and a whole caravan may pass within twenty yards of a tent without being heard by the occupants.

The winter of 1917-18 was a severe one for the camels. Lawrence's army was at Tafileh in January, at an altitude of five thousand feet. The snow drifted to a depth of four feet, impassable for the camels unless their riders dismounted and dug a path with their hands. Many of them, both camels and Arabs, perished from the cold.

Lawrence sent a request to headquarters, Cairo, for heavy clothing and boots for his men. Instead of receiving them, he got a wireless message telling him that Arabia was a "tropical country!"

One morning an Arab column awoke on a hillside to find that snow had drifted over their crouching camels. They dug them out with the iron spoons which are used for roasting coffee-beans, but all were dead. Lawrence and his men had to walk barefoot through the snow for miles before they reached a military encampment. Another time thirty-four men started from Akaba for Tafileh on camels, and only one man succeeded in getting through alive. The Arab army had plenty of camels at this time, thanks, partly, to Prince Zeid. Some months previous the Turks had sent a large caravan of supplies towards Medina from Hail, Ibn Rashid's capital in Central Arabia. Zeid and his men surprised it at Hanakieh, killed thirty Turks, captured two hundred and fifty more and also three thousand camels, two thousand sheep, four mountain-guns and several thousand rifles.

Although "the camel is an intricate animal and calls for skilled labour in the handling," according to Colonel Lawrence, "she yields a remarkable return. We had no system of supply: each man was self-contained and carried on the saddle from the sea base at which the raid started six weeks' food for himself. The six weeks' ration for ordinary men was a half-bag of flour, 45 lb. in weight. Luxurious feeders carried some rice also for variety. Each man baked for himself, kneading his own flour into unleavened cakes, and warming it in the ashes of a fire. We carried about a pint of drinking water each, since the camels had to come to water on an average of every three days, and there was no advantage in our being richer than our mounts. Some of us never drank between wells, but those were hardy men; most of us drank a lot at each well, and had a drink during the intermediate dry day. In the heat of summer Arabian camels will do about 250 miles comfortably between drinks: and this represents three days and nights of forced marching.

"The country is not so dry as it is painted, and this radius was always more than we needed. Wells are seldom more than 100 miles apart. An easy day's march was fifty miles: an emergency march might be up to 110 miles in a day.

"The six weeks' food gave us a range of over a thousand

miles out and home, and that (like the pint of water) was more than ever we needed, even in so large a country as Arabia. It was possible (for me, the camel novice in the army, 'painful' was a better word) to ride 1,500 miles in a month without revictualling, and there was never a fear of starvation, for each of us was riding on 200 lb. of potential meat, and when food lacked we would stop and eat the weakest of our camels. Exhausted camel is poor food, but cheaper killing than a fat one, and we had to remember that our future efficiency depended upon the number of good camels at our disposal. They lived on grazing as we marched (we never gave them grain or fodder), and after their six weeks on the road they would be worn thin and have to be sent to pasture for some months' rest, while we called out another tribe in replacement, or found fresh riding beasts."

Tradition says that the horse originated in Arabia. The most beautiful and symmetrical horses are found there. They do not, however, have the greatest powers of endurance; neither are they the fleetest.

The Arabs are very fond and proud of their horses. They are really domestic animals, and it is by no means uncommon for them to occupy the same tent as their master. The pedigrees of some of them can be traced back to the fifth century, and registered mares are seldom sold, although stallions are sometimes given away to distinguished foreigners. It is maintained that a female, whether horse or camel, has much more highly-developed powers of endurance. The Arabs oil the hoofs of their horses to keep them from slipping on the hot sand, and feed them on boiled goat's meat to give them staying powers. They are seldom given all the water they desire to drink. Even as colts they are continually stinted of water so that they may become inured to thirst and suffer as little as possible when crossing the dry parts of the Arabian Desert. Many of the water-holes of the desert are five days' travel apart. A horse, of course, cannot go so long without water; a camel can, however, and so an Arabian horse will travel by the side of a camel and drink the camel's milk, and in that manner make the distance from one water-hole to another.

The foregoing is but a small fraction of the horse and camel-lore familiar to a Bedouin expert. After years of experience in the Arabian and Syrian deserts, Lawrence confessed to me that often he could not size up his dromedary correctly.

CHAPTER XVI

ABDULLAH THE POCK-MARKED, AND THE STORY OF
FERRAJ AND DAOUD

ABDULLAH, the pock-marked, undersized, fiery little Bedouin who commanded Lawrence's personal bodyguard, although in appearance a dried-up stick of a man, is one of the most daring and chivalrous sons of Ishmael that ever rode a dromedary. He would take keen delight in tackling ten men by himself. Apart from his fearlessness, he was a valuable lieutenant, because he knew how to deal with unruly members of the body-guard. Lawrence would urge his followers on with the promise of extravagant rewards, gold, jewels and beautiful clothes, if they succeeded. Abdullah would promise them a sound beating if they failed, and the certainty that he would fulfil his threat carried at least as much weight with the body-guard as did Lawrence's milder method. As for Abdullah himself, his most frequent boast was that he had served under all the princes of the desert and had been imprisoned by every one of them.

The English shereef's personal bodyguard, consisting of eighty carefully-picked men, was the *corps d'élite* of the desert. All its men were famous fighters who possessed powers of endurance which would enable them to ride hard for a day and a night on end, if necessary. They were required to be ready for a raid on the Turks at any moment, and always to keep up with their leader on the trek. No man was accepted who could not, with one hand free, leap into the camel-saddle at the trot while carrying a rifle in the other. Taking it all round, the bodyguard was an extraordinary collection of mettlesome, gay-spirited, good-natured scallawags.

Its members were devoted to their Anglo-Bedouin shereef; but to guard against the possibility of a conspiracy among them, never more than two men were selected from each tribe, so that inter-tribal jealousy might prevent any group from plotting against their leader. Nearly every man in the Hedjaz army wanted to belong to the bodyguard, because Lawrence took it on all of his raiding, bridge-blowing, and train-wreck-ing expeditions, "stunts" which provided much loot and many thrills—gifts dear to the heart of the Bedouin. Then, too, the pay was greater than that given to any of the other volunteers in the Arabian army. Furthermore, they received a liberal allowance for costly raiment; for they spent all their money on clothes, and when gathered in a body they produced an effect similar to that of an Oriental flower garden.

A familiar saying among them was that they might as well spend their gold on clothes and a good time, since Allah might take them to paradise at any moment. Among Colonel Lawrence's personal retinue the percentage of casualties was far greater than among other regulars and irregulars of Feisal's army, for they were continually being sent across the desert on dangerous missions. Frequently they were despatched through the Turkish lines to act as spies, a service for which the bodyguard was especially suitable, since it contained at least one man from each district between Mecca and Aleppo. Lawrence always arrogated to himself more than his full share of these hazardous missions.

To accompany Lawrence and his bodyguard on an expedition was a fantastic experience. First rode the young shereef, incongruously picturesque with his Anglo-Saxon face, gorgeous head-dress and beautiful robes. Likely enough, if the party were moving at walking pace, he would be reading and smiling to himself over the brilliant satire of Aristophanes in the original. Then in a long, irregular column his Bedouin "sons" followed in their rainbow-coloured garments, swaying to the rhythm of the camel gait. And whether they were passing over the sands east of Akaba, or the stony hill-country of Edom and Moab, they always sang and jested.

At either end of the cavalcade was a warrior-poet. One of them would begin to chant a verse, and each man, all along the column, would take his turn to cap the poet's words with lines of the same metre. There were war-songs and songs that caused the camels to lower their heads and move at a faster pace. Often in the verses the men commented on each other's love affairs or on the Emir Feisal or Sidi (Lord) Lawrence.

"I wish he would pay us another pound a month." This, decorated with rhetorical flourishes in Arabic, was the theme of the bodyguard's song one day.

Another time it was: "I wonder if Allah has seen the head-cloth which has the good fortune to cover our Lord Lawrence's head? It is not a good head-cloth. The Lord Lawrence should give it me." As a matter of fact, the head-cloths that Shereef Lawrence wore were more resplendent than any they had ever seen. His playful "sons" coveted them.

The harmonic scale of Arabian music is different from ours, so that to Western ears unused to it Arabian singing sounds

like a medley of discords.   Yet the Bedouins delighted in
Western music churned out by a phonograph that Lawrence
brought from Cairo.   Its success encouraged a Scottish
sergeant in Akaba to provide some instruments and organize
a band.   He helped the Arab bandsmen to create an Arabian
national anthem, and taught them to play "Annie Laurie"
and "Auld Lang Syne" after a fashion.   The Scottish airs we
could stand for a time, even though every instrument was out
of tune and every man chose his own key; but whenever the
Arabs practised their own national anthem around the camp
we preferred swimming, and left at once for a deserted island
down the gulf for a dip in the surf, just below the ruin of a
Crusader castle, where Godfrey de Bouillon and his knights
had bathed a thousand years before us.

The Bedouin bodyguard's sense of humour sometimes took
the form of practical jokes.   If one of their number fell asleep
in his saddle, a companion would charge his camel straight at
the slumberer and knock him off.   Whenever their "Lord"
left them for a visit to Cairo, or to Allenby's headquarters,
most of his bodyguard managed to get themselves imprisoned
by the Emir Feisal as a result of their wild humour and general
unruliness.   Nobody but Lawrence could handle his devils,
as they were called.

Once, having just returned to Akaba from Egypt, he
wanted to set out on a secret mission without delay.   As usual,
he found the majority of his personal followers in the lock-up.
Among the prisoners were two specially daring men named
Ferraj and Daoud.   Lawrence immediately sent for Sheik
Yussef, the civil governor of Akaba, and asked what had
happened.   Yussef laughed and cursed, then laughed again.

"I had a beautiful white camel," he said, "and one night
she strayed away.   Next morning I heard a great commotion
in the street, and when I went out I found everyone in the
bazaar laughing uproariously at an animal with blue legs and
a red head.   Not without difficulty I recognized it as my camel.
Ferraj and Daoud were found at the waterfront washing red
henna and blue indigo dye off their arms, yet they denied all
knowledge of my beautiful white camel.   Allah will pardon
me for doubting them."

Ferraj and Daoud were well known as inseparable in a land
where lonely desert and the need for mutual protection called
for close friendships.   David and Jonathan were not more
intimate than Ferraj and Daoud, until, as an Eastern story-
teller might say, there came to them the Destroyer of Delights
and the Garnerer of Graveyards.   Daoud died of fever in

Akaba, whereupon Ferraj became intensely miserable and soon afterward committed suicide by galloping his camel headlong into the Turks.

Occasionally members of Lawrence's bodyguard accompanied him to Cairo. Those thus honoured would don their most vivid robes, rouge their lips, darken the hollows under their eyes with köhl, and saturate themselves with bottles of scent. Then, bristling with weapons, they swaggered contemptuously past the town Arabs of Cairo, ogling the veiled ladies, buying richly-brocaded garments, and causing much excitement, in which they revelled.

Abdullah, lieutenant of the bodyguard, once travelled with his leader to General Allenby's headquarters at Ramleh. While Lawrence was in consultation with the commander-in-chief, the Arab lieutenant roamed off alone. Six hours passed and he did not return. Then Lawrence was informed by telephone that the assistant provost-marshal had arrested the fiery little Arab because he looked liked a hired assassin who might be prowling around with the intention of shooting General Allenby. Abdullah, said the assistant provost-marshal, had explained through an interpreter that he was one of Sidi Lawrence's "sons," and demanded a ceremonious apology for having been arrested. Meantime, he was eating up all the oranges in the quarters of the head of the military police.

Punishment for the misdeeds of the various members of the bodyguard was difficult, for a nomad Arab can scarcely be imprisoned on his camel, and he cares naught for words of reproof. A conscientious beating from Abdullah was perhaps the most effective solution. A common form of punishment among the Bedouins is to throw at a man's head a short dagger so that it shall chop through the hair and cause a superficial but very painful scalp wound. Bedouins who are conscious of transgression sometimes wound themselves in this manner and then, with blood streaming over their faces, crave pardon of the person they have wronged.

CHAPTER XVII

AN EYE FOR AN EYE, AND A TOOTH FOR A TOOTH

IN Arabia the Old Testament law of an eye for an eye, a tooth for a tooth, a life for a life, still holds good, and complicated feuds drag on for centuries. A murderer can rarely escape the death penalty; it is almost impossible for him to avoid being found by the murdered man's relatives somewhere in the desert sooner or later. His only chance is to relinquish tent-dwelling and become a townsman; and since the Bedouin regards people who live in villages and cities as greatly inferior to him, he can seldom bring himself to such an indignity.

A peculiar feature of Arabian unwritten law is that for purposes of retribution no distinction is drawn between accidental and intentional manslaughter. If one Bedouin kills another, whether by chance or design, it is customary for him to flee and send regrets and explanations back by courier. Lawrence's bodyguard was involved in an affair of this sort. During a raid an Arab climbed through the window of a railway station and attempted to open the door from the inside. Meanwhile, some of his companions were trying to batter it open from without. One of them fired his rifle through a panel, and when the door finally was forced the man who had entered through the window was lying dead. The Bedouin who had fired the shot immediately dashed through the crowd, jumped on his horse, and galloped off.

Now, it is the custom that the slayer may avoid the penalty of death by paying damages if the lost man's relatives are willing to accept money in lieu of life. In this case the guards collected among themselves a sum of £100, which they sent to the relatives, and all was well. The rate of exchange on an ordinary life varies from £100 to £500. This particular fellow was rather a bad lot, and so his companions of the body-guard thought £100 was ample. Shereefs (members of the Prophet's family) have a far higher blood-value than other Arabs. Having killed one of them, a slayer must forfeit not less than £1,000, unless he has arranged a bargain price with his victim's family before committing the deed.

Lawrence never met a case of treachery against himself among the tribes with whom he established friendly relations, and even among unfriendly tribes he encountered only one serious violation of the laws of hospitality. Alone he had

passed through the Turkish lines for a tour of inspection among
the enemy's camps.   He called on a chieftain of the Beni-
Sakr, a tribe which had been co-operating with the Turks and
Germans.   The sheik broke the unwritten law of the desert
and attempted to double-cross his guest.   He sent a courier
to some Turkish forces that were ten miles distant and, in the
meantime, attempted to persuade Lawrence to remain in his tent.

His intention was to betray his valuable visitor and claim
the £50,000 reward.   But Lawrence surmised that there was
villainy afoot, and hurriedly left the Beni-Sakr camp.   The
fate that befell the sheik of the Beni-Sakr is instructive.
Although he was one of the leaders of a tribe considered hostile
to the Arabs co-operating with Lawrence, his own people gave
him a cup of poisoned coffee because he had been treacherous
to a guest.   The people of the Beni-Sakr felt themselves disgraced by the act of their sheik.

The strict observance of the rules of desert hospitality is
almost a religion.   If in his own district an Arab has a man
at his mercy and is about to kill him, the victim can usually
save himself by saying *dakhilak*—an Arab word implying:
"I have taken refuge with you," or "I am in your tent and
at your coffee-hearth as your guest."   Among the Bedouins
the protection is a sacred obligation.   The meaning of this
magic word *dakhilak* is one of the points of difference between
the nomad of Arabia and the town Arabs of Syria.   The Syrian
uses it as a variation of "please," which to a Bedouin is
a ghastly breach of etiquette.

In the gigantic task that he set himself, Lawrence had to
win the adherence not only of the wandering tribesmen but
of the less reliable Arabs of the towns and villages.   He accomplished this by taking into account the many differences
between the two types, and using correspondingly different
methods.   The Bedouin is of a pure breed, and to-day lives
in much the same manner as he did three thousand years ago,
when Abraham and Lot were wandering patriarchs.   The
townsman, a mixture of all the races in the East, has many a
bar sinister in his racial ancestry.   The nomad is a sportsman,
a lover of personal liberty, and a natural poet.   The villager
is often indolent, dirty, untrustworthy, and entirely mercen-
ary.   There are even differences in the everyday observances
of life, in the form of salutation, for instance.   The townsman
shows his respect for shereefs and other notables by kissing
the hand, but the Bedouin considers such action undignified
and only performs it when he wishes to convey the deepest
reverence.

SCOTTIES PREPARING BREAKFAST

Scene on board our floating ark, the S.S. *Ozarda.*

THE TRAMP STEAMER ON WHICH WE CROSS THE RED SEA FROM AFRICA TO ARABIA

Although Lawrence received support from many town Arabs, it was primarily the Bedouin who, under the guidance of Lawrence and Feisal, carried the Arabian revolution from small, localized beginnings to glorious success. The Bedouin passion for raiding and looting was a valuable asset in the guerilla campaign against the Turks. But the true Bedouin is nearly always content with booty and abhors the sight of blood. He will rob but will not otherwise abuse a stranger.

The pure Arab of the desert belongs to a race that has one of the oldest forms of civilization. They had a philosophy and a literature when the inhabitants of the British Isles were undeveloped savages. They are one of the few people of the world whom the Romans failed to conquer. Their primitiveness is due to the necessity of leading a nomadic life, as they are obliged to follow their herds from place to place in search of grass and water. They are wanderers on the face of the earth; creatures who trek behind their camels across the sanddunes, who sleep under starry skies, and who live as their forefathers lived when the human race was young.

Both the regulars and the irregulars in the Arabian army were paid wages just the same as other Allied troops in other parts of the world. They received their pay in gold coin, all of which was supplied by the British Government. Lawrence usually had a bag or two of sovereigns in his tent, and whenever a sheik came in and asked for money Lawrence would tell him to help himself. He allowed them to keep all that they could take out of the bag in one handful. A swarthy six-foot Howeitat giant dropped in for a cup of coffee and a cigarette one morning. In the richly-ornamented language of the people of the black tents he reminded Lawrence of the valuable assistance that he had been rendering King Hussein. Lawrence took the thinly-veiled hint, and, pointing to his gold bag in one corner, he asked his guest to help himself. The sheik broke all records by picking up one hundred and forty-three sovereigns in one hand !

The nomad tribes are amazed at the sordid lack of hospitality in the towns. They despise their settled kinsmen for their selfishness. In olden times, just as to-day, the Arabs prided themselves on four things: their poetry, their eloquence, their horsemanship, and their hospitality. Among Arab legends are many which glorify and keep alive the tradition of hospitality. One concerns three men who were disputing in the sacred mosque of the Kaaba as to who was the most liberal person in Mecca.

One extolled the virtues of a certain Abdullah, the son of

I

the nephew of Jaafar, the uncle of Mohammed. Another praised the generosity of Kais Ibn Said. The third proclaimed Arabah, the aged sheik, to be the most liberal. At last a bystander, to end the discussion and avoid bloodshed, suggested that each should go and ask for assistance from the one whose liberality he had extolled and return to the mosque, where the evidence would be weighed and judgment given. This agreed upon, they set forth. Abdullah's friend, going to him, found him mounting his dromedary for lands beyond the horizon, and thus accosted him: "Oh, son of the nephew of the uncle of the apostle of Allah and Father of Generosity, I am travelling and in dire necessity." Upon which Abdullah bade him take his camel with all that was upon her. So he took the camel and found on her some vests of silk and five thousand pieces of gold.

The second went to Kais Ibn Said. The latter's servant told him that his master was asleep, and desired to know his mission. The friend answered that being in want he came to ask Kais's assistance. The servant protested that he himself preferred to supply the necessity rather than wake his master; so saying, he gave him a purse of ten thousand pieces of gold, all the money in his master's house, and likewise directed him to go to the caravanserai with a certain token and take therefrom a camel and a slave. When Kais awoke, his servant informed him of what had occurred. Kais was so much pleased that he gave the servant his freedom, at the same time upbraiding him for not arousing him. "By my life!" he said, "would that thou hadst called me that I could have given him more."

The third man went to Arabah and met the old sheik coming out of his house on his way to noon-day prayers at the Kaaba. His eyesight having failed him, he was supported by two slaves. When the friend made known his plight, Arabah let go the slaves and, clapping his hands together, in the name of Allah loudly lamented his misfortune in having no money, but he offered to give him his two slaves. The man refused his offer, whereupon Arabah protested that since he would not accept them he must give them their liberty. Saying this, he left the slaves and groped his way along the wall. On the return of the adventurers a unanimous judgment was rendered in favour of Arabah as the most generous of the three. "May Allah reward him!" cried they with fervour.

This legend may well be founded on fact, for one sees many examples of this spirit of liberality, a liberality which increases one's admiration for these children of Allah.   Lawrence, recognizing generosity to be a cardinal virtue with the Arabs, made it a point to excel them in this as well as in bravery, physical endurance, and nimbleness of wit, which they so much admire.   After the first successes which enabled him to gain the confidence of his own Government, he brought caravans laden with presents rich and rare, and bewildered them with a prodigality surpassing even the legends in the classic poems recited round their camp-fires extolling the generosity of the caliphs of old.

The Bedouins were all particularly fond of wrist-watches, revolvers and field-glasses, so that Lawrence used to take two or three camels laden with trinkets of that sort to give away. He also gave his men from fifty to one hundred rounds of ammunition each day; and they always shot it off into the air regardless of whether they were fighting or not!   In most armies if a man fires off a single round of ammunition without the permission of his commanding officer he is court-mar- tialled.   The Arabs shot at every sparrow they saw, and one day, when a false rumour came in to us at Akaba that Maan had been captured by Feisal's chief of staff, General Nuri Bey, thousands of rounds were fired wildly into the sky.   If the Bedouins who came in to the supply-bases along the Red Sea coast happened to see a British officer strolling along with nothing but a riding-crop or a stick, they would shake their heads, stroke their beards, and say: "Mad Anglesi!   Mad Anglesi!"   But if the officer wandered about with a rifle, blazing away at every rock or bird in sight, they would remark in the Arabian equivalent: "I say, these blighters are not such silly asses after all.   Really, they are quite sane, don't you know."

Like the cow-worshipping sepoys of India, the Bedouins refused to clean their rifles with grease made from pork, because the Mohammedan religion teaches them that pork is unclean.   So Lawrence either had to clean all the rifles in the Arabian army himself, or provide rifles that would not have to be cleaned.   He solved this problem by equipping them with German nickel-steel rifles which Allenby had captured on the Palestine front, rifles that could survive a year's service without being cleaned.

The freedom of the desert has been his for thousands of years; so naturally the Bedouin is independent by nature. "Discipline" and "obedience" are unknown words to him. Probably none of Lawrence's men would have made a high record in the senior examinations at Sandhurst or West Point, but they did know how to fight the Turks—and how to whip them, and they regarded themselves as of equal rank with any general !

These, then, were the men Lawrence had to mould from an inchoate, inter-tribal conglomeration into a large army capable of defeating highly-trained and well-officered forces. All the organization had to be improvised on original lines. There was no commissariat department.   When the Bedouin irregulars started off on an expedition each man carried a small bag of flour and some coffee.   Every meal was the same. The entire army lived and fought on unleavened bread baked in ashes.   The Arabs could eat a pound or two at a time, but Lawrence usually carried a chunk in the folds of his gown and nibbled at it as he rode at the head of a column.

The Bedouins looked upon tinned food as a dubious institution.   One day, when Major Maynard was accompanying us on a journey over the desert north-east of Akaba, he handed a tin of bully beef to each of the men with us. They took the meat reluctantly and seemed to regard it as unholy. It was then we discovered how suspicious the Arab was of things in tins—but from religious not hygienic motives.   It is customary for an Arab when he cuts the throat of a sheep or of any other animal to say, as he inserts the knife: "In the name of Allah the Merciful and the Compassionate !"   When they opened the tins they repeated these same words, fearful lest the Chicago packers had not performed the ceremony according to the law of the Prophet.

Apart from a few such formal observances, the average Bedouin is by no means a religious fanatic. He refuses to take notice of the three cardinal principles of Mohammedanism. He never fasts, for, says he: "We never have enough to eat as it is !" He rarely bathes, using the excuse, "We have not even enough water to drink."   He seldom prays, for he maintains: "Our prayers are never answered, so why bother?"

But with all his looting and his lack of religion, the Bedouin is a man of honour and a man of humour.

CHAPTER XVIII

"A ROSE-RED CITY HALF AS OLD AS TIME"

ONE of the most colourful and romantic episodes of the War in the Land of the Arabian Nights was a battle fought in an ancient deserted city that had been asleep for a thousand years, only to wake to the booming of big guns and the spirited clash of Turks and Arabs. Here, among the immemorial and perfect ruins of a lost civilization, Lawrence the archæologist and Lawrence the military genius merged in one. To the few travellers who have ventured into that hidden corner of the Arabian desert it is known as a "rose-red city, half as old as time," carved out of the enchanted mountains of Edom. It lies deep in the wilderness of the desert, not far from Mount Hor, where the Israelites are believed to have buried their great leader, Aaron.

The battle took place on October 21, 1917, shortly after the fall of Akaba. It was important from a military stand-point because it definitely decided that the uprising against the Turks in Holy Arabia was to develop into an invasion of Syria, an affair of world-wide importance destined to revolutionize the history of the Near East. In this battle Lawrence and his Bedouins, fought the Turks on the same mountain-tops from which Amaziah, king of Israel, hurled ten thousand of the inhabitants to the cañons below. Lawrence successfully defended the city against the Turks in much the same way that the Nabatæans defended it against the armies of Alexander the Great three hundred years before Christ. He trapped the Turks in the same narrow gorge that resounded to the tramp of Trajan's conquering legions two thousand years ago.

After hearing Lawrence's enthusiastic description of the palaces carved out of the living rock, where he had camped with his Bedouins, I asked Emir Feisal if he would permit me to do a bit of exploring among the mountains of Edom. He not only granted the request but gave us a picked band of his wildest brigands as a bodyguard to protect us from robbers and enemy patrols. From Akaba we trekked thirty-eight miles through the Wadi Ithm to one of Feisal's outposts, at Gueirra. The Wadi Ithm is a narrow gorge hemmed in by jagged granite mountains, criss-crossed with black lava veins from twenty to two hundred feet wide caused by volcanic

eruption ages ago.   This weird Wadi pours out on to a mud
plain which reminded us of the Bad Lands of Dakota and the
high plateaux of Central Baluchistan.   Here we occupied a
deserted bell-tent for several days before continuing our trek
across arid mountain-ranges and sandy desert stretches.   Up
and up we went over a precipitous, rocky zig-zag trail, where
our camels, time after time, stumbled to their knees.   Reaching the summit of the Nagb, the camel-track led across a
grassy plateau to the battlefield around the wells of Abu el
Lissal.

General Nuri Pasha, one of the commanders of Feisal's
army, turned out his troops to welcome us.   We stopped a few
minutes for coffee, and as I left the general's tent he picked up
the princely Persian lamb rug on which he had been sitting
and threw it over my camel-saddle, insisting, in spite of all my
protests, that I should take it along and use it as a cushion.
He also lent me a hippopotamus-hide cane, presented to him
by the king of Abyssinia, with which to guide my dromedary.
A few miles beyond Abu el Lissal a courier from Feisal caught
up with us and handed me a letter of introduction from the
Emir to his commander at Busta.   The courier was a swarthy
rascal, who looked like Captain Kidd with his flashing black
eyes and fierce upturned moustachios.   His red head-cloth was
embroidered with huge yellow flowers, and his robes flashed
as many colours as Joseph's coat.   At his belt he wore a pearl-
handled revolver and two wicked-looking daggers.   To my
amazement he spoke typical New York Bowery English, and
dropped such remarks as "Say, cul, will youse slip me de can-
opener?"   He informed me that he had lived fourteen years
in America as a machine-operator in a cigarette factory.

He was born in the mountains of Lebanon, and his real
name was Hassan Khalil, but in New York he was plain
Charley Kelly.   At the outbreak of the World War he was
working for Thomas Cook & Son in Constantinople, and was
immediately conscripted into the Turkish army.   At the second
battle of Gaza he deserted and joined the Australian forces as
an interpreter.   After serving with the British in Egypt, he
was finally transferred to the Hedjaz army.   As soon as we
became better acquainted, Charley told me he was not a
Mohammedan, but an "R.C.," which he explained in a
whisper, stood for Roman Catholic.   But he begged me not
to reveal his secret to any of the other members of the caravan,
for he feared that he would be killed instantly by some of our
over-zealous Moslem companions, should they discover his
apostacy.

Charley Kelly entertained us around the camp fire with detective yarns. He had several Arabic translations of "Nick Carter" in his saddle-bags, and said the Egyptians believe Nick Carter to be the actual head of the American Secret Service. According to Charley, "Nick Carter" is a best seller in Egypt, where his exploits are regarded as authentic history. If an Egyptian cannot read himself, he hires a public reader to entertain him with one of these detective tales. Another member of our column was a silent Egyptian with an immobile face that might have been chiselled out of stone. We dubbed him Rameses because he looked so much like the statues of that mighty potentate along the Nile. The rest of our picturesque bodyguard was made up of Lawrence's Bedouins. All these Beau Brummels used khol-sticks under their eyebrows and rouge on their lips and cheeks. The Prophet Mohammed is said to have remarked on one occasion that there were two things no true believer should ever lend to his brother—his kohl-stick and his wife.

Every morning Charley had to help Chase, who is a little man, mount his camel. Practically every camel Chase rode died in its tracks before the end of the journey. He was singled out as the special object of attraction by all the insects of the desert. Several mornings when we crawled out of our sleeping-bags we found scorpions and centipedes between Chase's blankets. One morning Chase handed a treasured can of bacon to one of the members of our bodyguard with instructions to cook him a breakfast that would remind him of home. But he ended by frying his own bacon. As soon as the can was opened the Bedouin cook dropped it in horror and backed off, aghast that his Moslem nostrils had been profaned with the aroma of unclean meat. Like all Mohammedans, Arabs will not use pork in any form. They cook their food in butter made from goat's milk.

That day we passed a flock of white sheep, all of them fat as butter, with thick curly wool and cute little corkscrew horns. A Bedouin shepherd sat nearby on a lump of basalt, strumming an ancient Arab love-song on his lute. Some of these uplands of the Hedjaz are carpeted with barely enough grass for sheep pasture, and a few of the more settled tribes tend flocks and own very few camels and horses.

One schemer from Bagdad, hearing of the uprising in the Hedjaz, was far-sighted enough to realize that the Allies were bound to take an interest in the affair sooner or later and that British gold pieces would supplant the Turkish sovereigns which long had been the medium of exchange along the desert fringe. So, from lead gilded over, he made thousands of counterfeit British sovereigns, and as soon as the first gold began coming into the Hedjaz from Egypt, but before the Bedouins were familiar enough with it to detect the spurious from the genuine, he trekked across the country buying all the sheep he could find. Instead of the normal price of one pound for each animal, he offered two of his counterfeit pieces. Then, before the Bedouins had time to get into Jeddah, Yenbo and Wedj to spend their gold in the bazaars, the Bagdadi drove his sheep north to Palestine, and sold them at two pounds a head to the British army. When the hoax was discovered he had vanished into the blue.

Distances in Arabia are not gauged by miles, but by water-holes. The night after our unfortunate bacon incident, just as we had finished putting up our pup-tent at "third water," otherwise known as Busta, twenty Arab regulars came along mounted on Peruvian mules. The mules were camel-shy, and as soon as they saw our caravan they bolted at top speed in all directions, some of them bucking off their riders and disappearing into the mountains of Edom. These soldiers, who hailed from Mecca, sat up all night shouting and singing around our camp fire and firing their rifles into the dark. The Turkish lines were only a few miles away, and I had a presentiment that a Turkish patrol would slip up during the confusion and put a finish to the hilarity by scuppering the lot of us. Nothing happened, however, and after trekking eighty miles across country without a single skirmish with the Turks to make the expedition more lively, we came out on the top of a high plateau.

Spreading off to the north-west before us were magnificent ridges of white and red sandstone. About twenty miles to the north lay the valley of the Dead Sea, and beyond, disappearing in purple and grey haze, the Central Arabian Desert. The peaks ahead were the sacred mountains of Edom. Our problem was to penetrate that massive range of sandstone before us. We descended from the high plateau into a valley twelve miles wide that narrowed to twelve feet, a mere defile through the mountain wall. Through this gorge, or sik, as it is called by the Arabs, our camels and horses scrambled over boulders and pushed their way through thousands of oleander bushes, while the Arabs popped away with their pistols at the lizards creeping across the stones. As we wandered through this rent in the rock we marvelled at its beautiful walls towering hundreds of feet above us, at times almost shutting out the sky.

> And on each side, aloft and wild,
> Huge cliffs and toppling crags were piled.

Hassan Morgani, one of our Bedouins, who wore a purple jacket trimmed in green and a pair of cavalry boots that he had taken from a dead Turkish officer, told us that the gorge was the Wadi Musa, the Valley of Moses. Charley Kelly confirmed this with the assertion that it was here that Moses brought the water gushing from the rock. To-day every Arab family in this region has its little Moses. Through the narrow gorge a brook plunged in and out among the great boulders, the oleanders and the wild fig trees. High above, the sun warmed the tops of slender cathedral rocks to a wonderful rose-red.

After pushing our way through the gorge for more than an hour, we suddenly rounded the last bend and stood breathless and speechless. There, in front of us, many miles from any sign of civilized habitation, deep in the heart of the Arabian Desert, was one of the most bewildering sights ever revealed to the eye of man—a temple, a delicate and limpid rose, carved like a cameo from a solid mountain wall. It was even more beautiful than the Temple of Theseus at Athens or the Forum at Rome. After trekking nearly a hundred miles across the desert, to come suddenly face to face with such a marvellous structure fairly took our breath away. It was the first indication we had that we had at last reached the mysterious city of Petra, a city deserted and lost to history for fourteen hundred years and only rediscovered during the last century by the famous Swiss explorer, Burkhardt.

The secret of the enchantment of this first temple we saw lies partly in its position at one of the most unusual gateways in the world. The columns, pediments and friezes, have been richly carved, but it is difficult to distinguish many of the designs, which have been disfigured by time and Mohammedan iconoclasts. At one side are two rows of niches, evidently the traces of ladders used by the sculptors who carved their way down. These artistic artisans used a tooth tool that they might get the maximum effect out of the coloured strata, which seems to form a perfect quilt of ribbons and swirl like watered silk in the morning sunlight. Although the temple is wonderfully preserved, it shows the effects of the sand-blasts of the centuries. The auditorium within is almost a perfect cube, forty feet each way. The architecture is of a corrupt Roman-Grecian style.

The temple was carved from the cliff almost two thousand years ago, during the reign of the Roman Emperor Hadrian,

who visited Petra in A.D. 131. The desert Arabs who were
with me said it was called El Khazneh, or the Treasury,
because of the great urn that surmounts the edifice, which
the Bedouins believe is filled with the gold and precious jewels
of the Pharaohs. Many attempts have been made to crack
the urn, and it has been chipped by thousands of bullets. My
bodyguard also fired away at it, but fortunately it was nearly
a hundred feet above their heads. Colonel Lawrence is of
the opinion that the building was a temple dedicated to Isis,
a goddess popular during the reign of Hadrian. One traveller
had carved his name in letters a foot high on one of the pillars
of the temple, but Lawrence ordered his men to polish it out.

The city lay farther down on the plain of an oval valley,
a mile-and-a-half long and half-a-mile wide. How populous it
was there is no way of telling, but several hundred thousand
people must once have lived there. Only the more insignifi-
cant buildings have perished, and even of these some striking
ruins remain. The upper part of the valley is the site of
ancient fortresses, palaces, tombs, and amusement resorts—
all carved out of the solid rock. The lower part was
apparently a water circus where the people indulged in aquatic
sports and tournaments. Petra is a huge excavation made by
the forces of Nature. From the nine-thousand-foot plateau
from which we first saw the mountains of Edom, we had
dropped down to an altitude of one thousand feet when we
entered the ruined city.

All the travellers who have visited Petra have marvelled at
the wonderful tints of its sandstone cliffs. It is carved from rock
the colours of which beggar description at certain hours of
the day. In the morning sunlight they are like great rainbows
of stone flashing out white, vermilion, saffron, orange, pink
and crimson. Time and the forces of Nature have played the
magician, painting the different strata in rare tints and hues.
In places the layers of rock dip and swerve like waves. At
sunset they glow with strange radiance before sinking into the
sombre darkness of the desert night. We wondered at times
whether we were really awake or whether we had not been transported to fairyland on a magically-coloured Persian carpet.

Stairs carved from the rock, some more than a mile in
length, run to the top of nearly all the mountains around
Petra. We climbed one great staircase ascending to a height
of one thousand feet above the city to the temple which the
Arabs call El Deir, or the Convent, a most impressive grey
façade, one hundred and fifty feet high, surmounted by a
gigantic urn, and decorated with heads of Medusa. Most of the

steps cut into the mountains lead to sacrificial altars, where the people used to worship on the high places thousands of years ago.

An even greater staircase winds up to the Mount of Sacrifice, an isolated peak that dominates the whole basin. On the summit are two obelisks and two altars. One altar is hollowed out for making fires, and the other round and provided with a blood-pool for the slaughter of the victim offered to Dhu-shara and Allat, the chief god and goddess of ancient Petra. One of my Bedouin companions insisted upon taking off his raiment and bathing in the rain-water which had collected in the pool. The average Bedouin needs a little encouragement along these lines, and so we did not reprimand him for his sacrilegious act. Lawrence told me that it was supposed to be the most complete and perfect example in existence of an ancient Semitic high place. Near the altars are the two great monoliths, each about twenty-four feet high, which the people of Petra carved out of the solid rock and used in their Phallic worship, one of the oldest forms of worship known to man. The names of these monoliths and the nature of the worship do not admit of description. The mountain-top commands a view of all the surrounding valleys and mountains, as well as most of the ruins of the city. The outlook is sublime.

It is a scene to stir in one's heart those emotions which have ever led man to worship his Creator. On a peak nearby are the broken remains of a Crusader's castle. Farther off to the left rises a black lava mountain. On its summit, glistening beneath the burning rays of the Arabian sun, we saw a small white dome, white like the bleached skeletons we passed in crossing the desert between Akaba and the mountains of Edom. This peak is Mount Hor, and the dome a part of a mosque built by the Bedouins over the traditional tomb of Aaron, high priest of the Israelites and brother of Moses. We spent a day ascending it, and upon reaching the summit found a Turkish flag flying over Aaron's tomb. As a propitiation before any important event takes place, the desert Arabs climb Mount Hor with their sacrifice of a sheep and cut its throat before the tomb of Aaron. Although no news of it reached the outside world at the time, the far-flung battle-lines of the Great War reached even to the slopes of Mount Hor.

All the buildings of this city of ghosts have elaborate façades, but within they are simple and austere. The magnitude and beauty of them even now strikes one with awe. How much more they must have meant to beauty-worshippers in the days when the city pulsed with life! Most of the stone is rose-coloured when the sun falls upon it, and shot with blue and porphyry. The deserted streets are rich with laurels and oleanders, whose hues seem copied from the rock itself. In fact, the only inhabitants of this rose-red city for hundreds of years have been the countless millions of brilliant wild flowers that flourish in the cracks of the hundreds of former palaces and temples and wind themselves around half-ruined columns. Petra's mighty men and beautiful women have passed on to that undiscovered country from whose bourne no traveller returns. It is indeed a scene to impress one with the evanescence of all life.

> The worldly hopes men set their hearts upon
> Turn ashes, or they prosper;
> And anon like snow upon the desert's dusty face
> Lighting a little hour or two—are gone.

In the centre of the city, surrounded on all sides by temples and palaces and tombs, is a great amphitheatre, cut out of the base of the same mountain that leads to the great high place of sacrifice. Tiers and tiers of seats face the mountain avenues of tombs. The diameter of the stage is 120 feet, and the theatre is the one symbol of life and mirth in all this mysterious, deserted city. The laughter and cheers of thousands once rang here across this hollow cemetery of ancient hopes and ambitions. Here thousands of years ago the Irvings and Carusos of that bygone age performed and received the plaudits of their admiring thousands. Where now are all the gay throngs who occupied these tiers on feast-days and watched the games? The lizards are crawling over the exquisitely-coloured seats to-night, and the only sounds that have been heard in the theatre for centuries have been the desolate howls of jackals. Little did the ancient Edomites or Nabatæans imagine that a people called Americans from an unknown continent would one day wander among the ruins of their proud city.

> It seems no work of man's creative hand
> By labour wrought as wavering fancy planned;
> But from the rock as if by magic grown;
> Eternal, silent, beautiful, alone.
> All rosy-red, as if the blush of dawn
> That first beheld it were not yet withdrawn.
> The hues of youth upon a brow of woe
> Which man deemed old two thousand years ago.
> Match me such marvel, save in Eastern clime;
> A "rose-red city, half as old as Time." *

*By Dean Burgon (Fellow of Oriel and afterwards Vicar of St. Mary's), prize poem, Newdigate, 1845.

The Nabatæans, an ancient Arab tribe, conquered Edom, and by 100 B.C. had created a powerful kingdom extending north to Damascus, west to Gaza in Palestine, and far into Central Arabia. Lawrence told me that the Nabatæans were great pirates who sailed down the African coast and made devastating raids on the Sudan. They had reached a high stage of civilization, did beautiful glass-work, made fine cloth, and modelled pottery. They frequently visited Rome and Constantinople. Both King Solomon and the Queen of Sheba had employed the Nabatæans, who rivalled even the Palmyrians in organizing a rich caravan trade, and made Petra their principal commercial centre in Arabia. Antigonus visited Petra in 301 B.C. and found there large quantities of frankincense, myrrh and silver.

The Greeks, knowing of this fortress-city, impregnable in its mountains, were the first to name it Petra, which means rock. Tradition says that Alexander the Great conquered all the then known world and wept because there were no more worlds to conquer. But tradition is wrong. Here is one city that Alexander the Great failed to conquer. Diodurus Siculus tells us that Alexander considered Petra of such importance that he sent Demetrius with an army to capture it. Demetrius tried to force his way into it by the same narrow defile through which we entered. But the inhabitants shut themselves up in their mountain fastness and successfully defied both siege and assault. Although the city refused itself to the visitor who came with the sword, it welcomed him who came with the olive branch.

As the capital of the Nabatæans, it rose to its zenith in the second century before Christ. Greek geographers of those days called the land of Edom by the name "Arabia Petræa."

The presence of Egyptian architecture and symbols indicates that Petra must have been built by a race that had come in contact with the culture of the peoples who carved the Sphinx and piled up the Pyramids. Even the desert traditions of nomenclature support the belief that Petra was at some time identified with Egypt. The nomads believe that these rocks were carved by Jinn, under the order of one of the Pharaohs, and not only are they certain that the great urn on El Khazneh contains the wealth of the old Egyptian tyrants but they believe that they actually lived in Petra, and call a ruined temple down in the valley Kasra Firaun, the Palace of Pharaoh. But nobody knows when, or by whom, Petra was built. Some think that it had its beginning long

before the time of Abraham and was an old city when the
Israelites fled from Egyptian bondage.

As we stand there amid the ruins of this forgotten city, we
are reminded that:

> When you and I behind the veil are passed,
> Oh, but the long, long while the world shall last;
> Which of our coming and departure heeds
> As the seven seas shall heed a pebble cast.

The region around Petra was known as Mount Seir in the
time of Abraham, and it is said that Esau, with his followers,
came to this country after he had lost his birthright. We read
in the Old Testament about Petra. It is called Sela, which is
Hebrew for rock. It is believed that when the children of
Israel were wandering in the Wilderness they came upon Petra
and asked for permission to enter and rest. But the people
of Petra refused, and Israel's prophets predicted its desolation.
Obadiah accused it of being proud and haughty, saying:
"Though thou mount on high as the eagle, and though thy
nest be set among the stars, I will bring thee down from thence,
saith the Lord." In the time of Isaiah it was a proud and
voluptuous city, of which the stern old Jew predicted
destruction.

Under Aretas III, surnamed Philhellene, or friend of the
Greeks, the first royal coins were struck and Petra assumed
many of the aspects of Greek culture. Even in the age of
Rome, when Augustus sat on the throne of the Cæsars, the
fame of this far-away city had reached Europe. It was a
Mecca for tourists from all over the world, and it must have
had a population of several hundred thousand souls. It was
a seat of arts and learning to which the Praxiteles, the Michael
Angelos, and the Leonardo da Vincis of that day repaired.
Its hospitality was a byword among the ancients. It opened
its doors to the early Christians, who were permitted to have
their houses of worship there side by side with the temples
of Baal, Apollo, and Aphrodite. Petra was to this part of
Asia what Rome was to the Romans and Athens to the Greeks.
In A.D. 105 one of Trajan's generals conquered Petra and
created the Roman province of Arabia Petræa, but the city
continued to flourish as a trade centre under the strong peace
of Rome. In those days Petra was the focussing point on
the caravan routes from the interior of Arabia, Persia, and
India to Egypt, Palestine, and Syria. It was a great safe
deposit of fabulous wealth, fortressed by frowning cliffs. Both
Strabo and Pliny described it as a great city. But when

Roman power waned, the Romanized Nabatæans were unable
to withstand the desert hordes. The caravan trade was
diverted through other channels; Petra declined in importance,
and ultimately was forgotten. In the twelfth century the
Crusaders, under Baldwin I, sent an expedition through the
locality and built many castles; they were expelled by Saladin.

There are many indications that Petra was a pleasant and
pleasure-loving city. Its wealthier classes must have lived
in luxury such as even the luxurious East has not known in
many centuries. With its concert-halls, its circuses, its mystic
groves, its priests and priestesses of many sensual religions,
its wealth of flowers, its brilliant sunshine, and its delightful
climate, it must have been at the same time the Paris and the
Riviera of Asia Minor.

"Rose-red there lies, and vivid in the sun,
    A magic city, hid in Araby;
Of her no ancient legend has been spun;
And all her past the silent years have won
    To the deep coffers of antiquity.

"About her brooding stillnesses there blow
    The scarlet windflowers, as a carpet flung
Upon the stones. And oleanders grow
Where, in the night, the mourning jackals go
    A-prowl through temples of a god unsung.

"And so she stands, and centuries have kept
    Her olden secret, tragic or sublime;
Without her gates, what tides of men have swept,
Within her portals, race of kings have slept?
    This 'rose-red city, half as old as Time.'

"Was there no poet's voice to chant her pride,
    To clarion her magic down the years?
No warrior famed, to set her valorous stride?
No splendid lovers who for love's sake died,
    Gifting to song their passion and their tears?

"Was there no storied woman's golden face
    To glimmer down unnumbered years to come?
No prophet's vision to foretell her place,
Mysterious city of forgotten race?
    Only her beauty speaks, and it is dumb.

"And so she stands, while Time holds jealously
    Her olden secret, tragic or sublime;
Her sorrows, joys, her strength, her frailty
Are in the coffers of antiquity,
    This 'rose-red city, half as old as Time.' " *

*Mona Mackay, Christchurch, New Zealand.

A little more than a century ago, John Lewis Burckhardt, a Swiss traveller, who had heard rumours of a great city of rock lying far out on the fringe of the Arabian desert, penetrated the gorge and found once more this wonderful city of Petra, which had not been mentioned in any literary record since A.D. 536. In the century or more since Burckhardt wrote of his discovery of the rock city in a letter from Cairo, only a comparatively few travellers and archæologists from the West have visited Petra. The danger of violence from Bedouin nomads was so great that not many had the zeal to attempt it. The lion and the lizard kept the court where Jamshyd gloried and drank deep, until Lawrence brought his fighting Bedouins into this city of tombs and empty palaces.

A HIGHLAND LAD HOLDING A COUNCIL OF WAR WITH A FUZZY-WUZZY

"BATHING BERT," WHO TOOK A "SHOWER" OUT OF A BUCKET FIVE TIMES A DAY, TO THE DISGUST OF SOME OF THE OTHERS, WHO HAD NEVER HAD A BATH IN THEIR LIVES

CHAPTER XIX

A BEDOUIN BATTLE IN A CITY OF GHOSTS

THE possession of Petra is necessary to the holding of Akaba, the most important strategical point on the west coast of Arabia, where the great fleets of King Solomon rode at anchor three thousand years ago. But Lawrence's battle was the first fought in Petra in the last seven hundred years. The Crusaders, with their flashing spears and pennants blazoned with the coats-of-arms of half the medieval barons of Europe, were the last warriors to clank in armour through the ribbon-like gorge. Lawrence, the archæologist, garbed in Arab kit, had wandered over this country before the War, and knew every foot of the region from the driest water-hole to the most dilapidated column in Petra. After he had forced the Turks to surrender at Akaba, he was determined to capture all the approaches to the high plateau which begins fifty miles inland from the head of the Gulf of Akaba and crosses Arabia to the Persian Gulf. At the same time the Turks realized that they must either recapture Akaba or reconcile themselves to the loss of all Holy Arabia. So they brought ten thousand fresh troops from Syria and stationed them at the various strategical positions on this plateau.

But Lawrence was certain that the Turks would never be able to retake Akaba, because there is only one feasible avenue of approach for an army by land to that ancient seaport—down the Wadi Ithm. To be sure, he had marched his own irregular army through the same gorge a few weeks before, but he had caught the Turks napping, and swept down on Akaba before they were aware of their danger. He had no intention of giving the Turks a similar opportunity. The Wadi Ithm is one of the most formidable passes in the world for an armed force to enter; it is as difficult of access as the famous Khyber Pass between India and Afghanistan. It penetrates the barren volcanic range called King Solomon's Mountains, which extends along the eastern shore of the Gulf of Akaba and rises a sheer five thousand feet on either side of the pass. An invading army, if attacked from the tops of the peaks crowning its sides, would have no protection. Lawrence would have annihilated any Turkish force attempting to advance on Akaba through the Wadi Ithm.

From July until the middle of September, 1917, the Turks

K

were quiet. Then they made several reconnaissances around
Petra in an effort to dupe Lawrence and the Arabs into
believing they were going to attack Petra, although their real
intention was to advance direct on Akaba. The last of these
three reconnaissances was a gloomy affair for the Turks;
Lawrence and his men cut off and wiped out one hundred of
the scouting party.

Fifteen miles north-east of Petra an old Crusader castle
frowns down on the desert from a steep hill of white chalk.
It is known as Shobek. Baldwin I, king of Jerusalem, built
a great wall all the way round the crest of the mountain in
the days of the Crusaders. Both the castle and the modern
Arab village are within the wall, and the only approach to
the summit is up a winding, precipitous trail. Shobek was
still in the hands of the Turks, but Lawrence's spies brought
him word that the garrison was made up entirely of Syrians,
all men of Arabian blood, in sympathy with the new
Nationalist movement. So Lawrence sent Malud and ten of
his lieutenants to Shobek by night, followed by Shereef Abdul
Mu'in and two hundred Bedouins.

The Syrians in a body transferred their allegiance to him.
Next morning the combined Syrian and Arabian forces
descended the chalk mountain and destroyed three hundred
rails on a side-line of the Damascus-Medina Railway near
Aneiza. They also tried to capture the terminus of this spur,
where seven hundred Armenian wood-cutters, whom they
wanted to rescue, were at work. But this time the Turks had
erected such strong fortifications around the terminus that,
although the Arabs and Syrian deserters took the Turkish outposts, they were unable to capture the main positions. The
Turks, badly frightened, sent couriers to Maan and Abu el
Lissal asking for reinforcements. By weakening their garrison
at Abu el Lissal the Turks played directly into Lawrence's
hands, for as soon as the Turkish reserves arrived, Lawrence
called his men back to Petra from the railway.

After the desertion of the entire Shobek garrison and
Lawrence's bold sortie against the railway terminus, Djemal
Pasha, commander-in-chief of the Turkish armies in Syria,
Palestine, and Arabia, decided, against the advice of Field-
Marshal von Falkenhayn, then German generalissimo in the
Near East, that before he could hope to recapture Gueirra and
Akaba it would be necessary to retake Petra. Djemal trans-
ferred a crack cavalry regiment, an infantry brigade, and
several organizations of light artillery from Palestine down
the Hedjaz Railway to Maan.

This was a clever strategic coup for Lawrence. First, the Germans and Turks had to diminish their forces opposing Allenby in the Holy Land. Secondly, they were walking into the trap which had been set for them because it was Lawrence's belief that if a battle were fought by his irregular Bedouin troops in the mountain-fastnesses of ancient Edom, the superior mobility of his army would eventually enable him to defeat any division of methodically-trained regulars in the world.

Malud Bey, Lawrence's first in command at the battle of Petra, was one of the most interesting figures of the Arabian revolt, as well as one of the most picturesque. He wore very high purple-topped Kafir boots—like Jack the Giant Killer must have worn—also spurs that jangled musically as he strode about, a long medieval sword, and a long moustachio, which he tugged like the villain of a melodrama. But there was no more charming and gallant officer in the whole Arabian army. He was the son of a Bedouin sheik and a Circassian concubine, and from boyhood had been an ardent Arab nationalist. He made a thorough study of modern military science in order that some day he might help to overthrow the Turk, and he even went so far as to spend three years studying at the Turkish Staff College before they discovered his revolutionary leanings and expelled him.

Then he went into the desert and became secretary to Ibn Rashid, one of the potentates of Central Arabia. There Malud participated in scores of raids, and earned such a reputation as a fighter that the Turks forgave him his past sins and invited him to return and join their cavalry. At the outbreak of the World War he was raised to the rank of captain, but he was later court-martialled and imprisoned for taking part in a conspiracy against the Sultan. After his release he fought against the British in Mesopotamia, and was captured by them near Basra. Eventually, he was allowed to join Feisal. He was wounded in every single engagement in which he took part, because he was so foolhardy that he would not hesitate to charge the Turkish army by himself.

Djemal Pasha selected Maan, the most important station on the Hedjaz Railway between the Dead Sea and Medina, as the starting-point for three columns comprising over seven thousand men, several units of light artillery, and a squadron of German aeroplanes. One column made the Crusader's castle at Shobek its base; another came up from the south by way of Abu el Lissal and Busta; and the third moved direct from Maan on the east. The Turks directed the movements of their columns so that they would all converge on Petra on October 21.

In the meantime, Lawrence and his Bedouins were comfortably and safely lodged in the ancient capital of the Nabatæans, behind those mighty rocky ramparts which had defied the armies of Alexander the Great. For the first time in many centuries the silent avenues throbbed with life. Camp fires were lighted on the old altars of the gods, and sentinels stationed on the ancient great high places watched for the coming of the Turks. In the vast, echoing chambers of the tombs the Arabs sat around in circles until late at night, telling interminable stories and singing old chants of epic battles. Lawrence himself occupied princely headquarters: the Temple of Isis (El Khazneh), the rose-tinted palace at the entrance of the gorge. If he wished he could have used his archæological imagination and re-peopled the gloomy hall with the vision of handmaidens of Isis dancing before the shrine of their goddess.

Instead, he sent for Sheik Khallil of Elgi, a neighbouring village, and told him it would be necessary to summon all the able-bodied women for miles around to help reinforce his troops. Arabian women may not have gone in for Red Cross work and women's motor-corps or canteen service, as their Western sisters did during the War, but they have always encouraged their men to fight. In the incessant tribal warfare they are often in the rear, encouraging their men with praise, chanting songs of Bedouin heroes, and shrieking words of blame if their own men-folk are not gallantly charging into the thick of the fray. A few centuries ago the fighting forces of the desert always had two or three of their women dressed in resplendent robes to act as standard-bearers. This, however, was the first time in Arabian history that armed battalions of women actually engaged in battle.

The Bedouin women living in the vicinity of Petra rose magnificently to the emergency. They dropped their butter-making and their weaving and thronged to Lawrence's head-quarters under the leadership of Sheik Khallil's wife. No smart uniforms with braid and buttons for the Bedouin Amazons! Barefooted, with long blue cotton robes, wearing gold bracelets and rings in their ears and noses, they gathered from all quarters to form their Battalion of Death. Rallying to the call of Lawrence, who had few men at his disposal, they fought with as great valour as their husbands and brothers, and played a vital part in routing the Turks.

Lawrence, remembering the stout defence put up by the

old Nabatæan kings, when Alexander's army failed to capture
Petra, stationed the Bedouin women at the narrow gorge
opposite the Temple of Isis to defend the city. The women
were fierce in their enthusiasm and needed no coaching to
make them capable musketeers. They hid behind the pillars
of the temple, some of them with their half-grown children,
and covered with their rifles the gorge, which was so narrow
that only a few Turks and Germans could march through
abreast. The men held their ground and were not even panic-
stricken when German aeroplanes swooped down over the
rock temples and dropped bombs on the streets, theatre and
water-circus. They clutched their rifles only the more tightly
when one German bomb made a direct hit on an Arabian
machine-gun, causing the Maxim and its crew to vanish as
though spirited away.

Throughout the whole battle Lawrence commanded from
the top of the north ridge. He had with him a force of fifty
Bedouin youths, who were selected for their speed as runners,
and who proved most valuable as orderlies. They could sprint
like hares, and clamber about the rocks with the agility of
the oryx. If one had viewed the battle from the Arabian
positions and seen only the women and the Bedouin men
dressed in every conceivable desert costume, mounted on
horses and camels without saddles, and using nearly every
weapon invented by man from the dawn of time, if one could
have eliminated the modern note provided by the trench-
helmets and commonplace, lead-coloured uniforms of the
Turks and their squadron of aeroplanes, one might easily
have mistaken the battle of Petra for a clash between the
ancient Edomites and the kings of Israel.

Lawrence had only two mountain-guns and two machine-
guns, but with these he held the first ridge, five miles south
of Petra, for over six hours and killed sixty Turks, with
practically no casualties on his side. Then, when the enemy
attack had fully developed, when the Turks and Germans were
advancing straight up the ridge in spite of the fire of the Arabs,
Lawrence vacated it and sent half his men to occupy a ridge
a little nearer Petra to the south, and the other half to a ridge
on the opposite side of the valley on the north. Between his
two companies ran the wide part of the Wadi Musa, a mile
distant from the point where it narrows down and becomes a
mere cleft through the mountain wall south of the city.

The Turks, elated at having captured the trenches on the
first ridge, were certain that they had decisively beaten
Lawrence's forces; so they charged enthusiastically over the

summit and down into the valley, thinking the Arabs had surely retired all the way into Petra. Meanwhile, Lawrence and his men were hiding in ambush on the hills of Petra. He permitted at least a thousand of the enemy's troops to push headlong into the gorge before he gave the order to fire. When he had the Turks wedged into the narrowest part of the gorge, near the entrance to the city, one of his aides fired a rocket into the air as a signal for the Arabs to attack. A moment later pandemonium broke loose in the mountains of Edom. The Arabs poured in a stream of fire from all sides. The crack of rifles seemed to come from every rock. With shrill screams the women and children tumbled huge boulders over the edge on the heads of the Turks and Germans hundreds of feet below. Those stationed behind the columns of the Temple of Isis kept up a steady fire. Utterly bewildered, the invaders became panicky, and scattered in all possible directions, while the Arabs on the ridges continued to devastate their broken ranks.

A few minutes before the sun declined behind the rose-coloured mountains, Lawrence and Malud Bey sent up a second signal to their followers.

"Up, children of the desert!" shouted Malud.

Crouching figures sprang from behind the rocks on all sides. "Allah! Allah!" came the answer from the throats of hundreds of Bedouins as they swept down the ridges into the valley.

The Arabs captured the entire Turkish transport, a complete field-hospital, and hundreds of prisoners. One body of over a thousand Turks, who succeeded in retreating to Busta in fair order, fought their way back several days later to Abu el Lissal and to Maan.

After the battle, Lawrence slipped through the Turkish lines in disguise and returned with a copy of the Turkish communiqué describing the battle. It brought roars of laughter from the victorious Arabs. It ran:

"We have stormed the fortifications of Petra, losing twelve killed and ninety-four wounded. The Arab losses are one thousand dead and wounded, and we counted seventeen British officers among the bodies."

The only British officers, except Lawrence, who were in that part of Arabia at the time were many miles away, at Akaba. Lawrence himself had worn his Arab robes. His losses were twenty-eight killed and wounded. The Turks had made a little error of 972 in their estimate.

CHAPTER XX

"THE RELATIVE IN MY HOUSE"

"PERHAPS the reason why women played such a small part in the War in the Land of the Arabian Nights," explained Colonel Lawrence, "was because their men-folk wear the skirts and are prejudiced against petticoats." Then adding philosophically: "Perhaps that is one of the reasons why I am so fond of Arabia. So far as I know, it is the only country left where men rule!"

But Colonel Lawrence denies the assertion made by another authority on Arabia that man is the absolute master and woman a mere slave. Although "she is the object of his sensual pleasures, a toy with which he plays whenever and however he pleases"; although "knowledge is his, ignorance is hers"; although "the firmament and the light are his, darkness and the dungeon are hers"; and although "his is to command, hers is blindly to obey," she still wields a vast, indirect influence. But one sees and hears very little of her. Arabia is one country, indeed, where the equal suffrage propaganda of Mrs. Catt and Mrs. Pankhurst has made little headway.

Although the king of the Hedjaz figures in the cable news, his queen, Gellaleta el Melika, is never mentioned. Emir Feisal attended the Versailles Peace Conference as the head of the Arabian delegation, but his wife, who shortly afterward became the first queen of a new dynasty in Bagdad, did not accompany him.

Hussein Ibn Ali's capital is one city where European and American diplomatists and their wives are not welcome. Just imagine how dull life in London and New York would become if the customs of Mecca were suddenly adopted. There would be no charming stenographers, no coquettish midinettes, no dancing in hotels and restaurants, no charity bazaars, and no feminine politicians.

Where we rise when a woman enters the room, an Arab never does. In fact, he will not even eat with a woman, but, of course, she is expected to serve him. When an Arab prince goes out "to smell the air" on his camel, his wife does not accompany him. In fact, the women of the towns rarely leave the harem oftener than once a week. In Jeddah, for instance, on Thursday afternoon they stroll outside the city wall to the tomb of Mother Eve. But, in spite of their secluded lives, many a veiled beauty of Arabia has played a subtle part in politics and has by no means been satisfied with conquests of love. Many, indeed, have been the successors to the Queen of Sheba who, by their wisdom as well as their charm, have made their lords and masters kiss the dust beneath their feet.

The Koran permits a man to have four wives at a time, but a Moslem usually marries only one, unless he is rich enough to provide a separate house for others. Of course, this only refers to the townsmen. Hard as it may be to believe, it is nevertheless true that the average Mussulman actually finds it difficult to get along peacefully with four wives all under the same roof! The Koran also conveniently permits him to have as many concubines and slave girls as his right hand can hold. Mohammed himself is said to have had eleven wives and several concubines; and, although it may be difficult for a stream to rise higher than its source, it is nevertheless a fact that among the more intelligent city dwellers of to-day polygamy, concubinage, and slavery are dying out. King Hussein, King Feisal, Emir Ali, and the Sultan Abdullah of Transjordania, and most of the prominent present-day leaders in Arabia, have but one wife each.

An Arab woman can be divorced for not having a son; she not only can be, but frequently is. An Arab seldom speaks of a woman as his wife. He calls her "the relative in my house," or "the mother of my son Ali." Girl babies are usually not very welcome. But when a child is born, no matter what the sex, the first precaution taken is to protect the babe from the influence of the evil eye. This is done by hanging a charm about its neck. Mothers also have a prejudice against curly hair, and do everything possible to straighten out any stubborn kinks in a baby's locks.

In some parts of the desert there is an unwritten law that if a girl is attacked by a man between sunrise and noon, the man shall be flogged severely; if between noon and sunset, he is merely fined; and if during the night, when all are supposed to be in their tents under the protection of their families, the man is not subject to punishment.

A man usually marries between the ages of twenty and twenty-four, and a woman any time after she is twelve. Professional match-makers in Arabia do not perform their services gratuitously and unsolicited as they do in Europe and America. When a Moslem wants to take unto himself a help-mate he hires the services of a matronly lady who is an arranger of marriages by profession. He pays a certain sum for his bride; how much is always a matter of spirited argument. He never sees his fiancée until after the orange-blossoms and old shoes—and then it's too late. The bride's mother does not call in the neighbours and a professional dressmaker to study the trousseau patterns in *Vogue* or *The Ladies' Home Journal*. She merely borrows a cashmere shawl for her daughter.

One of the few careers open to a woman of the Near East to-day is that of acting as a professional mourner. Often the mourners wail for days; and the wail, which sounds like the cry of a lost soul, usually ends in a piercing shriek which makes your blood run cold.

The custom of immediate burial often results in complications. There is a bazaar story told in Jeddah to the effect that a Scot, who was stationed there early in the War, passed away as a result of some mysterious malady. He was carried a short distance outside the city and buried in the sand near the shore, wrapped in nothing but a Union Jack. A few hours before the funeral a boat left Jeddah Harbour and it carried an official memorandum to the Government in London telling of the death of the officer. After the ceremony the mourners were returning to the city when suddenly they heard shouts and, turning, were panic-stricken to see the corpse running toward them, swathed in the Union Jack. It seems that the Scot had merely been in a trance, and, a few moments after he was buried in the loose sand, land-crabs attacked him and brought him back to life. But, not satisfied at letting the yarn go at this, they tell how the Scot was afterward arrested in London for impersonating himself when he called at his bank to cash a cheque.

Between the nomad woman of the tents and the towns-woman there is even more difference than between a wiry desert patriarch and his corpulent city cousin. Townswomen are fat and white, while the Bedouin women are thin and tanned. Many Bedouin sheiks have four wives at a time. Some of the richest chieftains have as many as fifty wives during a lifetime, but never more than four at once. One reason why they so frequently indulge themselves in the luxury of three or four is because it means easier housework. The Bedouin women all live in the same tent, too; and, strangely enough, jealousy is uncommon. They do not regard a husband as exclusive property as we do.

Bedouin women are even more ignorant and prejudiced than their men-folk, and they spend no small part of their time urging the men to fight. It is they who keep the century-old blood-feuds alive.

The desert nomads have no way of marking time; no Sundays, no Mondays, no 1925's and no 1926's. They are born: "It is the will of Allah." They grow up and after a while they die: "It is the will of Allah." That is all there is to it: "It is the will of Allah." So it is not bad form to ask a Bedouin woman her age, for she does not know whether she is sweet sixteen or a Mrs. Methuselah.

They are all frightfully talkative, and whenever we were seated on the men's side of the thin partition which divides the goat's-hair home of a Bedouin sheik, talking about Western customs, such as women walking along city streets unveiled, or attending the theatre in company with their gentlemen friends, or playing golf, his wives would pop their heads up over the partition and remark: "How disgusting! How vulgar! How beastly!"

Despite the example set by the Arabs themselves, Colonel Lawrence scrupulously avoided free talk about women. It is as difficult a subject as religion.

On one occasion, when seated in Sheik Auda Abu Tayi's tent, Lawrence was in an unusually talkative frame of mind and was giving his host a racy description of cabaret life in London. Every few minutes Auda would slap his knee and roar: "By Jove! I wish I were there!" Then his wives would break in and upbraid him bitterly.

The Bedouin women usually retain their beauty until their thirties, but after that . . . ! They are all short and thin. They take all their pleasures in their tents. The Bedouin women of the desert are not veiled, but they tattoo their faces and paint their lips blue. On all occasions they wear a garment of dark blue cotton and keep their hair covered. Mohammed objected to women exposing their hair in public.

All Arabs are fond of buying pearls or trinkets of hammered gold for their women. Some of their wives wear gold ornaments worth £1,000 or more. According to the unwritten law of Arabia, all ornaments are the personal property of a woman, and if divorced she keeps them. If an Arab wants to divorce his wife, he simply says three times before witnesses: "I divorce thee! I divorce thee! I divorce thee!" Consequently, all the women are foresighted enough to insist on having their possessions in portable form.

The training of the Bedouin women is entirely in the tents. They spend much of their time milking their camels and goats and making butter. To do the latter they get the milk in curds, which they squeeze in their hands and put on the tent-roofs until all the moisture drops out. When it dries it becomes as hard as a rock. In fact, their butter is so hard that it will even turn the edge of a knife! Lawrence would pulverize it between stones and mix it with water until it resembled malted milk.

Many Bedouins regard women as the source of all evil, and say that Hell is full of them. The verses of a few desert poets breathe hatred for women rather than love. Here is a verse from one of Sir Richard Burton's translations:

> "They said, marry.
> I said I am free;
> Why take unto my bosom
> A sackful of snakes?
> May Allah never bless womankind!"

It is a simple matter for a Bedouin woman to clean house or move. The tribe leaves one bit of the desert as soon as the pasturage in the vicinity is exhausted. The more aristocratic Bedouins have neither sheep nor goats—only camels and horses. They limit themselves to the least possible amount of possessions and refuse to be tied down to any one spot. They have the fewest wants and are the freest of all the peoples of the earth.

Sheik Nuri Shalaan once asked to be told something about European customs. "Well, if you come to my house in England," said Lawrence, "my women will serve you with tea." Whereupon Nuri clapped his hands for one of his wives, ordered her to make tea, and invited Lawrence into the women's quarters to drink it, an act entirely contrary to the unwritten law of the desert.

The Bedouins are exceedingly courteous, and no matter how appalling your Arabic they will never presume to correct you. When you call at a Bedouin tent you make all of your polite speeches right away, and then when you leave you may get up and brush off without saying a word of farewell. I have seen Bedouins call on Lawrence in his tent when he was reading. He would greet them, and then they would crouch down on their heels and he would resume his book. After a while they would get up and silently walk out. But Lawrence himself would never leave so long as a guest was there.

Al Ghazzali, the great theologian of Islam of the eleventh century, said: "Marriage is a kind of slavery, for the wife becomes the slave of the husband, and it is her duty, absolutely, to obey him in everything he requires of her

except in what is contrary to the laws of Islam." Wife-beat-
ing is allowed by the Koran. All female slaves taken in war
may become the private property of the man who wins them.
There is an old tradition that a lie is excusable in three
circumstances: in war, to reconcile friends, and to women.

To the average Arab, heaven is an oasis with date-palms,
sparkling fountains and racing camels, where every male
angel may have as many concubines as he desires. So is it
any wonder that the Arab and the Turk are splendid fighters
when we realize that if they die in battle against the unbeliever
they will go direct to such a paradise?

In that land of romance and mystery, of palm-trees,
camels, and veiled women, custom, founded on the teachings
of the Prophet, relegates the gentler sex to an inferior position
not only in this world but in the hereafter as well. But, despite this, there are many Arabs who make love just as ardently
as their enslaved brethren in other lands, and nearly all
Arabian poets draw their inspiration from the loveliness of
woman.

> "My heart is firmer than the roots of mountains;
> My fame pervasive as the smell of musk.
> My pleasure is in hunting the wild lion;
> The beast of prey I visit in his den.
>   Yet all the while a gentle fawn has snared me,
> A heifer from the pastures of Khazam."

CHAPTER XXI

THROUGH THE TURKISH LINES IN DISGUISE

NEARLY all Arabs carry some sort of good-luck charm, and the belief in jinn or genii is still common. The talisman which Auda wore round his neck was probably one of the most extraordinary to be found in all Arabia. The amulet was a diminutive copy of the Koran about one inch square, for which he paid more than two hundred pounds. One day he displayed it with great pride, and Lawrence discovered it had been printed in Glasgow and, according to the price marked inside the cover, had been issued at eighteenpence. So far as we could make out, the only things Bedouins are afraid of are snakes, and they believe that the sole protection against them is such a charm worn round the neck.

There are thousands of reptiles in certain parts of the desert. The worst snake-belt in the Near East extends from Jauf to Azrak along a chain of shallow wells in the North Arabian Desert, where one finds, usually near the water, Indian cobras, puff-adders, black whip-snakes, and hosts of others—nearly all deadly. Lawrence once started out on an expedition with eighteen men, five of whom died on the way from snake-bite. Instead of relying on the usual alcoholic antidote, he, like his nomad companions, put his faith in Allah. In Arabia a snake will often snuggle up to a sleeping Bedouin at night for warmth, but it will not bite—unless the sleeper is unlucky enough to roll over and frighten it. Although their consciences are by no means clear, nearly all Bedouins, fortunately, are sound sleepers!

Whenever Lawrence and his men reconnoitred in the snake-belt at night they put on boots and were careful to beat every foot of ground and every bush in front of them. When an Arab is bitten his friends read certain chapters of the Koran over him. If they happen to choose correct passages, he lives; but if they have no Koran, the unfortunate one in all likelihood dies. 'Tis the will of Allah!

Although the Arabs knew Lawrence was a Christian, once he had gained their confidence they often invited him to pray with them. This he did only when he felt inclined to humour them, but he had completely memorized all the important Mohammedan prayers so as to be prepared for any unforeseen emergency when his declining to pray might cause

157

embarrassment to Emir Feisal and King Hussein in the presence of members of strange tribes. Fortunately, no such emergency ever arose.

But when he did pray with his Bedouins on several occasions, just to please them, the procedure was as follows: Lawrence and his bodyguard would kneel on their prayer-rugs with their faces toward Mecca. Then with one of the sheiks acting as leader they would go through a ceremony consisting of rhythmic prostrations and the repetition, in unison, of passages from the Koran. A certain number of bows are made in the morning, so many at noon, and still a different number at sunset, although the words repeated each time are much the same. At the end of all prayers Lawrence and his men would turn their heads to the right and then to the left before rising. Lawrence explained to me that two angels were supposed to be standing beside each person while praying. One angel records good deeds and the other bad deeds, and it is customary to salute them both. All good Moslems have five prayer services daily, but Lawrence and his men usually cut them down to three by telescoping two in the morning and two in the afternoon; otherwise the Arab army would have spent more time praying than fighting.

Lawrence overcame the two greatest prejudices of the Bedouins, namely, that he was a foreigner and a Christian. Most of the foreigners these nomads had met were Turks, whom they despised as barbarians, for the Arabs are intellectual snobs. The only Christians they know are the native Christians of the Syrian coast and the Armenians, who are more accustomed to show the other cheek than to show courage; the Arabs loathe them. It suited them for the most part to ignore the fact that Lawrence was a Christian, because they consider it a disgrace that any Christian should outdo them at the very things at which they ordinarily excel. Occasionally, however, they actually invited him to recite his Christian prayers aloud, which he did most eloquently.

Charles M. Doughty, the traveller and poet, so far as I know, was the only man other than Lawrence who ever wandered openly up and down Holy Arabia as a Christian. All other explorers in the forbidden country of the Prophet have disguised themselves as Moslems. Doughty had at least a score of narrow escapes from death, and that he escaped at all was due to the fact that he always went unarmed and did nothing covertly. He took no money with him, and made his way about by healing the sick with simple remedies and by vaccinating Arabs. An old man and a great scholar, he now lives at a watering-place on the south coast of England. He and Lawrence are close friends, and the younger man gives his predecessor full credit for "breaking the ice" and making it possible for him and his associates to work with the Bedouins during the War.   In fact Doughty's "Arabia Deserta" was both Lawrence's Bible and military text-book during the campaign.

The magnificent Bedouin clothes that Lawrence wore were not theatrical garb.   They were a part of his carefully worked-out plan to gain complete mastery over the Arabs.   Although he did not attempt to disguise either his religion or nationality, outwardly he was an Arab.   Except in certain areas, he found that being known as a British officer and a Christian was less of a hindrance than full disguise.   Had he desired to pass himself off as a Bedouin, he would have had to grow a beard, a feat he could not have achieved even if the fate of the British Empire had depended on it.   However, on a few occasions he did disguise himself as a Bedouin woman and made his way through the Turkish lines.   But to other British officers who desired to visit a tribe he recommended simply the Arab head-cloth, to be worn out of courtesy and not as a disguise.

Bedouins have a malignant prejudice against the hat, and believe our persistence in wearing it is founded on some irreligious principle.   If you were to wear this season's smartest Piccadilly bowler or Austrian velour in Mecca, your friends and relatives would disown you.

"Adopt the kuffieh, agal, and abba, and you will acquire the confidence and intimacy of the sons of Ishmael to a degree impossible in European garb," was a Lawrence maxim. "But to don Arab kit has its dangers as well as its advantages. Breaches of etiquette, excused in a foreigner, are not condoned if he is in Arab clothes.   You are like an English actor appearing for the first time in a German theatre.   Even that is not a parallel, because you are playing a part day and night, and for an anxious stake.   Complete success comes when the Arab forgets your strangeness and speaks naturally before you." So far as I know, Colonel Lawrence is the only European who was ever accepted by the Arabs as one of themselves.

His advice was that if you wear Arab dress, you shall always wear the best, for the reason that clothes are significant among the tribes.   "Dress like a shereef, if the people agree to it, and, if you use Arab costume at all, go the whole length. Leave your English friends and customs on the coast, and rely entirely on Arab habits.   If you can outdo the Arabs, you have taken an immense stride toward complete success, but the effort of living and thinking a foreign language, the rude fare, strange clothes, and stranger ways with the complete loss of privacy and quiet, and the impossibility of ever relaxing your watchful imitation of others for months on end, prove such an added strain that this course should not be taken without serious thought.''

Whenever Colonel Lawrence was not engaged in conducting major military operations or planting tulips along the Hedjaz Railway, he would disguise himself as an outcast Arab woman and slip through the enemy lines. This was the best disguise for a spy, for the Turkish sentinels usually considered it beneath their dignity to say: ''Stop, who goes there?'' to a woman. Time and again he penetrated hundreds of miles into enemy territory, where he obtained much of the data which finally enabled Field-Marshal Allenby's Palestine army and Emir Feisal's Arabian forces to overwhelm the Turks in the most dazzling and brilliant cavalry operation in history.

Lawrence once had a spare fortnight in which to make things lively for the Turks while he was waiting for Auda Abu Tayi to assemble his Howeitat warriors. Accompanied by a lone Bedouin of the Anazah tribe named Dahmi, he passed through the Turkish lines in his customary female disguise and made his way toward Palmyra, where he hoped to find an influential Bedouin sheik who was in sympathy with the Arabian revolt. This chief was a thousand miles away on the Euphrates, so Lawrence and Dahmi turned their camels toward Baalbek. In the desert near that ancient Syrian city, famous for its ruined temples, which rival the Acropolis at Athens, lives a tribe of semi-nomads, the Metawileh, who were friendly to King Hussein and Emir Feisal although they were compelled to co-operate with the Turks. Lawrence wanted to visit these Metawileh to assure himself of their assistance some months' later when the final advance would be launched and when he expected the Hedjaz forces and Allenby's troops to push the Turks north through Syria. His plan was to arouse all the nomad tribes in Syria, so that they would be constantly harassing the Turkish army from within their own lines.

Two miles outside Beelbek, Lawrence slid down from his camel, took off his Arab costume, and swaggered boldly into the little town in the uniform of a British officer without insignia. At this time Baalbek was still several hundred miles north of the line dividing Allenby's forces from the Turks. The British were only a few miles north of Jerusalem. The Turkish troops on the streets of Baalbek saluted Lawrence as though he had been a German officer. But there was nothing

LAWRENCE AND A PART OF HIS BODYGUARD READY TO SET FORTH ON A SECRET RAID

DURING THE WAR IN THE LAND OF THE "ARABIAN NIGHTS" LAWRENCE BLEW UP SEVENTY-NINE
TURKISH BRIDGES. HE ALSO DYNAMITED MANY TRAINS AND STATIONS

unusual in this, for if a Prussian officer of the Death's Head
Hussars had passed Whitehall in London during the War he,
no doubt, would have received the salute of the Horse Guards.
Lawrence's theory was that it was a much simpler matter to
go bodly and openly in uniform in rural Turkey than to dodge
about in a suspicious manner.   After hurriedly glancing over
the fortifications around Baalbek, Lawrence attempted to visit
the Turkish military school, where thousands of young officers
were being trained.   But when he reached the gates he
observed that officers barred the way and so he decided it
would be safer to retreat without exacting a salute.

Resuming his disguise, Lawrence went on to the tents of
the Metawileh, where he pulled aside his veil and revealed his
identity.   The sheiks gathered round the new English "Prince
of Mecca" and clamoured for a Syrian revolution at once.
Lawrence explained that the time was not yet ripe, and tried
to encourage them to future action by glowing accounts of the
victories farther south in the Hedjaz.   However, he found the
Metawileh so keen for a raid or a lark of some kind that he was
prevailed upon to join them in what he always referred to as
"a cinema show."   In his contact with the peoples of the
desert he made the discovery that noise is one of the best forms
of propaganda.   So that night, followed by every able-bodied
man, woman and child in the tribe, Lawrence went down to
the main line of the Turkish railway, which runs from
Constantinople and Aleppo through Baalbek to Beirut.   He
selected one of the largest steel and concrete bridges in the
Near East as the object of the evening's diversion.   After
planting his tulips under both ends of the bridge and all its
bastions, he carried an electric wire, connecting all charges,
to the summit of a nearby hill, which the people of the
Metawileh were occupying as a grandstand.   Then, at the
psychological moment, he threw in the switch and sent the
great bridge skyward in a mass of flame and smoke.   The
Metawileh to the last man were convinced of the might of the
Allies and swore oaths, by Allah the Most High and by the
Holy Koran, that they would join King Hussein's Faithful.

From here Lawrence and his solitary Bedouin companion
trekked across Syria to Damascus.   They rode through the
bazaars by night to the palace of Ali Riza Pasha, who was
acting as military governor for the Turks.   Ali Riza, although
one of the Sultan's highest officials in Syria, secretly sympathized with the Arabian Nationalist movement.   That evening
at dinner, over innumerable cups of sweetened coffee, Ali
Riza informed Lawrence that the growing dissension between

L

Turkish and German officials would assure the ultimate success of the Allies in Palestine and Arabia. The Germans had become so high and mighty in their own estimation that they were treating the Turks like dogs. Consequently, feeling against the Germans had become so bitter that whenever the German General Staff gave an order the Turks would do their best to prevent its execution.

According to Ali Riza, Falkenhayn a few weeks previously had advised the Turks to abandon both Palestine and Arabia and retire to a line across Syria to the Mediterranean from Deraa, the important railway junction south of Damascus. The German Field-Marshal had given the Turks sound and valuable advice, but the latter were as reluctant to accept it as they were to accept Field-Marshal Falkenhayn himself as their commander-in-chief. As a result of their having spurned his counsel, they were so overwhelmed a little later by the combined British and Arabian forces that they not only lost all the region which Falkenhayn had advised them to abandon but they also lost the city of Damascus and the entire territory of Syria which they otherwise might have saved.

After a bountiful dinner and this illuminating interview with the Ottoman governor of Damascus, Lawrence and Dahmi slipped into the desert and made their way south into the Hauran, the country of the Druses, a people who pitch their tents round a high mountain called Jebel Druz. The Druses owe much of their tribal solidarity to their peculiar religion, which is a secret faith built up around the worship of Hakim, a mad Sultan of Egypt of the Middle Ages. The Turks have always had great difficulty in getting this quarrelsome, independent tribe to recognize Ottoman authority or pay taxes to the Sultan. Most of the desert Arabs have carried on perpetual blood-feuds with them, but Lawrence called their chieftains together and, with his inimitable gift for winning friends, succeeded in convincing them that they should swear allegiance to Feisal and hold themselves ready to co-operate with his army when it approached Damascus.

There would have been no quarter for Lawrence had he made a single false step. With his companion Dahmi, and Tallal, a Bedouin sheik known to the far corners of Arabia, he rode all round Damascus, Deraa, and the Hauran, making a reconnaissance of the Turkish lines of defence. He explored the Turkish railway on three sides of the junction at Deraa and took a mental note of important points on the lines north, south, and west of the junction which it would be necessary for him to cut when he made his ultimate advance against

Damascus. All this was walking right into danger, and only the perfection of his disguise and his command of the dialects of the country saved him from being suspected by the Turks and shot as an ordinary spy.

He had one extremely narrow escape. When strolling nonchalantly along the streets of Deraa, dressed as Sheik Tallal's son, two soldiers of the Sultan's army stopped him at a bazaar and arrested him on the charge of being a deserter from the Turkish army. Every able-bodied Arab in the Ottoman Empire was supposed to be under arms. They took him to headquarters and flogged him until he fainted. Then they threw him out more dead than alive, and fearfully bruised. Some time later he regained consciousness and, barely able to crawl, he made his escape under cover of night.

Masquerading as a woman also entailed many difficulties. At Amman, in the hills of Moab, east of the Jordan, Lawrence went through the Turkish lines disguised as a Bedouin gipsy. He spent the afternoon prowling about the defences surrounding the railway station, and, after deciding that it would be futile for his Arabs to attempt to capture it on account of the size of the garrison and the strength of the artillery, he started toward the desert. A party of Turkish soldiers who had been looking with favourable eyes at the Bedouin "woman" started to trail him. For more than a mile they followed Lawrence, trying to flirt with him and jeering at him when he repulsed their advances.

One of the most important Turkish strongholds on the border of the Arabian Desert was the town of Kerak, near the south end of the Dead Sea. One night Lawrence, disguised as a Bedouin, went through the Turkish lines with Sheik Trad Ibn Nueiris of the Beni Sakr tribe and found that there happened to be only three hundred Turks in the garrison at the moment. Lawrence and the sheik banqueted that evening with one of Trad's Kerak friends. In honour of their distinguished visitors the Arab villagers dragged sheep and goats into the streets, built large fires, and feasted and circled in wild wardances until the witching hour. The members of the Turkish garrison were so frightened by this bold demonstration that they locked themselves in their barracks!

After the celebration, Lawrence and his companion left Kerak and returned to Akaba. The result of this unimportant little episode was that two thousand more Turkish troops were withdrawn from the forces opposing Allenby in Palestine and sent down to Kerak. Lawrence had attained the two objects that he had in mind in making this extended and adventurous

tour of enemy territory: he had spread broadcast propaganda
for the cause of Arabian nationalism among the tribes that
were still under Turkish jurisdiction, and he had obtained
information enough to fill a book regarding the plans of the
German High Command. He went over the territory behind
the Turkish lines so thoroughly that during the final drive of
the campaign he knew that part of the country almost as
intimately as the Turks themselves.

CHAPTER XXII

THE GREATEST HOAX SINCE THE TROJAN HORSE

WITH the capture of the ancient seaport of Akaba, which transformed the Shereefian Revolt into an invasion of Syria, and with the final recognition of the Hedjaz Army as the right wing of Allenby's forces, it became imperative that all Lawrence's movements should fit in with Allenby's plans.

Allenby by this time was in possession of all southern Palestine up to a zig-zag line extending across the country from the Jordan Valley to the shores of the Mediterranean just south of Mt. Carmel, the peak which since earliest times has been known as the Mountain of God. His first drive in the autumn of 1917 had resulted in the liberation of Beersheba, the ancient home of Abraham and Lot, of Gaza, the capital of the Philistines where Samson was betrayed by Delilah, and of Hebron, where Abraham, Isaac, Sarah, and Rebecca were buried in the cave of Machpelah. It had also resulted in the deliverance of Jaffa, the chief port of Palestine since the days of David and Solomon three thousand years ago, of the Plains of Philistia and the Plains of Sharon, and, more important still, had resulted in the liberation of the sacred cities of Bethlehem and Jerusalem from the Ottoman yoke.

But the ancient land of Samaria, the city of Nazareth and all Galilee, the coastal plain of northern Palestine and all of Syria still remained in the hands of the Turks, so that the campaign was only half completed. There were now two courses open to Allenby: either to push the Turks north by degrees, or to crush Turkish power in the East with one sweeping blow. The commander-in-chief elected to take the big risk, and he chose the latter.

He decided to launch his final attack north of Jaffa and Jerusalem in July, 1918. But in June, when Ludendorff was making his last drive toward Paris and the Channel ports, the Allies were so hard pressed in Western Europe that they were compelled to call upon Allenby to send many of his divisions to reinforce them in France.

This completely disrupted all Allenby's plans. It now became necessary for him to create a new army. The unexpected necessity for a complete reconstruction of the forces in the Holy Land was a staggering blow; but England's modern Cœur de Lion was not in the least disheartened and

immediately set to work to form a new army made up largely
of Indian divisions from Mesopotamia hitherto untried in
the War, and from his veteran Anzac cavalry under Light
Horse Harry Chauvel, the Australian general whom he had
placed in command of the largest body of mounted troops that
ever participated in modern warfare. Instead of attacking the
Turks in northern Palestine in June or July it now seemed
impossible for him to launch his final thunderbolt before
October or November. Lawrence was convinced that such a
long delay would make it difficult for him to give much
assistance on the right flank. By then his restive Bedouins
would be wanting to migrate with their flocks to their winter
pastures on the Central Arabian plateaux, and, in addition,
his many years' experience in the country led him to believe
that autumn rains would impede any military operation
attempted during that season.

He explained this to the commander-in-chief, who
immediately grasped the situation, and by superhuman effort
whipped his new army into shape so that his new divisions
were ready to take the field within eight weeks from the date
of their arrival from Mesopotamia ! Toward the end of August
he despatched an aeroplane to Arabia with a welcome
message for Lawrence, the announcement that he would be
ready for a joint attack early in September instead of October
or November.

Allenby, fully aware of the inexperience of most of his new
troops, realized that the Turks would have to be defeated by
strategy rather than by force. So he decided to dupe the Turks
with a colossal hoax, a sort of moving picture of the British
Army pushing straight up along the Jordan River from the
Dead Sea toward Galilee. But it was to be a bogus army ! In
preparing this hoax Allenby's first move was to shift all his
camel hospitals from southern Palestine to the Jordan Valley
within fifteen miles of the Turkish lines. Next, he had
hundreds of condemned and worn-out tents shipped up over
the Milk and Honey Railway from Egypt, and pitched them
on the banks of the Jordan. Then he hauled all his captured
Turkish cannon down into the Jordan Valley and started them
blazing away in the direction of the Turks encamped in the
hills of Moab. Ten thousand horse blankets were thrown over
bushes in the valley and tied up to look like horse lines. Five
new pontoon bridges were flung over the river.

The sacred valley of the Jordan was filled with all the
properties for a sham battle of the ages. Never since the
Greeks captured Troy with their famous wooden horse has

such a remarkable bit of camouflage been put over on a credulous enemy.

When the German reconnaissance aeroplanes flew over the Jordan they buzzed back to Turkish headquarters with the important news that Allenby had placed two new divisions in this sector! This camouflage army, arranged largely by General Bartholomew of Allenby's staff, was so realistic that the Germans and Turks never dreamed that it might all be a fake; and fortunately the lines were so carefully guarded that not a single German or Turkish spy got through. Lawrence, also, lent a helping hand in duping the Turks. Shortly before the date arranged for the big push three hundred members of the Imperial Camel Corps came down from Palestine to help him. They were under the command of Colonel "Robin" Buxton, a born soldier, who before the War was a prominent Lombard Street banker. Under the guidance of his tent-mate, Major W. E. Marshall, R.A.M.C., the fighting bacteriologist, Lawrence sent the camel corps to attack an important Turkish garrison at Mudawara, where a spectacular twenty-minute engagement was fought on August 8.

After the battle of Mudawara, Lawrence led a combined force of camel corps and Arabs against Amman, just east of the Jordan. This was merely a feint, but it confirmed the Turks in the belief that the valley of the historic Jordan River was swarming with the bulk of Allenby's forces. Lawrence sent one of the most prominent chiefs of the Beni Sakr toward Damascus with £7,000 in gold to buy barley. The sheik bought recklessly in every town and village on the eastern border of Syria. The Turks, knowing well that Emir Feisal's Bedouin cavalry could not use such vast quantities of grain, immediately decided that the barley must be intended for Allenby's forces in the Jordan Valley. Lawrence also started the rumour through the Arab army that Emir Feisal's host intended to launch its main attack against Deraa railway junction between Amman and Damascus.

"As a matter of fact," Lawrence remarked, "we had every intention of attacking Deraa, but we spread the news so far and wide that the Turks refused to believe it. Then in deadly secrecy we confided to a chosen few in the inner circle that we really were going to concentrate all of our forces against Amman. But we were not."

This "secret," of course, leaked out and was betrayed to the Turks, who immediately shifted the greater part of their forces to the vicinity of Amman, exactly as Allenby and Lawrence had planned.

When the advance of the Arab army actually started, none but Emir Feisal, Colonel Joyce, and Colonel Lawrence knew that the attack was to centre on Deraa. Early in September Lawrence started north from the head of the Gulf of Akaba to help Allenby in his historic final drive. But instead of taking his Bedouin followers from the Hedjaz, with the exception of his personal bodyguard, Lawrence recruited a new army from the tribes of the North Arabian Desert, and Joyce kept adding to his rapidly-increasing mob of deserters from the Turkish ranks.

When it started up the Wadi Araba from the head of the Gulf of Akaba, Lawrence's caravan consisted of two thousand baggage camels, four hundred and fifty Arab regulars mounted on racing camels, four Arab machine-gun units, two aeroplanes, three Rolls-Royce armoured cars, a demolition company of picked men from the Egyptian camel corps, a battalion of Gurkhas from India mounted on tall camels from the Sind Desert, and four mountain-guns manned by French Algerians. In addition he had his resplendent private bodyguard of one hundred picked Bedouins. His total force amounted to one thousand men mounted on camels.

Lawrence's motto on this expedition, as on all others, was: "No margin!" He faced a march of five hundred miles across unmapped desert under stupendous transport difficulties. During one stage they marched four days from one water-hole to another, carrying their entire water supply with them and suffering from thirst. When they reached the new water-hole they drank copiously, only to discover that the water was filled with leeches. These leeches fastened themselves on the inside of their nasal membranes and proved most painful. But the column made the trek in a fortnight. They were hurrying north to cut three Turkish railway lines and all the telegraph-wires around Deraa, Lawrence's primary mission being to prevent the Turks from communicating with Damascus, Aleppo, and Constantinople when Allenby started his advance.

The camouflage army of the Jordan was a complete success. As a matter of fact, there were only three battalions of able-bodied troops in that part of the Holy Land, two of which were made up of newly arrived Jewish troops from the British Isles and the United States.

If the Turks had known the truth they might have sent down one brigade, pushed up behind Allenby's lines, and recaptured Jerusalem!

Allenby was taking enormous chances, but great men usually do.

The commander-in-chief supplied his troops in the Jordan Valley with but three weeks' rations in order that he might use all of the transport for his main army. His supply people were frantic; they said the troops along the Jordan must be given eight weeks' food; but Allenby knew he was perfectly safe so long as his plan for one smash went through without a hitch.

Allenby felt that it would not be safe to engage the Turks in a pitched battle with his small and inadequately-trained army, and so his sole object was to lure all the Turkish reserves to the wrong place—the Jordan Valley.

Allenby's sham attack down near Jericho had been scheduled for September 18. The British Intelligence Corps carefully allowed this "secret" to get out, and of course the Turks were ready to meet it. Allenby's real attack was made not on the eighteenth but on the nineteenth, and when they woke up and discovered how they had been fooled, the War in the Near East was over, and most of them were British or Arab prisoners. Furthermore, it was not made in the Jordan Valley but away on the other side of Palestine to the north of Jaffa on the Mediterranean coast! He had transferred nearly all his infantry and cavalry there by night, and they remained concealed in the orange groves until the day of the real battle, the battle that broke the backbone of the Ottoman Empire.

CHAPTER XXIII

A CAVALRY-NAVAL ENGAGEMENT AND LAWRENCE'S LAST
GREAT RAID

ALL the Turkish ammunition and food had to be brought down from northern Syria over the Damascus-Palestine-Amman-Medina Railway. Lawrence's plan was to swing way out across the unmapped sea of sand, get clear around the eastern end of the Turkish lines, unexpectedly appear out of the desert, dash up behind the Turks, and cut all their communications round Deraa. One of Lawrence's most difficult problems during this manœuvre was to keep his column supplied. Even his armoured cars and aeroplanes could not carry enough petrol to pull through. From Akaba to the oases of Azarak is 290 miles across burning desert. There were wells at only three places where the camels could be watered, and the little band had to live from hand to mouth.

On its way the column rested at Tafileh, a village of six thousand inhabitants, near which the most unusual episode of the whole campaign had taken place. A body of Bedouin horse under Abu Irgeig of Beersheba, under cover of darkness, rode up to a small enemy naval-base, near the southern end of the Dead Sea, not far from the ancient cities of Sodom and Gomorrah. The so-called Turkish Dead Sea Fleet, consisting of a few ancient arks and motor-driven craft armed with light guns, was moored alongshore. The officers were having breakfast in a Turkish Army mess nearby, utterly unaware of the approach of a hostile force. Abu Irgeig saw at a glance that the decks were deserted except for a few sentries, so he ordered his followers to dismount. With a rush they clambered on board like Barbary corsairs, scuppered the crews, scuttled the boats, remounted their snorting thoroughbreds, and vanished into the desert-haze before the dazed Turks had time to realize what had happened. This is perhaps the only occasion in history in which a naval engagement has been won by cavalry.

Lawrence's original plan was to gather under his standard the enormous Rualla tribe, which fills a large part of the North Arabian Desert, and then descend in force upon the Hauran hill-country to make a direct assault on Deraa. This came to naught because of a little difference which unexpectedly arose between King Hussein and General Jaffer Pasha and the senior officers of the northern army, which ruffled the temper of an important part of Lawrence's forces. By the time harmony had been restored it was too late, and, as a result, the Rualla never came together, making it necessary for Lawrence to modify his scheme.

In the end he decided to carry out a flying attack on the railways north, west, and south of Deraa with his regular troops, assisted only by the wild Druses of the Hauran and a handful of the Rualla horse under Sheiks Khalid and Trad Shaalan. Before starting this attack, Lawrence arranged for another feint to be made on the eighteenth against Amman and El Salt, and for this purpose he sent word to the members of the Beni Sakr tribe to mass in the desert near Amman. The rumour of this, confirmed by Allenby's mobilization of his great camouflage army in the Jordan Valley, kept the eyes of the Turks fixed constantly on the Jordan instead of on the Mediterranean coastal region to the north of Jaffa.

For some days Lawrence made his headquarters here on the Oasis of Azarak where there is a magnificent old castle that dates back to somewhere between the sixth and fourteenth centuries, and is turreted and loopholed like the fortress of a Scottish baron. Evidently it was an outpost of the far-flung Roman Empire, for Colonel R. V. Buxton, of the Imperial Camel Corps, found a carved stone in the ruins on which there was an inscription stating that two legions of Antoninus Pius had been stationed here. So far as is known no other force visited it until Lawrence and his men came. The Arabs refuse to go near it because they say it is haunted by the mad hunting dogs of the Shepherd Kings that prowl round it o' nights. Lawrence at one time thought he would like to retire here and make Azarak Castle his home after the War.

On the thirteenth, Lawrence, accompanied by the small but mobile force which he had organized for his big attack on Deraa, left the oasis of Azarak and marched into the El Salt foothills. Two days later they arrived at Umtaiye, thirteen miles south-east of Deraa, where the male population of nearly all the villages of the Hauran joined the Shereefian army in a body. Among them was Sheik Tallal el Hareidhin of Tafas, the finest fighter in the Hauran, who had accompanied Lawrence on some of his spying expeditions behind the Turkish lines. He acted as guide for the expedition from this point, and sponsored Lawrence's cause in every village. Lawrence declared that if it had not been for this man's courage, energy, and honesty some of the tribes of the country through which they passed, who were blood-enemies of King Hussein and

Emir Feisal, might easily have wrecked all their plans. Probably twenty or thirty thousand Arab villagers and nomads joined Lawrence at different points in this grand finale of the Near Eastern campaign.

In addition to severing the lines of communication it was Lawrence's intention to place himself and his troops between the vital railway junction at Deraa and the Turkish armies in Palestine so as to lure the enemy into reinforcing the thus isolated garrison at Deraa with troops from the Palestine front who otherwise would be free to help stem Allenby's advance. At the same moment it was also necessary for Lawrence to cut the railway to the south and west of Deraa in order to add colour to the belief of the enemy that the entire Allied attack was coming against the Turkish Fourth Army in the upper Jordan Valley.

The only unit available for putting the railway out of business consisted of the armoured cars. The cars, plus Lawrence, whizzed gloriously down the railway line and captured one post before the open-mouthed Turks were aware of their danger. This post commanded an attractive railway bridge, 149 kilos south of Damascus, on which was inscribed a flattering dedication of the bridge to old Abdul Hamid, the Red Sultan.

Lawrence planted tulips containing one hundred and fifty pounds of gun-cotton at both ends and in the centre, and when he touched them off the bridge faded away on the autumn breeze. This job completed, the cars started on again at top speed, but became stranded in the sand, where they were delayed for several hours. On their way back to rejoin the army in the Hauran they crossed the railway five miles north of Deraa, where Lawrence suppressed another post, wiped out a Kurdish cavalry detachment, blew up another bridge, and ripped up six hundred pairs of rails.

After blowing up enough of the railway in the vicinity of Deraa to throw the whole Turkish service of supply into complete chaos, Lawrence and his men ascended a high promontory called Mount Tell Ara, which commanded a panoramic view of Deraa four miles away. Through his field-glasses he made out nine planes on the enemy's aerodrome. During that morning the German aviators had had it all their own way in the air. They had been playing mischief with Lawrence's troops by dropping their eggs and raking the Arabs with their machine-guns. The Shereefian forces tried to defend themselves from the ground with their light artillery, but they were getting the worst of it until Lawrence's one surviving machine, an antiquated old bus, piloted by Captain Junor came trundling up from Azarak and sailed square into the middle of the whole German squadron.

Lawrence and his followers watched this fracas with mixed feelings, for each of the four enemy two-seaters and four scout-planes was more than the equal of the one prehistoric British machine. With both skill and good luck Captain Junor cruised right through the German bird-men and led the whole circus off to the westward.

Twenty minutes later the plucky Junor came tearing back through the air with his attendant swarm of enemy planes and signalled down to Lawrence that he had run out of petrol. He landed within fifty yards of the Arab column and his B.E. flopped over on its back. A German Halberstad dived on it at once and scored a direct hit with a bomb that blew the little British machine into bits. Fortunately, Junor had jumped out of his seat a moment before. The only part of his B.E. that was not destroyed was the Lewis machine-gun. Within half-an-hour the plucky pilot had transferred it to a Ford truck and was tearing around outside Deraa, raking the Turks with his tracer bullets.

Meanwhile, Lawrence dashed off to join the detachment of troops he had sent on in the direction of Mezerib. An hour after reaching it he helped them cut the main Turkish telegraph-lines between Palestine and Syria. It would be difficult to over-estimate the importance of this, because it completely cut the Turkish armies off from all hope of relief from Northern Syria and Turkey proper.

At Mezerib several thousand more natives of the Hauran joined the Arab forces, and the following day Lawrence and his column marched on along the railway toward Palestine, right into the heart of the Turkish back area. They spent most of that day planting tulips, and near Nasib Lawrence blew up his seventy-ninth bridge, a rather large one with three fine arches, thus bringing to a close this long and successful career of demolition. Knowing it might be his last, he planted twice as many tulips under it as necessary.

The column slept soundly at Nasib on the night of the eighteenth after a good day's work. The next morning, bright and early, Lawrence marched his camels, horses, and Arabs off to Umtaiye, where he was joined by the armoured cars. During the morning another enemy aerodrome was sighted near the railway, and Lawrence, with two of the armoured cars, sped across open country for a near view. They found three German two-seaters in front of the hangars. Had it not been for a deep gully intervening, the two armoured cars would have rushed them. As it was, two of the Germans took off and circled around like great birds, pouring streams of lead down on the Rolls-Royce machines, whilst at the same time Lawrence and the crews inside the turrets finished the third aeroplane with fifteen hundred bullets. As the armoured cars started back to Umtaiye, the Germans swooped down on them four times; but all their bombs were badly placed, and the cars escaped unhurt, except for a bit of shrapnel that wounded the colonel in the hand. Speaking of his impression of armoured-car work, Lawrence remarked that he considered it fighting de luxe.

This same day the Arab regulars, under Jaffer Pasha, and the armoured and French detachment and the Rualla horse under Nuri Shallan gave a fine account of themselves.

Jaffer Pasha, who also slashed his way brilliantly through this engagement, comes of a rich and noble Bagdad family. His history is full of romantic vicissitudes. At the outbreak of the War Jaffer el Askari, as a general on the Turkish staff, was sent across in a submarine from Constantinople to North Africa to organize an uprising in the Sahara among the Senussi Arabs. He led the Senussi in their short but spectacular campaign against the British. In the first battle he defeated the British; the second battle was a draw; and in the third he was badly wounded, defeated, and captured by the Dorset Yeomanry at Agagia near Sollum, and imprisoned in the great citadel at Cairo.

In trying to escape at the end of three months he broke his ankle and was recaptured in the moat under the citadel. He was as fat as a barrel, full of the joy of life, and such a gentlemanly, likeable fellow that a little later the British put him on parole and allowed him to wander about Cairo. Being an Arab himself he sympathized with the Arab Nationalist cause, and one day asked his British captors to permit him to volunteer as a private with Feisal. His request was granted, and he did such remarkable work that before many months had passed he had risen to the post of commander-in-chief of Feisal's regular army, which was composed mainly of deserters from the Turkish ranks who had known Jaffer as a general in Turkey.

Jaffer Pasha had received the Kaiser's Iron Cross at the Dardanelles and the Turkish Crescent for his work in the Senussi campaign, and after he had been with the Arabs for a while he was made a Commander of the Order of St. Michael and St. George by the British! Allenby accorded him this last honour at his Ramleh headquarters in Palestine. The guard of honour on this occasion was the same Dorset Yeomanry that had captured the Pasha just a year before. Jaffer was tremendously pleased and amused at this subtle touch of humour on Allenby's part.

Nuri Said, Jaffer Pasha's brother-in-law, played an equally brilliant part in the War. He was Emir Feisal's chief of staff, and remained in this position when Feisal became King in Damascus, and later in Bagdad. Like Jaffer, he had attended the Turkish Staff College. In the Balkan War he was an aviator. Afterwards he acted as secretary of the Arab officers' secret society which plotted to overthrow the Turks. He is reckless and loves a hot fight. In fact, the hotter the action the cooler was Nuri Said. He was one of the few Arab townsmen whom the Bedouins admired and respected.

All had gone well with the preliminary plans for Allenby's drive in Palestine. But until twenty-four hours before the attack was launched, on the nineteenth, the commander-in-chief himself was not certain whether he was going to succeed or not. If the Turks and Germans had discovered his real plan and had not been deceived into thinking that both the British and Arabian forces were concentrating on Amman with the intention of attempting to push north up the Jordan Valley, and if the enemy had withdrawn its right wing only about half-way across Palestine from the Mediterranean coast and the River Auja to the hills of Samaria, which would merely have been a retirement of ten miles along the entire front, the Turks could have played safe, Allenby's whole blow would have been wasted, and Lawrence's brilliant operations around Deraa would have been all in vain.

Lawrence did not even have sufficient supplies to last his column for two extra days, so that failure would have been nothing short of a catastrophe for him. Of course, neither Allenby nor Lawrence would have suffered heavy losses, but on the other hand they would not have rung the curtain down in Arabia and Palestine so soon. The entire World War might have dragged on for several months longer, and an additional hundred thousand lives or more might have been sacrificed on the Western Front. But there were no "ifs"; the enemy walked into the prepared trap like lambs to the slaughter.

CHAPTER XXIV

THE DOWNFALL OF THE OTTOMAN EMPIRE

On the whole, this last joint operation of the British and Arabian forces was one of the most marvellous pieces of staff-planning in all military annals. It was a game of chess played by experts on an international board. Never before was there a similar campaign. It was a complete reversal of all Marshal Foch's principles. Allenby and Lawrence went back to the Napoleonic wars, to the battles of the eighteenth century, when generals won by manœuvre and strategy instead of by tactics (the term "tactics" referring to the science of handling men under fire).

In this, the most brilliant and spectacular military operation in the world's history, Allenby and Lawrence lost only four hundred and fifty men, although they completely annihilated the Turkish army, captured over one hundred thousand Turks, advanced more than three hundred miles in less than a month, and broke the backbone of the Turkish Empire. Part of the credit should go to Brigadier-General Bartholomew. Allenby is colossal; he needs a needle-sharp man to complete him. He had such an officer and strategist in General Bartholomew.

Allenby's complete plan, which involved the destruction of all the Turkish effectives with one sweeping blow, was known only to four people: the commander-in-chief himself, his chief of staff (Major-General Boles), General Bartholomew, and Colonel Lawrence. Not even Emir Feisal or King Hussein knew what was going to happen.

At five o'clock on the morning of September 18, 1917, General Bartholomew came to his office at headquarters in Ramleh and anxiously said to the staff officer on duty: "Has there been any change?"

"No, the Turks are still there," replied the latter.

"Good!" said Bartholomew. "We will take at least thirty thousand prisoners before this show is over."

He did not dream that the Allied forces would capture three times thirty thousand Turks.

The deception of the enemy had been perfect in every detail. When Allenby's forces entered Nazareth, which had been the German and Turkish Palestine headquarters, they found papers indicating that the German High Command had

THE RECKLESS MALUD BEY AND HIS STAFF

TOMMIES AND ARABS MEET IN THE DESERT

been certain the attack would take place in the Jordan Valley. Field-Marshal von Sanders had been taken in down to the last point.

Meanwhile, Lawrence, Joyce, General Nuri, and their associates had received no news of what was going on in Palestine, but they were busy day and night demolishing sections of the railway. One night Lord Winterton, who played an active part in this final stage of the desert campaign, went out on a demolition expedition and placed some thirty parties at work along the line. The earl himself dashed about in the dark from point to point in an armoured car. While walking along the railway he met a soldier who said: "How are things?"

"Fine!" replied Winterton; "we have twenty-eight charges planted and will be ready to touch them off in a few minutes." The soldier remarked that this was splendid, and then disappeared. A moment later machine-guns blazed forth on all sides, and the earl had to run for it. His questioner had either been a German or a Turk, and had the incident occurred an hour earlier it might have spoiled Lord Winterton's work for that night. But the tulips were duly touched off, and the show was a success.

The following day Lawrence dashed back to Azarak in an armoured car, then flew across the desert and northern Palestine to Allenby's headquarters at Ramleh. A hurried conference with the commander-in-chief secured for him three more Bristol fighters, the best battle-planes that the British were using in the Holy Land. He also brought back the astounding news that more than twenty thousand prisoners had already been taken by Allenby's forces, that Nazareth, Nablus, and many other important centres had fallen, and that they were advancing toward Deraa and Damascus. This meant that the Arabian army would be called upon by Allenby to play a still greater part from now on, because it was the only force between the crumbling Turkish divisions and Anatolia, toward which they must retreat.

Lawrence had flown to Palestine for aeroplanes because the Germans had nine of them near Deraa, with which they were bombing Feisal's followers out of the ground. One of the pilots was a Captain Peters, and another was a Captain Ross Smith, who later became world-famous and was knighted for flying from England to Australia. Lord Winterton gives us a graphic picture of the events of that morning in a scintillating article in "Blackwood's";

"While L. and the airmen were having breakfast with us,

M

a Turkish plane was observed, making straight for us. One of the airmen . . . hurried off to down the intruder. This he successfully did, and the Turkish plane fell in flames near the railway. He then returned and finished his porridge, which had been kept hot for him meanwhile. But not for him a peaceful breakfast that morning. He had barely reached the marmalade stage when another Turkish plane appeared. Up hurried the Australian again; but this Turk was too wily and scuttled back to Deraa, only to be chased by P. on another machine, which sent him down in flames.''

That night the Germans burnt all of their remaining machines, and from that moment the British airmen had the air above North Arabia, Palestine, and Syria to themselves.

That afternoon a giant Handley-Page arrived from Palestine with General Borton, commander of Allenby's air squadrons, as the passenger, and Ross Smith as the pilot. They brought forty-seven tins of petrol and also a supply of tea for Lawrence, Winterton and companions. This was the first time that a great night-bombing plane ever flew over the enemy lines by day. The purpose was for propaganda, and so profoundly were the tribesmen impressed by this vast bird, which was several times larger than any they had thus far seen, that all of the peoples of the Hauran, who had been reluctant to co-operate with Emir Feisal, immediately swore allegiance to the Arab cause and galloped in on their horses, with their rifles popping off into the air, eager to charge the Turks, or at least make a noisy display of valour.

The next day the infantry under General Jaffer Pasha, the jovial commander-in-chief of Colonel Joyce's regulars, went down to have a look at the first large bridge which Lawrence had dynamited in the vicinity of Deraa. They found it nearly repaired, but after a sharp fight they drove off its guards, who were persistent and game German machine-gunners, destroyed more of the line, and then proceeded to burn the great timber framework which had been erected by the Turks and Germans during the intervening seven days. In this rather sharp encounter the armoured cars, the French detachment under Captain Pisani, and the Rualla horse under Nuri Shaalan plunged into the heart of things.

Nuri is a quiet, retiring man of few words and plenty of deeds. He turned out to be unusually intelligent, well informed, decisive, and full of quiet humour. Lawrence once remarked to me that he not only was the chief of the largest tribe in all the desert, but one of the finest Arab sheiks he had ever met, and that the members of his tribe were like wax in his hands because "he knows what should be done and does it."

When Lawrence started his operations around Deraa, von Sanders did exactly what his opponents wanted him to do. He sent his last reserves up to Deraa, so that when Allenby's troops once smashed through the Turkish front lines they had fairly clear going ahead of them. At the important railway junction of Afuleh, on the evening of the nineteenth, the Turkish motor-lorries came streaming in for supplies, not knowing that all their great depots were in the hands of Allenby's men. As they rumbled into the supply-station, a British officer remarked politely to one and all: "Would you mind going this way, please?" That lasted for four hours, until the news spread through the Turkish back area that Allenby's troops had taken Afuleh, the railway junction in the centre of the plain of Esdraelon, where the Turkish railway which connects Constantinople, Damascus and the Holy Land branches out, one line extending down into Samaria and the other east to Haifa on the Mediterranean.

Afuleh was the main supply-base of the whole Turkish army. After Allenby had occupied Afuleh for fully six hours, a German plane came down with orders to von Sanders from Hindenburg. The occupants of the plane did not discover their predicament until they left their machine and walked over to local headquarters to report. To their chagrin they found themselves turning over their orders to Allenby's staff.

By September 24, Allenby's forces had advanced so far that the entire Turkish Fourth Army, concentrated around Amman and the Jordan on the mission of attacking empty tents and horse-blankets, had been ordered back to defend Deraa and Damascus. The Turkish Fourth Army generals were infuriated when they discovered that the railway line had been cut behind them, and attempted to retreat north along their motor-roads with all their guns and transport. Lawrence and his cavalry did not intend to pave their retreat with roses. Stationed on the hills they poured down such an incessant stream of bullets that the Turks were forced to abandon all their guns and carts between Mafrak and Nasib.

Hundreds were slaughtered. The formal column of retreat broke up into a confused mass of fugitives, who never had a minute's peace to re-form their lines. British aeroplanes added the finishing touch by dropping bombs, and the Turkish Fourth Army scattered panic-stricken in all directions.

Lawrence now decided to put himself between Deraa and Damascus, hoping to force the immediate evacuation of Deraa and thus pick up the sorry fragments of the crack Turkish Fourth Army as it emerged from Deraa, and also harass other remnants of the Turkish armies in Palestine that might attempt to escape north. Accordingly, at the head of his camel corps, he made a hurried forced march northward on the twenty-fifth, and by the afternoon of the twenty-sixth swept down on the Turkish railway near Ghazale and Ezrya on the road to Damascus.

With him were Nasir, Nuri, Auda, and the Druses—"names with which to hush children even in the daytime," to quote Lawrence himself. His rapid manœuvre took the panic-stricken Turks completely by surprise. Just the previous day they had worked feverishly on the railway line and had reopened it for traffic at the points where Lawrence had damaged it a week earlier. He planted a few hundred tulips, putting the line out of commission permanently and penning six complete trains in Deraa. Fantastic reports of disaster spread like wildfire throughout Syria, and the Turks at once began the evacuation of Deraa by road.

By dawn of the twenty-seventh, Lawrence and his cavalry were already out scouting the surrounding country and had captured two Austro-Turk machine-gun companies placed across a road to oppose Allenby's approaching columns. Then Lawrence climbed to the summit of a high hill in the vicinity called Sheik Saad, whence he could sweep the countryside with his glasses. Whenever he saw a small enemy column appearing on the horizon, he jumped on his horse and, accompanied by some nine hundred picked men, he swooped down upon the stragglers. If from his observation-station on the hill he saw a column that was too large to tackle, he lay low and let it pass.

About noon an aeroplane dropped Lawrence a message stating that two columns of Turks were advancing on him. One, six thousand strong, was coming from Deraa; the other, two thousand strong, from Mezerib. Lawrence decided that the second was about his size. Sending for some of his regulars, who were gathering stray Turks like daisies a few miles away, he dashed off to intercept the enemy near Tafas. At the same time he sent the Hauran horsemen in the other direction to get around behind them and hang on the skirts of the column in order to annoy them. The Turks reached Tafas a short time before Lawrence and brutally mistreated all the women and children of the village. Shereef Bey, commander of the Turkish Lancers, at the rearguard of the column, ordered all the people to be massacred, including women and children.

Tallal, head sheik of this village of Tafas, who had been a great tower of strength with Lawrence from the beginning and one of the boldest horsemen in North Arabia, was riding at the front of the Arab column with Lawrence and Auda Abu Tayi when he came upon the wives and children of his kinsmen lying in pools of blood in the road.

Several years after the War one of Lawrence's poet friends in England got married, and when Lawrence expressed regret at not having enough money to buy an appropriate wedding-present the poet suggested that he might let him have a few pages of his diary instead. The wish was granted, and the poet disposed of the pages to "The World's Work" for publication in America. The portion sold happened to include Lawrence's story of the death of the gallant Sheik Tallal el Hareidhin:

"We left Abd el Main there and rode on past the other bodies, now seen clearly in the sunlight to be men, women, and four babies, toward the village whose loneliness we knew meant that it was full of death and horror. On the outskirts were the low mud-walls of some sheepfolds, and on one lay something red and white. I looked nearer, and saw the body of a woman folded across it, face downward, nailed there by a sword-bayonet whose haft stuck hideously into the air from between naked legs. She had been pregnant, and about her were others, perhaps twenty in all, variously killed, but laid out to accord with an obscene taste. The Zaagi burst out in wild peals of laughter, in which some of those who were not sick joined hysterically. It was a sight near madness, the more desolate for the warm sunshine and the clean air of this upland afternoon. I said: 'The best of you brings me the most Turkish dead'; and we turned and rode as fast as we might in the direction of the fading enemy. On our way we shot down those of them fallen out by the roadside who came imploring our pity.

"Tallal had seen something of what we had seen. He gave one moan like a hurt animal, and then slowly rode to the higher ground, and sat there a long while on his mare, shivering and looking fixedly after the Turks. I moved toward him to speak to him, but Auda caught my rein and stayed me. After some minutes Tallal very slowly drew his head-cloth about his face, and then seemed to take hold of himself, for he dashed his stirrups into his horse's flanks and galloped headlong, bending low in the saddle as though he would fall, straight at the main body of the enemy.

"It was a long ride, down the gentle slope and across the hollow, and we all sat there like stone while he rushed forward, the drumming of his horse's hoofs sounding unnaturally loud in our ears. We had stopped shooting and the Turks had stopped shooting; both armies waited for him. He flew on in this hushed evening, till he was only a few lengths from the enemy. Then he sat up in the saddle and cried his war-cry: 'Tallal, Tallal!' twice, in a tremendous voice. Instantly, all their rifles and machine-guns crashed out together, and he and his mare, riddled through and through with bullets, fell dead among their lance-points.

"Auda looked very cold and grim. 'God give him mercy! We will take his price.' He shook his rein and moved slowly forward after the enemy. We called up the peasantry, now all drunk with fear and blood, and sent them from this side and from that against the retreating column. Auda led them like the old lion of battle that he is. By a skilful turn he drove the enemy into bad ground and split their column into three parts. The third part, the smallest, was mostly made up of German and Austrian gunners, grouped round three motor-cars which presumably carried high officers. They fought magnificently and drove off our attacks time and again, despite our desperation. The Arabs were fighting like devils, the sweat blinding our eyes, our throats parched with dust, and the agony of cruelty and revenge which was burning in our bodies and twisting our hands about so that we could hardly shoot. By my orders they were to take no prisoners—for the first time in the War."

This account of the death of Tallal el Hareidhin of Tafas, in Lawrence's own words, shows us what marvellous descriptive powers this young soldier-scholar has at his command, and gives us a hint of the masterpiece that the world should one day receive from his pen.

Two German machine-gun companies had resisted magnificently and escaped, with the Turkish commander-in-chief, Djemal Pasha, in his car in their midst. The Arabs wiped out the second section completely after a bitter hand-to-hand struggle. No prisoners were taken, because the Arabs were wild with rage over the Tafas massacre. Two hundred and fifty German prisoners had been captured during the day; but when the Arabs discovered one of Lawrence's men with a fractured thigh pinned to the ground with two German bayonets, they acted like enraged bulls. Turning their machine-guns on the remaining prisoners they wiped them out.

After the encounter, Nuri Shaalan, at the head of the Rualla horse, rode straight into the main street of Deraa. There were two or three fights on the way, but they took the town in a whirlwind gallop. The next morning Nuri returned to Lawrence at Tafas with five hundred infantry prisoners and the freedom of the town of Deraa. Some of Allenby's troops arrived in Deraa that day also.

Lawrence and his army spent that night—and a very uneasy night it was—on Sheik Saad hill. He did not feel certain of victory since there was always a risk of his small force being washed away by a great wave of the enemy in retreat. All that night the Hauran horsemen clung tenaciously to the great Turkish column from Deraa, made up of six thousand men, which Lawrence had not dared engage in pitched battle. Instead of sleeping with the regular troops at Sheik Saad, Lawrence spent part of the night helping the Hauran cavalry, and at dawn he rode off to the westward with a handful of men until he met the outposts of the fourth cavalry division of the British army.

After guiding them into Deraa and starting them off on their northward march toward Damascus, Lawrence galloped back full speed to the Hauran cavalry. Although the Turkish column when it left Deraa was six thousand strong, at the end of twenty-four hours only five thousand remained. One thousand had been picked off by the Bedouins. Eighteen hours more and there were three thousand, and after a point called Kiswe, where Lawrence headed off the remnant of the Turkish Fourth Army and flung them into one of Allenby's cavalry brigades coming from the south-west, only two thousand remained.

In all, Lawrence, Joyce, Jaffer and Nuri, and their scattered force of wild Bedouins and regular camel corps had killed about five thousand of the Turks in this last phase of the campaign and captured more than eight thousand of them, as well as one hundred and fifty machine-guns and thirty cannon. In addition to the column of less than one thousand men who had started north from Akaba with Lawrence, Auda Abu Tayi and two hundred of the best fighting-men of the Howeitat tribe took part in Lawrence's war-dance around Deraa, also two thousand Beni Sakhr, "the Sons of Hawks," from the east of the Dead Sea, four thousand Rualla under Nuri Shaalan from the North Arabian Desert, one thousand Druses from the Hauran, and eight thousand Arab villagers from the Hauran.

In a letter which he wrote to me more than a year after the War, Colonel Stirling, who had played a prominent role in this final raid, summed up the effects of what the Arabs had done to help Allenby overwhelm the Turks:

"This, after all," wrote Colonel Stirling, "was the main justification of our existence and of the money and time we had spent on the Arab revolt. The raid itself was really very dramatic in that we started out, a small regular force of Arabs 400 strong, and marched 600 miles in twenty-three days through unmapped Arabia and came in out of the blue—miles behind the Turkish main armies, and as an absolute surprise.

"Two days before the British advance in Palestine began, we had cut three lines of railways and for five days allowed no trains to get through to the Turkish armies. The result was that when their retreat commenced they found all their advance food depots and ammunition dumps were exhausted. During these days we, of course, led a somewhat precarious existence, generally shifting camp twice in a night to avoid being surprised. We were only a very weak force then, you see, though by the time we got on and rushed Damascus, something like 11,000 mounted Arabs had joined us."

Some of the Arab horsemen rode right on that evening into Damascus, where the burning ammunition dumps turned night into day. Back at Kiswe, just a few miles south of Damascus, and not far from where Saul of Tarsus was dazzled by the light that transformed him into Paul the interpreter of Christianity, the glare of the fires from Damascus and the roar and reverberation of explosives kept Lawrence awake most of the night. He was completely worn out. From September 13 to 30, he had caught only occasional snatches of sleep. Mounted on a racing-camel or dashing about the country on an Arab steed, riding inside the turret of an armoured car or flying about in one of the fighting planes, he had led the relentless existence demanded of him in this great emergency of the War. Now the end of the War was in sight in the Land of the Arabian Nights. But sleep was difficult because all night long the Turks and Germans were blowing up their ammunition-dumps eight miles north in Damascus. With each explosion the earth shook, the sky went white, and splashes of red tore great gaps in the night as shells went off in the air. "They are burning Damascus," Lawrence remarked to Stirling. Then he rolled over in the sand and fell asleep.

CHAPTER XXV

LAWRENCE RULES IN DAMASCUS, AND THE TREACHERY OF THE ALGERIAN EMIR

THE next morning they saw Damascus in the centre of its gardens as green and beautiful as any city in the world. The enchantment of the scene, "like a dream that visits the light slumbers of the morning—a dream dreamed but to vanish," reminded Lawrence of the Arab story that when Mohammed first came here as a camel-driver, upon seeing Damascus from a distance, he refused to enter, saying that man could only hope to enter Paradise once. Coming out of the desert and beholding this view, than which there is none more enchanting and alluring in the world, it is no wonder Mohammed was sorely tempted and even trembled for his soul. Seen from afar, this oasis of verdure, rimmed round by yellow desert against a background of snow-capped mountains, is indeed a pearl in an emerald setting. So it is only natural that the desert-dweller should look upon it as an earthly paradise.

As the sun-rays fell aslant, weaving a fairy gossamer veil over the minarets and cupolas of this dream city, Lawrence and Stirling drove into Damascus in their famous Rolls-Royce, the Blue Mist. They went straight to the town-hall, and there called a meeting of all the leading sheiks. Lawrence selected Shukri Ibn Ayubi, a descendant of Saladin, to act as the first military governor under the new régime. Then he appointed a chief of police, a director of local transportation, and numerous other officials. These details arranged, Shukri, Nuri Said, Auda Abu Tayi, Nuri Shalaan, and Lawrence, at the head of their Bedouin irregulars, proceeded through the streets of Damascus.

The twenty-nine-year-old commander-in-chief of the greatest army that had been raised in Arabia for five centuries, who in less than a year had made himself the most important man in Arabia since the days of the great Caliph Haroun al Rashid, made his official entry into this ancient capital of the old Arabian Empire at seven o'clock on the morning of October 31. The entire population, together with tens of thousands of Bedouins from the fringes of the desert, packed the "street that is called straight" as Lawrence entered the gate, dressed in the garb of a prince of Mecca.

All realized that at last their glorious city had been freed from the Turkish yoke. Howling dervishes ran in front of him, dancing and sticking knives into their flesh, while behind him came his flying column of picturesque Arabian knights. For months they had heard of the exploits of Shereef Lawrence, but now for the first time they saw the mysterious Englishman who had united the desert tribes and driven the Turks from Arabia. As they saw him come swinging along through the bazaars on the back of his camel, it seemed as though all the people of Damascus shouted his name and Feisal's in one joyful chorus. For ten miles and more along the streets of this, the oldest city in the world that still remains standing, the crowds gave the young Englishman one of the greatest ovations ever given to any man.

Dr. John Finley, of the American Red Cross, who came north with Allenby, said, in describing it, that "there were scenes of joy and ecstasy such as may never be witnessed on this earth again. The bazaars were lined with hundreds of thousands of people. The 'street that is called straight' was so packed that the horses and camels could hardly squirm through. The house-tops were crowded. The people hung priceless Oriental carpets from their balconies and showered Lawrence and his companions with silken head-cloths, flowers and attar of roses."

Fortunately for the Arabs, Allenby had ordered Light Horse Harry Chauvel to hold his Australians back and let Feisal's advance-guard enter the city first, and Allenby also had not given any arbitrary orders regarding the establishment of a temporary government in Damascus. So Lawrence was astute enough to see to it that representatives of the Arabian army entered just ahead of the British, thereby giving Emir Feisal first possession.

Colonel Lawrence remained in Damascus only four days. But during that time he was the virtual ruler of the city, and one of his first moves was to visit the tomb of Saladin, where the Kaiser, back in 1898, had placed a satin flag and a bronze laurel wreath inscribed in Turkish and Arabic: "From one great emperor to another." The wreath and inscription adorned with the Prussian Eagle had irritated Lawrence on his pre-War visits to Damascus, and early in the campaign, when they were far south at Yenbo, Lawrence and Feisal had vowed that they would not forget Saladin's tomb. The bronze wreath now adorns the office of the curator of the British War Museum, while the Kaiser's flag returned with me to America.

During Lawrence's brief rule of Damascus, the kaleido-scopic bazaars of that most orthodox of all Oriental cities were seething with excitement. Only his intimate acquaintance with the personal caprices of the conspirators behind the innumerable intrigues and counter-intrigues made it possible for him to control the situation. Even then there were thrill-ing incidents and danger from assassins.

On November 2, a riot broke out in Damascus, a dis-turbance that might easily have blossomed into a counter-revolution. The moving spirit in it was an Algerian emir, one Abd el Keder, who had long been an arch-enemy of King Hussein and his sons. This blackguard was the grandson of the celebrated Emir Abd el Keder, who for many years had fought the French in Algiers and, when finally defeated, had fled to Damascus. His two grandsons, Emir Muhammad Said and Emir Abd el Keder, played an unsavory part in the War in the Near East. The former served as an agent of the Germans and Turks in Africa, where he exhorted the Senussi of the Sahara to invade Egypt, while his younger and even more truculent brother, Abd el Keder, as a super-spy for Enver Pasha, joined the Shereefian army.

A mock escape from Constantinople gave Abd el Keder all the alibi needed for him to get into the good graces of the Arabs, and when he arrived across the desert at Feisal's head-quarters in Akaba he posed as an ardent Arab Nationalist. In fact, so plausible and eloquent was he, and so seemingly genuine were the promises of co-operation which he made, that even King Hussein welcomed him to Mecca and gave him an honorary title.

Then when Allenby launched his first great drive which resulted in the capture of Beersheba, Gaza, Jerusalem, and Jericho, Lawrence was asked to co-operate by destroying an important railway bridge between the Turkish army and its Damascus base. It so happened that Abd el Keder was the feudal lord controlling much of the region round about the bridge, and when Feisal discussed the project with him he at once begged to be allowed to take part in the raid. But after accompanying Lawrence on his trek north for many days, until the party was actually within a few miles of the bridge, Abd el Keder and his cavalcade of followers galloped off in the desert night and delivered the details of Lawrence's plan to the German and Turkish staff. Although this left him with only a few men, Lawrence nevertheless made a desperate but unsuccessful attempt to destroy the bridge, an adventure from which he barely escaped with his life.

The Turks at first suspected their Algerian spy of double-crossing them and of really having turned pro-Arab, but they finally released him and then showered him with honours. Later on, when Allenby made his last great drive toward Damascus, Abd el Keder was sent among the Syrian villagers to cajole them into remaining loyal to their Ottoman rulers. But when the cunning Algerian and his brother saw that the Turkish retreat was degenerating into a debacle, their enthusiasm for their friends Enver, Talaat and Djemal vanished, and they galloped to Damascus several hours ahead of Allenby and Lawrence, hurriedly organized an Arab civil government, with themselves as the heads, and prepared a triumphal welcome for the approaching British and Hedjaz armies.

But, naturally, they were a bit nonplussed to find the victors led by Colonel Lawrence, who peremptorily ordered them to resign, and then appointed men of Emir Feisal's choice in their stead. This so upset and enraged the intriguing brothers that they drew their weapons and would have attacked Lawrence had the others present at the council not disarmed them. Then these two unpleasant but immensely rich Algerian emirs collected together the members of their own personal bodyguard, who were mainly exiles like themselves, and paraded through the streets making impassioned speeches denouncing Emir Feisal and King Hussein as puppets of Lawrence and the British. They called upon the Damascenes to strike a blow for the faith and launch a new rebellion.

Rioting soon broke out, and it took Lawrence's men six hours to clear the town. The rioting soon degenerated into pure looting, and it was necessary for Lawrence, General Nuri Pasha, Shukri Ayubi, and the other leaders of the Shereefian force to resort to machine-gunning in the central square of Damascus and impose peace by force, after killing and wounding a score or more.

The two turbulent Algerian emirs managed to hide, and for a month they kept under cover, while they planned a new rebellion. But Abd el Keder's restless and impulsive spirit got the better of his discretion, and in a moment of passion, he seized his rifle, leaped on his charger, and galloped down to Feisal's palace, shouting for Feisal to come out and fight him, and then started shooting. So persistent was he that one of the Arab sentries, who had taken to cover, sent a rifle ball through his head and thus abruptly ended the adventures of the Algerian emir.

After the fall of Damascus, the combined British and Arabian forces occupied the Syrian seaport of Beyrouth, where the famous American university is located that has done so much to inoculate the Near East with the spirit of democracy. Here an incident occurred that warned the Arabs of the diplomatic troubles ahead of them. As in the case of Damascus, the Shereefian forces, through the local people, took over the reins of government, but a few days later a French representative (accompanied by a British officer) came along and demanded that the Arab flag be hauled down from the town hall so that the French tricolour could be raised in its stead. Whereupon the Arab governor laid his pistol on the table and said:

"There is my revolver. You may shoot me if you like, but I will not take down our flag!" However, after another three days, Allenby wired that no flag at all should fly over Beyrouth, and that a French officer should rule the city in the name of all the Allies. From that date the Arabs had to fight an all-uphill battle on the field of diplomacy to keep from losing what they had fought for on the field of war. And once again their champion was young Lawrence.

From Beyrouth the united British and Arab forces pushed on north to Baalbek, the City of the Sun, where, in the days of the decline of the Roman Empire, men had erected the mightiest temple on earth, the columns of which still remain one of the wonders of the world.

Still unsatisfied, Allenby's armoured cars and Feisal's racing-camel men under the dashing Arab general, Nuri Said, swept on north until they had driven the Turks out of Aleppo, one of the most important strategical points in the East so far as the Great War was concerned. And then, if the Turks had not put down their arms, they would have been driven north into the Golden Horn.

When Allenby and Lawrence captured Damascus and Aleppo and then cut the Berlin to Bagdad Railway, the dream of the Kaiser and the Junkers for a Mittel-Europa reaching from the Baltic to the Persian Gulf vanished into thin air!

When Turkey threw in her lot with the Kaiser, she asserted that she could mobilize an army of over a million men. But of that million some fifty per cent were of Arab stock, and from the outbreak of the Arabian revolution to the final collapse of Turkey it is estimated that approximately four hundred thousand of them deserted. The phenomenal number of desertions was due mainly to two factors: the Arab

Nationalist propaganda which Lawrence and his associates had spread throughout the Near East, and the brilliant success of the Arabian revolution. In fact, the desertions alone more than repaid the Allies for backing the Shereefian cause.

In our swift journey north from Akaba to Aleppo with Lawrence, we have made no reference to the sacred city of Medina and the fate of the important Turkish garrison there. Although Holy Arabia was now no longer under Turkish rule, Ottoman forces still occupied the city famed for the Tomb of the Prophet. To be sure, Feisal's brother, Emir Abdullah, had long kept it surrounded with an army and indeed the fact that the Turks had managed to hold on to Medina had proved to be one of the blessings of Allah for the Arabs, because all of the supplies required by the garrison were shipped across the desert from Syria; and Lawrence had seen to it that a very considerable part went to the Arabs instead of to the intended destination. In fact Lawrence's crop of tulips, planted along the Damascus-Medina railway, had brought forth a bountiful harvest of Turkish food supplies, ammunition and other military stores.

In explaining the reasons for not driving the Turks out of Medina, writing in The Army Quarterly, Colonel Lawrence said: "We were so weak physically that we could not let the metaphysical weapon rust unused. We had won a province when we had taught the civilians in it to die for our ideal of freedom; the presence or absence of the enemy was a secondary matter.

"These reasonings showed me that the idea of assaulting Medina, or even starving it quickly into surrender, was not in accord with our best strategy. We wanted the enemy to stay in Medina and in every other harmless place in the largest numbers. The factor of food would eventually confine him to the railways, but he was welcome to the Hedjaz railway, and the trans-Jordan railway, and the Palestine and Damascus and Aleppo railways, for the duration of the War, so long as he gave us the other nine hundred and ninety-nine thousandths of the Arab world. If he showed a disposition to evacuate too soon, as a step to concentrating in the small area which his numbers would dominate effectively, then we would have to try and restore his confidence, not harshly, but by reducing our enterprises against him. Our ideal was to keep his railway just working, but only just, with the maximum of loss and discomfort to him."

In fact so little of what was sent down from Syria ever

reached the garrison that for months prior to the armistice this isolated Turkish force in Medina had been reduced to a diet of nothing but dates, gathered from the palms for which the oasis is celebrated. Even the roofs of all the houses in the city had been torn down and used for fuel. But still the garrison would not give in, for the commander, Fakhri ed din, was a courageous, determined, stubborn, and fanatical general.

Even when the news reached him that the combined British and Arab armies had captured Damascus and Aleppo, and the Turkish forces in Syria had been completely overwhelmed and compelled to sign an armistice, and even though Fakhri Pasha knew that it was futile for him to attempt to hold out any longer, since the War was all over and he and his garrison were isolated in the midst of the desert a thousand miles from Constantinople, this Turkish tiger refused to acknowledge defeat.

Days went by, and then weeks elapsed. The Medina garrison was now reduced to worse straits than the British at Kut-el-Amara before the surrender of Townsend. Of the 20,000 men who had made up the defending force, less than eleven thousand now remained. But still Fakhri Pasha swore on the Koran that rather than surrender to the Arabs and British he would blow up the Tomb of Mohammed and wipe out himself and all of his men. The British even guaranteed Fakhri that he and his troops would be protected from any possible rapacity of the Bedouins. But still the old tiger stood adamant.

However, his troops were not so fanatical, and longed to get back to their homes in Anatolia. So they finally mutinied, arrested their gallant commander-in-chief and surrendered the city to Emir Abdullah on January 10, 1919—months after the War was all over.

Surely the name of General Fakhri ed din deserves a high place in Turkish history, and for generations to come Arab mothers of Medina will use it as a means of hushing their babies.

After the dramatic surrender of Medina, Fakhri Pasha was no longer heard of in the Near East and seemed to have completely vanished from the picture. But some time afterwards, when we were travelling in little-known parts of Central Asia, I encountered the defender of Medina in the city of Kabul, at the court of the Amir of Afghanistan. He apparently had lost none of his fire, and in his capacity of Turkish ambassador to the Afghans was reported to be doing his utmost to keep the

Amir of Afghanistan from becoming friendly with the British in India.

If Turkey had a million fighting-men with the fighting-spirit of Fakhri ed din, she not only could regain all of her old provinces, but she could conquer the Near East and build up an Empire that would surpass the ancient glory of the Great Moguls.

A BABY CAMEL ONE DAY OLD

SOME OF THE BRITISH OFFICERS WHO HELPED THE ARABS
WIN THEIR FREEDOM

Colonel Lawrence is seated in the chair. Standing directly behind him is
Captain H. S. Hornby, an expert at dynamiting trains, and the other officer
standing is Major William E. Marshall, the fighting surgeon and bacteriologist.
Sitting on the rug in front of Lawrence is Major T. H. Scott, who looked after
the boxes of gold; seated on the left is Major P. G. W. Maynard, a judge from
Central Africa; and the officer with the dog is Captain Raymond Goslett, czar
of the Arab army commissariat.

CHAPTER XXVI

TALES OF THE SECRET CORPS

ALTHOUGH none played quite so spectacular a part as Lawrence, there were at least a score of other dashing officers who distinguished themselves in Arabia, and a volume might well be, and, in fact, should be, written about the exploits of each.

All of Britain's co-operation with the Arabs was arranged by a secret-service department: the Near Eastern Intelligence Corps, created in the days when Sir Henry McMahon was still High Commissioner for Egypt. Upon his retirement, the control of this branch of the service passed on to his successor, Sir Reginald Wingate, and to Sir Edmund (now Field-Marshal Viscount) Allenby. Although these three distinguished men each personally encouraged the Arabs and took an active interest in the Shereefian revolt, no man among those who did not actually visit Arabia deserves more credit for the success of the revolution than Sir Gilbert F. Clayton, the organizer of this secret corps.

During the early days of the operations in the Near East, General Clayton made his headquarters in Cairo. There he gathered together a group of brilliant men who were each intimately acquainted with some corner of the Near East, and with some one particular group of its bewildering mosaic of peoples. Among them were students of political affairs, men like Mark Sykes and Aubrey Herbert; then there was Hogarth, the famous antiquarian and geographer; Cornwallis and Joyce, veterans from the Sudan; Woolley and Lawrence, who were engaged in archæology in Mesopotamia; and many others, including an engineer-adventurer of reckless daring by the name of Newcombe, whom Lawrence described to me as "the most devastating energetic person in the world."

Although Colonel Lawrence had more train demolitions to his credit than anyone else, he was not the man who first introduced the gentle sport of tulip-planting in Arabia. That honour must go to Lieutenant-Colonel S. F. Newcombe, who might even have exceeded Lawrence's record as a train-wrecker and railway-demolisher had not his fearless spirit and love of fighting resulted in his spending the final stages of the War in a Turkish prison.

Prior to 1914, Newcombe had earned the reputation of

N

being the ablest engineer in the British army. The railway
line which crosses the Sudan Desert from the valley of the
Nile to the Red Sea was one of his efforts. Always a pioneer,
he had surveyed and blazed trails in Abyssinia, Persia, and
various other regions that are mere blobs on the map to most
of us.

So engrossed did he become in each job that he also gained
renown for his forgetfulness as well as for his daring. After
the capture of El Wedj, in the early days of the Hedjaz revolt,
he was placed in temporary command of that port. Living
with him were several other officials, but as the colonel
happened to be the only one who had a servant they were all
obliged to depend upon him for mess arrangements. But
Newcombe attended to this unimportant phase of his day's
activity in the most casual manner, if at all, and when one
o'clock came around and someone suggested: "Now for a bit
of lunch," it usually developed that Newcombe had forgotten
to give instructions; and as a result they would have to compromise by telescoping lunch and tea at two o'clock.

Colonel Newcombe played a meteoric part in Arabian
affairs for seven months, and initiated the methods of railway
destruction which Lawrence afterward applied so effectively.
Although he donned Arab garb, he was utterly un-Oriental in
his ways, and plunged headlong into his work both day and
night at such a furious pace that no one could keep up with
him. Then at the end of seven months in the desert he
rejoined the British army in Palestine, and in the attack on
Beersheba carried out one of the most daring actions of the
War.

Allenby's cavalry and infantry were closing in on
Beersheba from the west, south, and east. But to the north
of that ancient home of Abraham runs the Beersheba-Hebron-
Jerusalem Road, in those days the main artery of the Turkish
line of communications. Newcombe, and one hundred
Australians who had volunteered to follow him, crept through
the Turkish lines by night just before the attack on Beersheba
was launched. Their job was to attempt to cut the Hebron
Road and hold up all Turkish supplies and reinforcements
until Allenby and his army had routed the Turkish forces and
taken Beersheba. It was a desperate thing to attempt, but
for three days and nights Newcombe and his band of
Australians remained astride that road and outfought fifty
times their number. Eventually they were surrounded on a
hill-top, and the few lucky enough to be still alive were
captured.

It happened that Colonel Newcombe was the highest rank-
ing British officer whom the Turks had thus far captured in
Palestine, and so they made quite a fuss over him when he
was paraded through the streets of Jerusalem on his way to
prison in Anatolia.

But months later, after having survived small-pox and all
of the other luxuries of Turkish prison life, the colonel escaped
from his cell in Constantinople through the aid of a beautiful
Syrian girl, who then concealed him in her home. This was
shortly before the Turkish collapse, and Newcombe, preferring
the thrills of life in disguise in Constantinople to the monotony
that might follow complete escape from Turkey, remained in
Stamboul in order to start an underground bureau of propaganda right in the heart of enemy territory. So successful
was he that eventually he got into touch with a group of
prominent Turks who were opposed to the pan-German policy
of Talaat and Enver, and he even helped them arrange the
armistice which resulted in Turkey's dropping out of the War.
Then, as any born hero of melodrama would be expected to
do as the climax to his romantic career, he married the beautiful Syrian girl who had helped him escape—and, we hope,
lived happily ever after.

Among the men most actively engaged in arranging British
aid for the Arabs and in advising them on military matters
were Colonel C. E. Wilson, Colonel K. Cornwallis, Lieutenant-
Colonel Allan Dawnay, and Commander D. G. Hogarth.
Colonel Wilson was the governor of the Red Sea Province of
the Sudan when Shereef Hussein and his sons first overthrew
the Turks in Mecca, and he engineered considerable surrepti-
tious gun-running to keep the revolt alive until the Allies had
time to make up their minds officially to help the Arabs.
Colonel Wilson loaded British ships with ammunition and
rifles at Port Sudan and then transferred them to sailing dhows
in the middle of the Red Sea.

These dhows then landed the supplies secretly along the
Arabian coast, where they were distributed to the Bedouins.
But after the fall of Mecca and Jeddah he left his administrative work in the Sudan and crossed over to Jeddah, where he
remained in charge of British activities in the Southern Hedjaz
and as adviser to Shereef Hussein until the termination of the
War. In fact it was Colonel Wilson, in company with General
Clayton and Ronald Storrs, the Oriental secretary to the High
Commissioner for Egypt, who opened up the first negotiations
between Britain and the leaders of the Arab revolt. In spite
of poor health, Colonel Wilson did particularly fine work.

Cornwallis, Dawnay, and Hogarth spent most of their time at headquarters in Cairo at what was known as the Arab Bureau. Colonel Cornwallis, who after the War was sent to Mesopotamia as one of the principal British advisers to Feisal when that Emir was proclaimed King of Bagdad, was in charge of the Arab Bureau. He personally superintended the political side of the work which co-operation with the Arabs entailed, such as official negotiations between Britain and the newly-established government of the kingdom of the Hedjaz, and the important business of the subsidy which was granted to King Hussein to enable him to continue his campaign. In addition Colonel Cornwallis supervised the extremely important work of winning recruits for the Shereefian army from the Ottoman troops of Arab blood who were in the prison camps of Syria, Palestine, Egypt, and Mesopotamia. Lawrence often referred to the genius of Cornwallis and seemed to regard him as indispensable to Arab success.

Another brilliant officer who divided his time between the Arab Bureau in Cairo, the desert, and Allenby's headquarters in Palestine was Lieutenant-Colonel Allan Dawnay of the Coldstream Guards. Although responsible for putting the Arabian campaign on a proper and efficient military basis for personnel and service of supply, Dawnay's main task was that of keeping Emir Feisal, Colonel Lawrence, and the other leaders in Arabia in constant touch with Allenby. Lawrence and he were intimate friends and worked in perfect harmony. Dawnay did everything possible to wangle the equipment and everything else that Lawrence required. He also saw to it that his own visits to Arabia allowed him enough time to take part in a raid or two, for he, too, was an ardent "tulip-planter."

But so unusual was the nature of the desert war that it required the diplomatic genius of at least one man to act as an intermediary between Arabia and the Imperial Government in London. This delicate task was left to a scholarly man of international renown whose suggestions could therefore hardly be disregarded even by a Prime Minister and his War Cabinet. Sir Gilbert Clayton here again proved himself a genius at selecting men by choosing D. G. Hogarth, head of the Ashmolean Museum of Oxford, for this post, and in Hogarth he not only picked a man famous as an antiquarian and archæologist but one who had long been looked upon as the foremost living authority on Arabia. Here again Lawrence was favoured by fortune in being associated with one who could hardly have been more ideally qualified, for

Commander Hogarth (he was given an honorary naval commission to increase his official prestige) had known Lawrence from childhood, and had given him his start in the field of archæology.

Throughout the campaign Commander Hogarth was looked upon by Lawrence and his colleagues as their counsellor, philosopher and mediator, whose delicate task it was to justify the various steps taken in Arabia to the General Staff and the War Cabinet. He also edited the secret publication at headquarters in Cairo called *The Arab Bulletin*, of which only about four copies per edition were printed: one for Lloyd George and his Cabinet, one for Allenby and staff, one for Lawrence and associates in the desert, and one for the file at the Arab Bureau.

CHAPTER XXVII

JOYCE & CO. AND THE ARABIAN KNIGHTS OF THE AIR

THE forces of the King of the Hedjaz, as previously stated, included both regulars and irregulars; the latter were the Bedouins mounted on camels and horses, while the former were deserters from the Turkish army, men Arab of blood conscripted into the Ottoman armies and afterward captured by the British in Palestine and Mesopotamia. There were nearly twenty thousand regulars specially trained as infantry to attack those fortified positions which could not be taken by Lawrence's irregulars. They were under the leadership of Lieutenant-Colonel P. C. Joyce, who, like Lawrence, was an Irishman, and who next to Lawrence probably played a more important role in the campaign than anyone else.

Unlike Lawrence, Joyce was a soldier by profession, an officer in the Connaught Rangers with a splendid record for service in the Boer War and in Egypt and the Sudan. Physically there was a further difference between them, for while Lawrence stood barely five feet three, his colleague loomed well over six feet three. None but the largest ship of the desert could navigate under Joyce's bulk, hence he seldom mounted a camel. But when he did, it looked like one mountain on top of another.

Colonel Joyce spent nearly a year building up an army to send against the strongly-fortified city of Medina. It was to be under the leadership of Emir Ali. At last, when by the grace of Allah all seemed in readiness, a courier from Emir Ali handed a message to Joyce to be forwarded on to His Majesty the King in Mecca with all possible despatch. The message read:

"O Father of Mercies and Lord of the Earth, greetings from thy son:
Thy heroic army awaits but the command for its victorious advance upon the Turks. Yet for lack of one mere detail are we delayed. Our valorous officers swear that it would be futile for them to advance without swords. Wherefore I implore thee to send thirty of thy Damascus blades in scabbards of beaten gold in order that they may be satisfied.
"THY SLAVE."

But fortunately Colonel Joyce proved himself capable of coping with the thousand and one unexpected difficulties that arose, for in addition to his ability to speak Arabic he had many other valuable qualifications. For instance, he was tactful and cool and utterly imperturbable, could not be hustled under any circumstances, was painstaking, and, above all, patient beyond the normal vanishing-point of patience as practised in the Occident. So while Lawrence spent his time with his Bedouin rabble, Joyce demonstrated his military ability by building up the auxiliary force of regulars from the medley of Syrians, Palestinians, and Bagdadis who were attracted to the Shereefian banner. But he also now and then found time to join Lawrence on a raid or to lead a demolition expedition of his own. In fact on one occasion he destroyed seven small bridges and tore up two thousand rails on the Turkish railway between the stations of Toweira and Hedia.

There were a number of other officers who fought with the Arabs and took part in the fascinating game of planting tulips and blowing up the Turkish railway. Among these were Lieutenant-Colonel W. F. Stirling, Major P. G. W. Maynard of the Irish Rifles, who had been a judge in a remote corner of the Sudan, Major H. W. Young, Major Wm. E. Marshall, Captain E. Scott Higgins, Captain H. S. Hornby, and Lieutenant H. Garland, who taught demolition to the Arabs. Nearly all of the men who fought in Arabia had annexed various military honours long before they were selected to play a part in the War in the Land of the Arabian Nights, but none had been quite so generously decorated as Stirling, who not only was a veteran of the South African War but had found time to serve with high distinction in the Royal Flying Corps before he crashed and nearly lost his life while on a reconnaissance flight over one of the most inhospitable corners of Arabia. Doomed to serve the remainder of the War on the ground, he was selected as the right type of man for the Hedjaz show.

He joined the Arabs just as they were about to invade Syria and was with Lawrence when the latter reached Damascus. Young, formerly of the Intelligence Department in Mesopotamia, was another who revelled in the manipulation of high explosives. During the final stage of the campaign he took over the all-important job of organizing the transport system; but among his numerous achievements, by no means the least was the success he met in raising a silky beard that was the envy of his less manly colleagues and which transformed him into an ideal sheik.

Perhaps the most universally liked, both by British and Arabs, of all the Europeans who took part in the desert war was Lawrence's tent-mate and intimate friend, an optimistic

Scot of the Royal Army Medical Corps with a Highland brogue thicker than Harry Lauder's, who divided his affections between his bacillus menagerie and tulip-planting. Under him were two other medical men, Captains Ramsay and McKibbin. But Major Marshall, although a quiet, shy man of science, whose whole life had been devoted to the realm of test-tubes, microscopes, and a search for mysterious microbes in the jungles of tropical Africa, had proved himself enough of a soldier to win the Military Cross in the battle of the Somme and other honours in Arabia.

When Lawrence was away on an expedition Marshall would transform their tent at Akaba into a Zoo for cholera typhus and plague bacillus. Incidentally he usually managed to contract most of the diseases, the mysteries of which he sought to solve. Then on his trip into the desert he would fill his stretchers with high explosives, and after a raid would throw out all the remaining dynamite and substitute the wounded. After inflicting casualties among the Turks he would proceed to bandage them up. So successful was he as a combined medical officer and soldier that after the War he was appointed adviser to the King of the Hedjaz, and for several years remained at Jeddah as the British Resident.

But of all the tulip-planters there was certainly none more daring than Captain H. S. Hornby, who, like Newcombe, had been an engineer. He had received his preliminary schooling in adventure on the Gold Coast, in the heart of the Congo, and in other out-of-the-way corners of the earth, and so reckless was he that even the wild Bedouins regarded him as stark mad. But his career as a dynamiter of trains came to an untimely end when a part of a mine exploded in his face, leaving him partially blind and deaf. The Arabs who were with him had great difficulty in getting him back to Akaba alive, and from then on he spent his time in administrative work.

At the base-camp in Akaba were two other officers, Major T. H. Scott, of the Inniskilling Fusiliers, and Captain Raymond Goslett. Scott specialized in mirth and money, while Goslett dispensed everything from boots to flour. In Scott's tent were boxes of sovereigns, gold conscripted from every corner of the Empire to help arouse enthusiasm in the breasts of the temperamental Bedouins whenever the spirits of those rather fickle gentlemen began to flag. The only guardian of all these boxes of golden "goblins" was a dog about the size of a squirrel, which Major Scott called his Bulgarian weasel hound. His associate, Captain Goslett, was the czar of the supply and commissary department, excepting when Auda Abu Tayi or some of Lawrence's other brigands could no longer resist the temptation of looting their own base-camp.

Then there were the officers in command of the armoured cars and light mobile artillery: Captains Gillman, Dowsett, and Brodie, and Lieutenants Greenhill, Wade, and Pascoe. Although seriously handicapped by lack of roads, they somehow managed to scale the barren mountains and get into action on many occasions, and they were mixed up in innumerable thrilling adventures during the later stages of the campaign.

But of all the unpleasant jobs, surely the airmen who were sent down to satisfy the Arabs, who insisted that their army like the Turks should have birds that laid explosive eggs, were the least to be envied. With Akaba as their base-camp, they would sally forth to locate approaching Turkish patrols and bomb the enemy garrisons along the Damascus-Medina Railway. Nowhere in the world have aviators ever taken greater risks, except perhaps in East Africa and on the Afghan frontier. When a plane left Akaba the pilot and observer knew full well that if they encountered engine-trouble they were for it, because they were constantly flying over unexplored, unmapped country, as uninviting as the mountains of the moon. On one occasion, when we were trekking across the mountains of the Edom on our way to the "rose-red city of Petra," we heard the drone of a battle-plane overhead, and as we gazed about at that jagged, unfriendly landscape, with the blue Arabian sky punctured everywhere by sharp lava mountains, our admiration for those reckless British Elijahs, soaring thousands of feet above us, increased appreciably.

These sheiks of the air were first under a Captain Harold Furness-Williams, although during the later stages of the campaign an embryo parson, Captain Victor Siddons, became the flight commander. On one occasion Furness-Williams flew from Egypt to Arabia, by way of the Sinai Desert. Hung around the fuselage and back struts he carried a precious cargo consisting of four dozen bottles of Bass, which his fellow sufferers in that thirsty land had commissioned him to bring. But under the eyes of his expectant friends the unfortunate aviator made a bad landing, the plane turned over, and every bottle was smashed. They told him that they would sooner have seen his blood soaking into the sands of the desert than that priceless liquid.

Captain Furness-Williams and his associates spent a portion of their spare time in taking the Arab chiefs for joy-rides. They gave Auda Abu Tayi his first "flip," and that cheerful

old sheik, who had already demonstrated his courage by
marrying twenty-eight wives, with the inborn poetic spirit of
the desert declared upon his return to earth that he deeply
regretted he had failed to take his rifle aloft with him. Never,
he said, had he had such a splendid opportunity for taking
pot-shots at all his "friends" in Akaba.

Among the Arabian knights of the air were Lieutenants
Divers, Makins, Oldfield, Sefi, and several others, but the only
one of them who went right through the campaign to Damascus
was Lieutenant Junor, who dropped bombs during nearly
every Arab battle, and survived to play a similar role on the
equally wild Afghan frontier in India, long after the World
War.

In the southern area were a number of other officers of
whom I saw little or nothing: men like Colonel A. C. Parker,
a nephew of Kitchener, who was on the Red Sea coast for a
short time and then appointed governor of the vast mountain
and desert region called the Sinai Peninsula; here the children
of Israel wandered for forty years. There also was Lieutenant-
Colonel J. R. Bassett, transferred to Arabia from the War
Office in London, who was second in command to Colonel
Wilson at Jeddah; Major H. J. Goldie, who described his
headquarters in Jeddah as so hot that nothing could live there
but human beings, and they could just gasp. Around Medina,
where Emir Abdullah's army made things lively for the large
Turkish garrison, were two more demolition experts, Majors
W. A. Davenport and H. St. J. Garrood.

But this brief enumeration of the other Europeans who
played a part in the desert war would not be complete without
reference to the French. Early in September, 1916, the
French indicated their faith in the Arab cause by sending a
mission to Jeddah under the leadership of a Colonel Bremond.
The French were at a great disadvantage simply because their
Government could not give them sufficient backing, and the
British had to furnish nearly everything for them. This made
it difficult for them to get a strong hold over the Arabs, because
the latter were aware of the circumstances. But Captain
Pisani, who led a detachment of French Algerians throughout
the campaign, had had unlimited experience in the Moroccan
Desert and did splendid sporting work against the Turkish
railway in 1917, and again in the final operations around
Deraa in 1918.

The only other foreigners in the Hedjaz were some mixed
Egyptian troops and a Mohammedan machine-gun section
from India.

One of the finest sporting achievements during the War in the Near East was accomplished by a British civilian official, a Mr. H. St. John Philby, who played no part in the Hedjaz campaign, but who startled King Hussein one day by turning up in Bedouin costume at his summer capital of Taif. Philby had been sent on a secret mission to the court of Ibn Saud in the very heart of Central Arabia, and he had accomplished the remarkable feat of trekking right across Arabia from the Persian Gulf to the Red Sea through a totally unknown region. Lawrence was so impressed with Philby's achievement and his skill in dealing with the Bedouins, that after the War he was instrumental in having Philby appointed adviser to the Sultan of Transjordania.

Perhaps the most genuine-looking brigand of all the Europeans who fought in the Arab rebellion was the Earl of Winterton. He wore a huge beard and an Arab head-cloth, and rode a tall racing-camel bedecked with gorgeous trappings. Lord Winterton turned out to be as much of a fire-eater in the field as he was back home in the House of Commons. When on one occasion a member from the Whitechapel district interrupted him while he was making a speech, the earl wheeled round, gave the disturber a withering look, and shouted "Silence in the Ghetto," and the House simply howled.

In the desert the noble earl managed to look as disreputable as possible, and in appearance was as successful a brigand as Auda Abu Tayi himself. One day Lord Winterton in his sheik's regalia came riding along on his camel on his way from Jaffa to Allenby's headquarters near Ramleh. There is a fairly attractive stretch of road between those two Palestinian cities, but during the War all natives on camels or donkeys or on foot were instructed to take a side-path, so that the road could be reserved for the interminable caravans of motor-lorries and whizzing staff-cars. Right up the middle of that sacred motor-highway came Lord Winterton, ambling along on his camel on a mission from the Arab army to Allenby.

A military police-sergeant on point duty directing traffic saw him, and shouted: "Get off the road, you black bounder!" Winterton placidly continued on his way; he was not accustomed to being addressed with such levity, and naturally assumed that the sergeant was speaking to someone else. But the latter shouted again: "I say you black beggar, —, —, can't you hear me talking to you? I said get off this road and over there where you belong."

Winterton pulled up his dromedary at this and replied as

only one of his social standing could reply: "Evidently, old chap, you don't know who I am. I am a major, a Member of Parliament, and an earl!" Whereupon the sergeant nearly collapsed, but managed to salute weakly and stammer: "Proceed, my lord, proceed," or words to that effect.

Most of the officers in Arabia were either colonels, lieutenant-colonels, or majors. But rank made very little difference, and there was a freemasonry among them such as did not exist on any other front. Saluting was taboo, and in addressing each other titles were dispensed with. Even when Lawrence had the opportunity to become a General he declined the honour and gave as his reason that he preferred not to be elevated in rank beyond his associates. Each man had his own task and went his own way. Each was a free-lance and conducted himself with much the same freedom as did the knights of old.

In a letter written home from Arabia during the latter part of the desert war Colonel R. V. ("Robin") Buxton, in command of the Camel Corps sent over from Palestine to co-operate with the Shereefian force, said of Lawrence: "He is the most wonderful of fellows, and is our guide, philosopher and friend. Although only a boy to look at, and with a very quiet manner, he is known to every Arab in the country for his exploits. He lives entirely with them, wears their clothes, always travels in spotless white, eats only their food, and in fact reminds one of the Prophet. He is a wonderful enthusiast, and has practically started all this movement."

CHAPTER XXVIII

FEISAL AND LAWRENCE AT THE BATTLE OF PARIS

AFTER the fall of Damascus and the complete overthrow of the Turkish armies, and after he had helped establish a provisional government for Emir Feisal, Lawrence laid aside the curved gold sword of a prince of Mecca, packed his pure white robes and his richly-brocaded ones, in which he had been received with all the honour due to an Arab shereef, and hurried to London. His penetrating eyes had pierced to the end of an epoch-making perspective, involving empires and dynasties and a new balance of power in the Near East. He had achieved the seemingly impossible; had united desert tribes that had sworn eternal enmity to one another; had won them over to the Allied cause, and helped Allenby put an end to German and Turkish ambitions for Near Eastern mastery.

But Lawrence realized that his work was not yet finished. He was determined that the great Powers should not forget the promises made to their Arab allies. The battle of the Peace Conferences was still to be fought. So Lawrence returned to Europe to prepare for the arrival of the Arab delegates.

An amusing incident occurred when Lawrence passed through Marseilles, where he landed in order to proceed overland to London. He stepped into the British railway transport officer's headquarters at the station to inquire the time of the next through train to Le Havre. It was a drizzly day, and Lawrence was wearing a dingy trench coat, without insignia, over his uniform. Although a full colonel at this time he still looked like a shave-tail lieutenant. The R.T.O. happened to be a lieutenant-colonel, a huge fellow, with a fierce moustache. When his visitor asked quietly about trains, the R.T.O. glanced up, gave Lawrence a withering look, and blusteringly told him that he couldn't be bothered, and to see his assistant. Without a word Lawrence walked out, but in the next room he took off his waterproof, and strolled right back into the R.T.O.'s august presence again, this time saying, even more quietly than before: "What time did you say the next *rapide* leaves for Le Havre?" For a moment the R.T.O. looked as though he would like to wring Lawrence's neck, but, catching a glimpse of the crown and two stars on his caller's shoulder, he jumped to his feet, saluted, and stammered:

"I beg your pardon, sir. I beg your pardon."

Nothing delights Lawrence more than to take a self-important man down a peg or two. There is no fuss and flurry or pomposity in his own make-up, and it amuses him when he occasionally encounters a blusterer who tries to play up stage.

Emir Feisal and staff were transported across the Mediterranean on board H.M.S. *Gloucester* as the guests of His Imperial Britannic Majesty. The French were considerably perturbed when they heard that an Arabian delegation was on its way to the Peace Conference, and they objected to its being recognized. France coveted Syria, and realized that Feisal and his persistent young British grand vizier would attempt to thwart them. But Feisal started for Paris despite the coolness of the French.

Like all orthodox Mohammedans, the Emir never touches intoxicants, and complications were narrowly averted on board the *Gloucester* because of the fact that several of the members of Feisal's staff, unlike their prince, were not ardent prohibitionists. Although they could not regale themselves publicly for fear of incurring the Emir's displeasure, they would spend half-an-hour or so in the ward-room with the ship's officers before dinner, and General Nuri Bey, who had been Feisal's foremost strategist during the desert war, even ventured to take his glass to the table, and, although he sat opposite the Emir, he cleverly concealed it behind the water-bottle so that Feisal couldn't see it.

On the voyage from Alexandria to Marseilles the Arab delegation was accompanied by Lawrence's tent-mate, Major Marshall, who wondered just how the French were going to receive his charges upon arrival in port. When the *Gloucester* steamed into Marseilles there was an official French mission on the dock, but no British representatives, and the French indicated by their attitude to Marshall that further British interest in Feisal would not be welcomed, and that all matters concerning Syria were purely the affair of France. So Marshall sent a wire of inquiry to the British Embassy in Paris, and a few hours later Lawrence turned up. With his usual tact he avoided friction with the French by borrowing Marshall's Arabian head-dress and attaching himself to Feisal's delegation as a member of the Emir's personal staff and not as a British officer.

When the delegates assembled in Paris, Emir Feisal took

up his headquarters at the Hôtel Continental on the rue de Rivoli. Wherever the Emir went, whether to an informal meeting or to an official conference, he was usually accompanied by the slightly-built, insignificant-looking youth in the uniform of a British colonel. Few people at the Peace Conference, however, were aware that this young man had virtually led the Arabian armies during the War and was almost as important a figure in the Arab delegation as Emir Feisal himself.

Prince Feisal was quite the most imposing figure at Paris. In his flowing robes he was the centre of attention wherever he went and continually sought by artists, photographers and writers. But publicity was almost as distasteful to Feisal as it was to Lawrence, and so they would get up at six o'clock in the morning, throughout the Conference, in order to go rowing in the Bois de Boulogne and escape the curious crowd, which, attracted by the picturesque dress and stately figure of the Arabian Emir, followed always at his heels.

Flattery he was quick to detect. A distinguished Frenchman, M. Dubost, eulogised him somewhat fulsomely in the course of an after-dinner speech at the Hôtel de Ville. When it was over a Moroccan interpreter asked the Emir how he liked it. Feisal's only reply was: "Hasn't he beautiful teeth?"

To induce the Arabs to fight in the World War, Britain had made certain promises which French interests made it extremely difficult to fulfil. But during the Peace Conference Feisal's tact and personal charm did much to win friends for the Arabian cause in Paris. No one ever came away from him in an angry mood. On one occasion, at a meeting of the Council of Ten, M. Pichon referred to the claims of France in Syria, which he said were based on the Crusades. Emir Feisal listened respectfully, and when the French statesman had finished his address he turned toward him and inquired politely: "I am not a profound student of history, but would you kindly tell me just which one of us *won* the Crusades?"

Lawrence's personal attitude regarding the Peace Conference was straightforward and simple: if Great Britain was not going to guarantee independence to the Arabs, and if she proposed to leave them in the hands of the French so far as their Syrian aspirations were concerned, for his part he intended to devote his energies and talents to helping his Arab comrades-in-arms contest France's claims and obtain the rights for which they had so valiantly fought.

During the War the British had sponsored the Arabian

movement for independence and made it possible for King
Hussein and his sons to maintain their army against the Turks.
The French, on the other hand, had merely sent a small
detachment to Arabia, which could hardly even have survived
had it not been for the supplies it received from Lawrence and
his British colleagues. But the embarrassing fly in the oint-
ment was the "you-take-this-and-I'll-take-that" compact
between the British and French in which it had previously
been decided that France was to have Syria as her sphere of
influence. Emir Feisal and Colonel Lawrence felt sure if that
compact was adhered to in the face of Arab claims, that Syria
would become a French colony despite the fact that the bulk
of her population wanted neither French control nor French
co-operation.

In presenting the Arabian case and in coaching Emir Feisal
to meet the delegates on their own ground, Lawrence was a
match for any diplomat at the Peace Conference. He had the
geography of Arabia, Syria, and Palestine at his finger-tips.
He spoke many of the dialects of the Near East. He had
lived with the Ansariya, the Yezedis, the Ismailia, the
Metawileh, the Christian Maronites of the Lebanon. He had
broken bread with the Druses and sat around the coffee-
hearths of nearly every tribe of the desert. He could hold
forth for hours on the intricate political relations, religions,
and tribal feuds of the Arabs and their neighbours. The cities
of Syria were as familiar to him as London and Oxford.
Sitting in an hotel room overlooking the garden of the Tuileries
in Paris, he made the ancient cities of the East live in vivid
phrases for frock-coated gentlemen who had never deviated
from the straight streets of continental capitals.

Lawrence admitted that Beyrouth, the foreign door of
Syria, was French in feeling and in language, in spite of its
Greek harbour and its great American university. But he
insisted that Damascus, the historic city of Syria, long the seat
of lay government and the religious centre, was pure Arab,
whose sheiks were orthodox "Meccan" in their opinions, and
exceedingly anxious to be free from alien rule. He also
argued that the great industrial cities of Hamah and Homs
were more jealously native than any other Syrian centres.

He maintained that the Arabian case rested on four important documents, which he described as follows:

"First: The British promise to King Hussein of October,
1915, which undertook, conditional on an Arabian revolt, to
recognize the 'independence of the Arabs' south of latitude
37 degrees, except in the Mesopotamian provinces of Bagdad

AN ANCIENT PATRIARCH OF ARABY

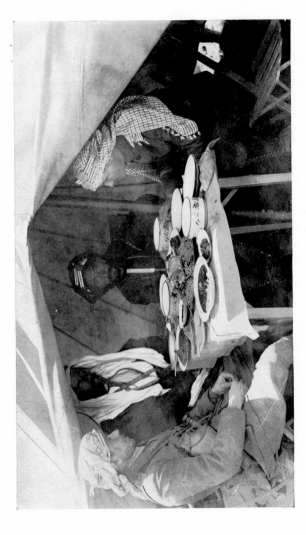

LUNCHEON IN EMIR FEISAL'S TENT AT WAHEIDA DURING THE BATTLE AROUND MA'AN

Reading from left to right: General Nuri Said, Sheik Auda Abu Tayi, Emir Feisal, and the author.

and Basra, and except where Great Britain might not consider herself 'free to act without detriment to the interests of
France.'

"Second: The Sykes-Picot Agreement made between
England and France in May, 1916, which divided the Arabian
provinces of Turkey into five zones, roughly: (a) Palestine
from the Jordan to the Mediterranean, to be 'international';
(b) Haifa and Mesopotamia from near Tekrit to the Gulf, to
be 'British'; (c) the Syrian coast from Tyre to Alexandretta,
Cilicia, and almost all southern Armenia from Sivas to
Diarbekir, to be 'French'; (d) the interior (mainly the provinces of Aleppo, Damascus, Urfa, Deir and Mosul) to be
'independent Arab' under two shades of influence: (1)
between the lines Akaba-Kuweit and Haifa-Tekrit, the French
to seek no 'political influence' and the British to have
economic and political priority, and the right to supply 'such
advisers as the Arabs desire'; (2) between the line Haifa-
Tekrit and the southern edge of French Armenia or Kurdistan,
Great Britain to seek 'no political influence' and the French to
have economic and political priority and the right to supply
'such advisers as the Arabs desire.'

"Third: The British statement to the seven Syrians of
Cairo, dated June 11, 1917. This assured the Syrians that
pre-War Arabian states, and Arabian areas freed by military
action of their inhabitants during the War, should remain
entirely independent.

"Fourth: The Anglo-French Declaration of November 9,
1918, in which Great Britain and France agreed to encourage
native governments in Syria and Mesopotamia, and without
imposition to assure the normal working of such governments
as the people themselves should adopt."

All these documents were produced under stress of military
urgency to induce the Arabs to fight on our side.

"I can find no inconsistencies or incompatibilities in these
four documents," said Lawrence, "and I know nobody else
who can. It may then be asked what is the cause of the difficulties among the British, French and Arabs. It is mainly
because the agreement of 1916, the second document, is
unworkable and no longer satisfies the British and French
Governments. As, however, it is, in a sense, the 'charter' of
the Arabs, giving them Damascus, Homs, Hamah, Aleppo,
and Mosul for their own, with such advisers as they themselves judge they need, the necessary revision of this agreement is a delicate matter, and can hardly be made satisfactorily
by England and France without giving weight and expression

o

also to the opinion of the third interest—the Arabs—which is created.''

The problem was, indeed, a delicate and intricate one to handle. Great Britain had entered into certain agreements with France, and had made definite promises to the Arabs, and other promises to the Zionists. Emir Feisal was frankly opposed to France. He claimed that the new Arabian Kingdom should include all of Syria, Mesopotamia and Palestine. France, by all the etiquette of old diplomacy, considered that she had special and incontestable rights in Syria, dating from the Crusaders. The French had founded educational institutions throughout the country, financed railways, and engaged in other forms of peaceful penetration. They considered themselves the historical protectors of the Christians in Syria. The Zionists were looking forward to a cultural state in Palestine under the protection of the British. All these varied and in some cases conflicting interests, had to be considered and, if possible, satisfied.

Emir Feisal, backed up by Lawrence's advice, insisted that the new Arabian state should include, not only the Hedjaz, but all Mesopotamia, Syria, and Palestine as well. Feisal would not listen to any proposal that Palestine should ever become a Jewish state. From his point of view, and in this he represented the opinion of the whole Arab world, Palestine could not be looked upon as a separate country, but as a province which should remain part and parcel of Syria. He maintained that, as there was no natural boundary and no frontier between the two countries, what affected one must affect the other, and that both from a geographical and a racial standpoint Palestine, Syria, and Mesopotamia were inseparable. At the same time he raised no objection to the Zionist proposal to encourage the immigration of Jews into the country, and to allow the Jews to have full control of their own schools, establish a Jewish cultural centre, and participate in the government of Palestine.

"The Jews, like ourselves, are Semites,'' agreed Emir Feisal. "And instead of relying upon any of the great powers, we should like to have the co-operation of the Jewish people for assistance in building up a great Semitic state. I appreciate fully Zionist aspirations, even extreme Zionist aspirations. I understand the desire of Jews to acquire a home-land. But so far as Palestine is concerned, if they have made up their minds that it is to be Palestine or nothing, then it must be Palestine subject to the rights and aspirations of the present possessors of the land. Palestine is still in effect the land of the Arabs and must remain an integral part of the Arabian state.''

Feisal, quite naturally, took an immediate and intimate view of the territorial rights and political aspirations of the Arabs. He was personally concerned in the establishment of an Arabian state and in all the problems that might threaten its success. But Lawrence, with his sixth sense and his imaginative understanding of the rise and fall of empires, appraised events in terms of rounded periods rather than of years. The Arabian question, the Palestine question, the Syrian question, must all sift and change with the sands of time.

In spite of all the diplomatic circumlocution, red tape and super-politeness that veneered the proceedings in Paris, Emir Feisal was under no delusion as to the true spirit that permeated the Peace Conference, and before he and Lawrence would start out to attend one of the meetings Feisal would playfully unsheath his gold dagger and whet it a few times on his boot.

The Emir is a keen wit, and many stories are told of his clever retorts in Paris. After he had been at the Conference for a few weeks someone asked him to give his opinion of modern statesmen as a result of what he had thus far seen of them. He replied: "They are like modern paintings. They should be hung in a gallery and viewed from a distance!"

The final outcome of the battle of the Peace Conference was a partial victory for Emir Feisal and Colonel Lawrence. They did not get all that they had asked for, nor did they expect to. France was given control of Beyrouth and the Syrian coast, Britain accepted a mandate over Palestine, but the Arabs were allowed to retain control of the interior of Syria and to make their beloved Damascus the capital of their new state.

CHAPTER XXIX

LAWRENCE NARROWLY ESCAPES DEATH; ADVENTURES
OF FEISAL AND HUSSEIN

During a lull in the long siege in the council-chambers at Paris, Lawrence had one more adventure. He had left his diaries and nearly all of his important papers relating to the campaign in a vault in Cairo, because the Mediterranean was still infested with German U-boats when the Turkish armistice was signed and when he returned from the Near East. So, after the preliminary work of the Peace Conference had been completed, Lawrence found himself in need of his notes and papers.

He heard that ten British machines—giant Handley-Page planes, with Rolls-Royce engines, that had seen service in many a night raid over Germany—were leaving for Egypt to blaze a new air route from London to Cairo. Lawrence promptly arranged to accompany them. But the machines were old and nearly worn out, and the pilots were dare-devil chaps who literally ran their planes to pieces. In fact some of the pilots had never flown a Handley-Page, and some of their mechanics had never even worked on a Rolls-Royce engine. On the way from Cologne to Lyons five forced landings were made. Nearly all the planes had to be rebuilt several times during the journey to Egypt.

The Air Ministry in London had vaguely directed the squadron to an aerodrome at Rome. When the pilots reached the Eternal City, they flew back and forth across the Tiber, over St. Peter's, the Coliseum, the Forum, and up and down the Appian Way, but nowhere on any of the Seven Hills could they spot a landing-ground. Finally the pilot of Lawrence's plane saw what he thought might be an aerodrome. But when he swooped down it turned out to be a stone quarry. Just before reaching the quarry he saw his mistake, switched on the engine, and tried to ascend again. Unluckily he was unable to get up sufficient flying speed. The machine raced along the ground, then bolted over the edge of the quarry, and crashed down into a tree-top.

Lawrence was seated in the gun-pit. The occupants had a vague impression of a tree coming toward them at amazing speed. Suddenly there was a noise like the crack of a machine-gun. In the flash of a second the great plane toppled over on its nose and right wing and splintered into matchwood. Both pilots were killed outright. The two mechanics, who were seated with Lawrence in the rear in the machine-gunner's compartment, were pitched out on their heads. One suffered concussion of the brain; the other was merely stunned. As soon as the second recovered consciousness he began to dig Lawrence out of the debris. The colonel's shoulder-blade, collar-bone, and three ribs were broken. In the excavating process, which took ten minutes, the mechanic kept spluttering excitedly that the plane might catch fire any minute. Lawrence replied: "Well, if she does, when I arrive in the other world I may find it chilly."

In spite of the accident, however, Lawrence jumped into another plane a few days later and continued his flight to Egypt. "Our strangest sensation," he afterward told me in Paris, "was breakfasting on the Isle of Crete and dining the same day in Cairo, seven hundred miles away." After he had gathered up his papers, and still somewhat shaken as a result of his aerial interlude, he returned to the seats of the mighty in Paris.

At the conclusion of the Peace Conference, Emir Feisal and staff visited London and then made a tour of the British Isles. Colonel Lawrence took delight in showing his Arab friends around. Everything was new to several of the sheiks who had just arrived from Arabia, and one would have expected them to be tremendously impressed by the subways, the motor-cars, and the countless wonders of the capital of the British Empire. But these things merely excited a supercilious, sheik-like smile. They were too proud to ever show any signs of surprise, except on one occasion in their room at the Ritz. They were dumbfounded when they turned on the water faucets, and found that one ran hot and the other cold.

In the holy Koran, they said, they had been told of the fountains of paradise, which flow with milk or with honey at will; but they had never heard of earthly fountains such as these in the Ritz. After alternating them a bit and making quite sure that they themselves were not dreaming, they told Lawrence they wanted to take some of those magic faucets back to Arabia so that they could carry them in their camel-bags to supply them with hot and cold water while trekking across the desert!

On one occasion Emir Feisal visited Glasgow and was entertained at a great civic banquet. He had been so busy seeing the sights along the Clyde that when it came time to respond to the toast in his honour he was unprepared. The

only other person present who could understand Arabic was
Colonel Lawrence, who sat beside him to act as his interpreter;
and so Emir Feisal leaned over and whispered in his ear: "I
haven't a thing to say, so I am going to repeat the passage
from the Koran on the cow. When you get up to interpret
you can tell them anything you like!" It happens that the
passage on the cow is one of the most sonorous and euphonious
parts of the Koran, and the business men of Glasgow were
tremendously impressed by the marvellous flow of eloquence
that rolled like Niagara from the lips of the Oriental monarch,
never dreaming that he was simply reeling off the Prophet
Mohammed's dissertation on the cow.

Shortly before he returned to the Near East the Emir was
entertained at a banquet in London, and Lord Balfour during
the course of a conversation tried to find out what Emir Feisal
thought of the British Government. He succeeded. "It
reminds me of a caravan in the desert," replied the George
Washington of Arabia. "If you see a caravan from afar off,
when you are approaching it from the rear, it looks like one
camel. But, riding on, you see that camel tied to the tail of
the next, and that one to the tail of the next, and so on until
you come to the head of the caravan, where you find a little
donkey leading the whole string of camels." Lord Balfour
wondered to just whom the Emir was referring!

When Feisal returned to Syria the people again welcomed
him as their liberator, and after a few weeks they proclaimed
him King of Syria, with Damascus as his capital. But this
new state was short-lived, for without foreign co-operation to
help him finance his government his position soon became
impossible. After using up his own private fortune in a vain
attempt to develop order out of chaos, he was obliged to leave
Damascus, and the French at once arbitrarily occupied the
whole of Syria. For the moment it seemed as though Feisal's
hopes were shattered. But Lawrence and the other British
leaders who had been associated with the Arabian Revolution
still had another card to play.

All through these turbulent days Emir Feisal's father had
continued to strengthen his position in the Hedjaz. Galloping
out of Mecca in the gorgeous Arabian twilight, a slight, lean
figure was often seen by the Bedouins of the desert; it was
Hussein, their king, on a night journey to Jeddah, forty miles
away. No music preceded him, nor stately pageantry; he
rode alone and a-muleback.

Until ousted in 1924 by the fanatical warriors of Ibn Sa'ud
from the oases of Central Arabia, the former Grand Shereef

not only ruled as King of the Hedjaz, but he assumed the title of caliph, or spiritual leader of over two hundred million Mohammedans. He was a monarch of simple tastes, and even preferred a mule to any other conveyance. But for mules he is a connoisseur and a fan. South America, Australia, and Abyssinia are combed for his favourite steeds; but the best of all, according to King Hussein, is the good Missouri "hard-tail."

Simple, even severe in his tastes, Hussein was a rigid upholder of the Volstead clauses in Al Qu'ran. After a gloriously successful train-wrecking expedition, two of Lawrence's Arab officers went up to Mecca on a week's leave, taking along in their grips something stronger than rose-water with which to celebrate. This breach of piety reached the ears of the king, who had the officers beaten in public. After that no one chose Mecca as an Arabian Montreal.

The Arabs are inordinately fond of talking-machines, but King Hussein has prohibited them in Mecca, believing them to be the invention not of Edison but of the devil. Although he himself prefers the life of a nomad, and his real sympathies are with the Bedouins, he is even more severe with the tribesmen of the black tents than with the Arab townsfolk.

One day he was resting in the cool shelter of date-palms in an oasis with a circle of Bedouins squatting around him on their prayer-rugs. Out of the corner of his eye he observed one of these Arabs slip the kuffieh belonging to his neighbour under the folds of his robes. A moment later, the owner returned and missed his handsome head-dress. Everyone denied seeing it, including the culprit. Hussein stood up, terrible in his wrath, and strode over to the guilty man.

"Varlet, where is thy brother's kuffieh?" he demanded.

"Master of mercies, I know nothing of it," stammered the terrified man.

"Thou liest!" growled Hussein, and, picking up the gnarled club that formed part of his regal trappings, he dealt the man a terrific blow in the ribs. The thief collapsed in a heap and died next day.

Hussein, as the Grand Shereef of Mecca, was the sixty-eighth of his dynasty. As king he was the first of a new line. As caliph of the Mohammedan world he attempted to revive the supremacy of his ancient clan, the Qu'reish, from whom the Prophet himself was descended. He showed himself to be a man of keen intelligence, and those who knew him best said that he had a mutual gift for diplomacy. But his advancing age made it more and more difficult for him to maintain

the difficult position as caliph over the divided and distracted
Moslem world of to-day. Many did not acknowledge him. In
his own Arabia the powerful schism of the Wahabis paid him
but scant attention. In fact Ibn Sa'ud, sultan of the Central
Desert, and head of the puritanical Wahabis, finally overthrew
Hussein and forced him to abdicate in favour of his son Ali.

Early in the War, according to Mr. H. St. John Philby,
"Sir Percy Cox, who accompanied the Mesopotamian Expeditionary Force as Chief Political Officer, immediately sent
Captain Shakespeare to spur Ibn Sa'ud into active operations
against the Turks and their natural ally, Ibn Rashid. The
campaign was launched in January, 1915, and I have always
thought that, had it not been for the unfortunate accident of
Shakespeare's death in the very first battle between the rival
forces, Colonel Lawrence might never have had the opportunity of initiating and carrying through the brilliant campaigns with which his name is associated, and as the result
of which he entered Damascus in triumph at the head of the
army of the Hedjaz."

Mr. Philby followed Captain Shakespeare into the Central
Desert ruled over by Ibn Sa'ud, and he had a tremendous
admiration for that potentate. But by the time Mr. Philby
was sent to the Wahabi country the Hedjaz revolt was at its
height and Colonel Lawrence was well on his way toward
Damascus. Mr. Philby made an extraordinary journey
through the unknown heart of Arabia and turned up rather
unexpectedly at the summer capital of King Hussein in the
mountains near Mecca. The aged monarch in greeting the
explorer called him the Lawrence of Nejd.

In the Wahabi sect sons can kill fathers or fathers can kill
sons who do not join. A man may also lose his head for
smoking a cigarette. These puritans want to abolish the
pilgrimage to Mecca and blot out all shrines such as the sacred
Kaaba and the Tomb of the Prophet in Medina. Ibn Sa'ud
is the head of a powerful force of fighting-men, and after the
World War he captured the city of Hail, his old enemy Ibn
Rashid's capital, and now rules the whole of Central Arabia.

King Hussein also had other rivals. The Emir of Morocco
claimed the pontificate by virtue of descent through another
branch of the illustrious Koreish. The Turks proclaimed a
republic, and Ghazi Mustafa Kemel Pasha undoubtedly hopes
to seize the sceptre of the Ottomans and become in fact if not
in name the supreme ruler in Islam. India is puzzled, and the
doctors of Al Azhar have up to date made no pronouncement
on the question of the caliphate.

Much, no doubt, is going on behind the scenes. We of the West are prone to under-estimate the importance of Mohammedanism; one day there may be a rude awakening, for it is the creed of one-fifth of the world and is an active and proselytizing creed, making converts in London as well as equatorial Africa.

Like the waves of unrest and religious fervour and splendid hope that passed through Christendom at the time of the Crusades, so now, from Sudan to Sumatra, there are ominous signs of another and darker movement. Men are muttering: "Verily those who disbelieve our signs we will surely cast to be broiled in hell-fire; so often as their skins shall be well burned we will give them other skins in exchange, that they may taste the sharper torment, for God is mighty and wise. But those who believe and do right, we will bring them into gardens watered by rivers."

The times are difficult for a ruler of Islam, but no one has a better claim than Hussein to the great inheritance to which he was vainly called by popular acclamation at Bagdad.

Although he is only five feet two inches in height, his regal bearing does not belie his ancient lineage and his high ambition. At sixty he is still a man of exceptional vigour, although that is not common in men of his age in the Southern Arabian Desert. His hands, delicate and beautiful as a musician's, impress one with a sense of power and finesse.

But the real hope for the future of Arabia now centres in his son, King Feisal, who realizes that the Arabs need European and American assistance in educational and industrial fields, and Feisal is eager to inaugurate many changes that may revolutionize Arabia.

Feisal, like his father, is a man of great personal courage. Were he not, he would never have united his ignorant and fanatical followers in a common brotherhood as he did. In the early days of the revolt, he was by turns rifleman, company commander, and army commander. The Bedouins were the only men he had, and they were meeting artillery-fire for the first time in their lives and didn't like it a bit. Feisal had to lead them in camel charges, bring up the rear in retreat, and defend narrow places in the mountains with his own rifle. At the time, they had few rifles and no stores, and Lawrence has revealed the fact that he kept up the spirit of his men with the thought of material rewards to follow by filling his treasure-chest with stones and ostentatiously loading it on a camel.

Lawrence believes that Feisal has a combination of qualities admirably fitting him for the leadership of the new

Arab state which may rise out of the ashes of the old Ottoman Empire. Lawrence is of the opinion that Feisal will go down in history, next to Mohammed and Saladin, as the greatest Arab who ever lived. He was and still is the soul of the Arab movement. He lives only for his ideals and for his country. His only thought is for the future of Arabia. That he and his father were liberal-minded enough to take advantage of the genius and unique ability of a European unbeliever, a mere youth many years their junior, seems incredible to anyone who knows the Mohammedans of the Near East, because to the average Moslem Arab all Christians are dogs; but King Hussein and his enlightened son even went so far as to accept their fair-headed British adviser as a fellow Arabian prince and an honorary shereef of Mecca, a title which had always been reserved in the past for direct descendants of the Prophet, and which had never before been awarded to any other person, either Moslem or Christian.

CHAPTER XXX

LAWRENCE FLEES FROM LONDON, AND FEISAL BECOMES KING IN BAGDAD

AFTER the Peace Conference, and after Emir Feisal had returned to Damascus, Lawrence vanished. Many of his friends thought that he had returned to Arabia to resume the role of mystery man. But I doubted this, for when I had last talked to him in Paris I had asked him point-blank if he intended to go back to the East in order to help the Arabs build up their new state. His answer was most emphatically in the negative.

"I will not return for some years—perhaps never," he said. "It would not be for the good of the Arabs for me to be there. As a matter of fact, I haven't the remotest idea what I will do. The War has so completely upset my life that it may take me several years to find myself. In the meantime I hope to discover a secluded corner somewhere in England far from war, politics and diplomacy, where I can read a bit of Greek without being interrupted."

His attitude regarding return to the Near East seemed to me another indication of his far-sightedness. During their war of liberation, the Arabs had followed Lawrence partly because of his own personality but mainly because he offered them a substitute for Turkish oppression. He well knew that as soon as the excitement of war disappeared his power over them would diminish. What would have happened if he had returned to the Near East? What would have been the outcome if he had temporarily gained a good position of political authority equivalent to the military position he had attained in Arabia? It is conceivable that, because of his tremendous influence over the Arabs during the War, he might at the outset have had a large following. But in a few months someone would have raised the cry: "Away with the infidel!" If he had returned to Damascus simply in the capacity of adviser to Feisal, that alone might have undermined the Emir's hold over his people. The Arabs are jealous, fickle, and suspicious, and they would have accused Feisal of being a mere puppet. If Lawrence had craved power he might conceivably have made himself an Arabian dictator by turning Moslem. But nothing could have been more remote from his mind. He had not led the Arabs to gratify personal ambition. His sole motive

was to defeat the Germans and Turks, and at the same time
to help his friends the Arabs win their freedom.

While the Peace Conference was still in session, many
people said to me that young Lawrence was the person best
equipped to represent Great Britain in the Near East, and that
he no doubt would return to Syria and Arabia in an official
capacity. But Lawrence's one ambition was to take off his
uniform, drop out of political and military life, and return to
his archæological studies.

I asked Nuri Pasha, one of the generals on Emir Feisal's
staff in Paris, how the Arabs intended to repay Colonel
Lawrence for his great service to their country. He replied:
"We have offered him everything we have, but he refuses
to accept anything. But if he will consent we wish to give
him the exclusive archæological rights to all the buried cities
of Arabia and Syria." Lawrence had other plans, however.

For many months after the Peace Conference not even his
most intimate friends knew what had become of him. Meanwhile I had returned to America and started a tour of the
continent presenting the pictorial records of the Allied campaigns which Mr. Chase and I had prepared. But we were
unexpectedly invited to appear for a season at Covent Garden
Royal Opera House, London, a thing we had never dreamed
might occur, because our material had been obtained solely
for America. Naturally one of the first things I endeavoured
to do upon arrival in England was to find Colonel Lawrence.
I wanted to show him what Auda Abu Tayi and the rest of
his Arabian knights looked like on the screen. Both at the
War Office and the Foreign Office no one seemed to know
what had become of him. He had apparently vanished into
the blue just as he used to do in the desert. But a fortnight
later I received a note from him. All it said was:

MY DEAR LOWELL THOMAS,
    I saw your show last night. And thank God the lights
were out!
                                    T. E. LAWRENCE.

I discovered that this man, whom all London would have
been delighted to honour, was living incognito in a modest
furnished room in a side street over the Dover Street tube-
station. Not even his landlady had any suspicion of his
identity. But he could not long keep it a secret.

A few days later he came round and had tea with us.
When he discovered that I was married and that my wife was

with me, he seemed very much embarrassed and blushed all over. He implored me to stop telling the public about his exploits and return to America. He said that if I stayed in London any longer life would not be worth living for him, because as a result of my production at Covent Garden he was being hounded night and day by autograph-fiends, reporters, magazine editors, book publishers, and representatives of the gentler sex, whom he feared more than a Turkish army corps. He said that as a result of the two weeks I had been speaking in London he had received some twenty-eight proposals of marriage, and they were arriving on every mail, most of them via Oxford.

When he came to call I noticed that he had two books under his arm. One was a volume of Persian poems, and the other, judging by its title, was about the last book in the world that you would have expected this young man to be reading—this man who had been called the Uncrowned King of the Arabs, who had achieved what no Sultan and no Caliph had been able to do in more than five hundred years, who had refused some of the highest honours at the disposition of the greatest governments of the world, who had been made an honorary descendant of the Prophet, and who will live in history as one of the most romantic and picturesque figures of all time. It was "The Diary of a Disappointed Man."

But when Lawrence found out that there was little immediate prospect of my sailing for America, and when he discovered that he was being followed by an Italian countess, who wore a wrist watch on her ankle, he fled from London.

It was not long after this that Emir Feisal lost his throne in Syria, and there was a good deal of propaganda work being done by the French in order to encourage the British not to sponsor the Arab cause. So, despite the fact that he had gone into retirement and was trying to keep out of political affairs, Lawrence could not refrain from defending Feisal. Without appearing personally, he began writing articles to the London papers presenting the Arab side of the controversy. I will quote from one or two of them because they give one an idea of the versatility of this youth, who could wield a pen as ably as he could lead an army.

"There is a feeling in England [wrote Lawrence] that the French occupation of Damascus and their expulsion of Feisal from the throne to which the grateful Syrians had elected him is, after all, a poor return for Feisal's gift to us during the War: and the idea of falling short of an Oriental friend in generosity leaves an unpleasantness in our mouths. Feisal's courage and statesmanship made the Mecca revolt spread beyond the Holy cities, until it became a very active help to the Allies in Palestine. The Arab army, created in the field, grew from a mob of Bedouins into an organized and well-equipped body of troops. They captured thirty-five thousand Turks, disabled as many more, took a hundred and fifty guns, and a hundred thousand square miles of Ottoman territory. This was great service in our extreme need, and we felt we owed the Arabs a reward: and to Feisal, their leader, we owed double for the loyal way in which we had arranged the main Arab activity when and where Allenby directed.

"Yet we have really no competence in this matter to criticize the French. They have only followed in very humble fashion, in their sphere of Syria, the example we set them in Mesopotamia. England controls nine parts out of ten of the Arab world; and inevitably calls the tune to which the French must dance. If we follow an Arab policy, they must be Arab. If we fight the Arabs, they must fight the Arabs. It would show a lack of humour if we reproved them for a battle near Damascus and the blotting out of the Syrian essay in self-government, while we were fighting battles near Bagdad, and trying to render the Mesopotamians incapable of self-government, by smashing every head that raised itself among them."

Britain was having a turbulent time in Mesopotamia just when the French had ousted Feisal from Syria. Lawrence felt that there ought to be a way of putting Feisal's talents to some use in Bagdad, and this article was his diplomatic way of introducing the plan which afterward was developed and adopted.

"A few weeks ago," continued Lawrence, "the chief of our administration in Bagdad was asked to receive some Arab notables who wanted to urge their case for partial autonomy. He packed the delegation with some nominees of his own, and in replying, told them that it would be long before they were fit for responsibility. Brave words—but the burden of them has been heavy on the Manchester men this week at Hillah.

"These risings take a regular course. There is a preliminary Arab success, then British reinforcements go out as a punitive force. They fight their way (our losses are slight, the Arab losses heavy) to their objective, which is meanwhile bombarded by artillery, aeroplanes, or gunboats. Finally, perhaps a village is burnt and the district pacified. It is odd that we do not use poison-gas on these occasions. Bombing the houses is a patchy way of getting the women and children, and our infantry always incur losses in shooting down the

Arab men. By gas attacks the whole population of offending districts could be wiped out neatly; and as a method of government it would be no more immoral than the present system.

"We realize the burden the army in Mesopotamia is to the Imperial Exchequer, but we do not see as clearly the burden it is to Mesopotamia. It has to be fed, and all its animals have to be fed. The fighting forces are now eighty-three thousand strong, but the ration strength is three hundred thousand. There are three labourers to every soldier, to supply and serve him. One in ten of the souls in Mesopotamia to-day belongs to our army. The greenness of the country is being eaten up by them, and the process is not yet at its height. To be sure they demand that we double our existing garrison. As local resources are exhausted this increase of troops will increase the cost by more than an arithmetical progression.

"These troops are just for police work to hold down the subjects of whom the House of Lords was told two weeks ago that they were longing for our continued presence in their country. No one can imagine what will be our state there if one of Mesopotamia's three envious neighbours (all nursing plans against us) attacks us from outside, while there is still disloyalty within. Our communications are very bad, our defence positions all have both flanks in the air, and there seems to have been two incidents lately. We do not trust our troops as we did during the War.

"Then there are the military works. Great barracks and camps have had to be constructed, and hundreds of miles of military roads. Great bridges, to carry motor-lorries, exist in remote places, where the only local transport is by pack. The bridges are made of temporary materials, and their upkeep is enormous. They are useless to the civil Government, which yet has to take them over at a high valuation; and so the new State will begin its career with an enforced debt.

"English statesmen, from the Premier downwards, weep tears over the burden thrust on us in Mesopotamia. 'If only we could raise a local army,' said Lord Curzon, 'but they will not serve (except against us, his lordship no doubt added to himself). If only we could find Arabs qualified to fill executive posts.'

"In this dearth of local talent the parallel of Syria is illuminating. Feisal had no difficulty in raising troops, though he had great difficulty in paying them. However, the conditions were not the same, for he was arbitrarily deprived of his

Customs revenue. Feisal had no difficulty in setting up an administration, in which the five leading spirits were all natives of Bagdad. It was not a very good administration, but in the East the people are less exigent than we are. Even in Athens Solon gave them not the best laws, but the best they would accept.

"The British in Mesopotamia cannot find one competent person, but I maintain that the history of the last few months has shown their political bankruptcy, and their opinion should not weigh with us at all. I know ten British officials with tried and honourable reputations in the Sudan, Sinai, Arabia, Palestine, each and all of whom could set up an Arab Government comparable to Feisal's, in Bagdad, next month. It also would not be a perfect government, but it would be better than Feisal's, for he, poor man, to pull him down, was forbidden foreign advisers. The Mesopotamian effort would have the British Government behind it, and would be child's play for a decent man to run, so long as he ran it like Cromer's Egypt, not like the Egypt of the Protectorate. Cromer dominated Egypt, not because England gave him force, or because Egypt loved us, or for any outside reason, but because he was so good a man. England has stacks of first-class men. The last thing you need out there is a genius. What is required is a tearing up of what we have done, and beginning again on advisory lines. It is no good patching with the present system. 'Concessions to local feeling' and suchlike rubbish are only weakness-concessions, incentives to more violence. We are big enough to admit a fault and turn a new page; and we ought to do it with a hoot of joy, because it will save us a million pounds a week."

Even while fighting in the desert, Lawrence had foreseen the complications that were going to arise after the War was over, and, as noted before, in his advance on Damascus he was extremely anxious that Emir Feisal's men should enter the city ahead of the British and French, because he realized this would make it doubly difficult for the Allies to disregard their friends the Arabs when the tumult and shouting was over.

Lord Winterton, who was with the Arab forces during the fighting around Damascus, in an article in *Blackwood's Magazine*, pays an eloquent tribute to Lawrence, and tells us how he was always thinking far in advance of the problem of the moment.

"I am of opinion," writes the Earl, "that we owed much in those days, before we finally effected a junction with the British, to the good generalship displayed by General Nuri,

THE ARMOURED CAR AND MOUNTED GUN SECTION THAT SPED BACK AND FORTH ACROSS THE DESERT HELPING THE ARABS WIN THEIR WAR

CHASE "SHOOTING" MOVIES FROM THE TURRET OF AN ARMOURED CAR

backed by L.'s advice and genius for thinking ahead of nine people out of ten." Then in another place Lord Winterton adds: "He had no intention that the Arabs should take a back seat in the final destruction of the Turkish army. There were political as well as military considerations at stake, as the Arabs knew well, and L. was only playing on a highly keyed-up instrument. L. infected us all with his enthusiasm, and I began to feel, despite my temperamental dislike of adventure *qua* adventure, that it would be monstrous, if, when the Turkish fox came to be broken up, the British got the body, head, and brush, and the Arabs, who had helped to hunt him for three and a half years, only got a bit of the pad. If we were in at the military death of Turkey, 'Brer Fox,' it would make it the more difficult to refuse the Arabs a big share of the results—spoils, if you will—of the victory."

During his seven years' wandering through the desert, dressing like an Arab, living with Arabs in their tents, observing their customs, talking to them in their own dialects, riding on his camel across a broad expanse of lonely country unbroken except by the long purple line of the horizon, lying down at night under a silent dome of stars, Thomas Edward Lawrence drank the cup of Arabian wisdom and absorbed the spirit of the nomad peoples. Few Westerners ever acquired greater influence over an Oriental people. He had united the scattered tribes of Arabia and induced chieftains who had been bitter enemies for generations to forget their feuds and fight side by side for the same cause. From remote parts of Arabia swarthy sons of the desert had swarmed to his standard as if he had been a new prophet. Largely by reason of his genius, Feisal and his followers had freed Arabia from Turkish oppression. Lawrence had contributed new life and soul to the movement for Arabian independence. The far-reaching results of his spectacular and successful campaign were destined to play an important part in the final adjustment of Near Eastern affairs, and half-way measures made no more appeal to Colonel Lawrence in time of peace than in time of war.

In another of his communications to the Press, when he was trying to mould public opinion in favour of the Arabs, we catch a further glimpse of his views.

"The Arabs rebelled against the Turks," said Lawrence in a letter to *The Times*, "not because the Turk Government was notably bad, but because they wanted independence. They did not risk their lives in battle to change masters, to

P

become British subjects or French citizens, but to win a show of their own.

"Whether they are fit for independence or not remains to be tried. Merit is no qualification for freedom. Bulgars, Afghans, and Tahitans have it. Freedom is enjoyed when you are so well armed, or so turbulent, or inhabit a country so thorny that the expense of your neighbour's occupying you is greater than the profit."

But Colonel Lawrence has no illusions as to the capacity of the Arabs for organization and administration. He fully appreciates that these are not their strong points. But he has faith in them and believes they have a message to give the West.

"History is against the probability of the creation of an Arabic empire," he once said to me in Arabia. "The Semitic mind does not lean toward system or organization. It is practically impossible to fuse the diverse elements among the Semites into a modern, closely-knit state. On the other hand, the Semites have been more fertile in ideas than any other people. The Arabian movement has presented itself to me as the latest expression of the influence of the desert upon the settled peoples; the Semitic spirit has again exercised its influence over the Mediterranean basin. Emir Feisal is the last of the line of Semitic prophets. His campaign for Arabian independence, which made some five million converts among the Arabic-speaking peoples of the Near East, is by no means the least of those revelations by which the Semites have so profoundly affected the Western world.

"The Semites are represented by very little art, architecture, philosophy. There have been few Jewish artists or philosophers. But we find an amazing fertility among the Semites in the creation of creeds and religions. Three of these creeds—Judaism, Christianity and Mohammedanism—have become great world movements. The broken fragments of countless other religions which have failed are found to-day on the fringes of the desert.

"The desert seems to produce only one idea, the universality of God. We who have gone out to discover the meaning of the desert have found only emptiness; nothing but sand, wind, soil, and empty space. The Bedouins leave behind them every extraneous comfort and go to live in the desert, in the very arms of starvation, that they may be free. The desert exacts a price for its secret. It makes the Bedouins entirely useless to their fellow-men. There has never been a Bedouin prophet. On the other hand, there has never been a Semitic prophet who has not, before preaching his message, gone into the desert and caught from the desert-dwellers a reflection of their belief. The idea of the absolute worthlessness of the present world is a pure desert conception at the root of every Semitic religion, which must be filtered through the screen of a non-nomad prophet before it can be accepted by settled peoples.''

With his exuberant imagination and his vista down the centuries, it was an easy matter for Lawrence to throw himself heart and soul into the Arabian movement. He remembered the time when the Arab Empire controlled most of the Mediterranean world, when its philosophers, poets, and scientists enriched the culture of Europe. ''There are some people who have dreams at night and wake to find them all rot. There are others who have dreams in the daytime, and occasionally they come true,'' he said to me one day in London. It is Lawrence's conviction that the Arabs still have something to give the world, something that the world, particularly the materialistic Western world, sorely needs. It has been a fortunate thing for the Arabs that he had the genius to make his dreams come true.

I should like to use Lawrence's own words in defining just what the Arabian movement means. ''There is no reason to expect from the Arabian movement,'' Lawrence told me, ''any new developments of law or economics. But Feisal has succeeded in restating forcibly the vital doctrines of the Semites, Other Worldliness, and his ideals will have a profound effect on the growing nationalist movements in Syria, Mesopotamia, Arabia, and Palestine, which are the present homes of Semitic political life.

''It is like watching the waves of the Atlantic coming in and breaking themselves against the cliffs of the west coast of Ireland. To look at them you would say the cliffs were made of iron, and the waves quite futile. But when you study a map you see that the whole coast is torn open by the wearing of the sea, and you realize that it is only a matter of time before there will cease to be an Irish question. In the same way the successive Semitic protests against the material world may seem simply so much waste effort, but some day the Semitic conviction of the other world may roll unchecked over the place where this world has been.

''I rank Feisal's movements as one more protest against the utter uselessness of material things. I was only trying to help roll up the wave, which came to its crest and toppled over when we took Damascus. It was just rolling up the

Arabs in a tremendous effort and joining the whole nation together in pursuit of an ideal object that had no practical shape or value. We were expressing our entire contempt for the material pursuits exalted by others from money-making to making statues."

Lawrence expresses the conviction that the Arabian movement is nothing more than a protest against outside interference. This time the protest has been directed against Turkey, but the next time it may be launched against France, Italy, Britain, or any Western nation that develops a tendency to be disregardful of another people's deep-seated racial sentiments.

"When you can understand the point of view of another race, you are a civilized being," Lawrence once remarked to me in the desert. "I think that England (out of sheer conceit, and not because of any inherent virtue in my countrymen) has been less guilty in its contacts than other nations. We do not wish other people to be like us, or to conform to our customs, because we regard imitation of ourselves as blasphemous."

Later on, in Paris, Lawrence summed up the whole Near Eastern situation for me in a few words. He is of the opinion that France, in receiving the mandatory for Syria, is merely obtaining control of a temporary phase of the Arabian movement.

"The Hedjaz will be absorbed in a few years by an Arabian state to the north of it. Damascus has always been the centre of Arabian self-determination, but Syria is a small country and too poor to look forward to a great agricultural or industrial future. It acts merely as a front door to Kurdistan, Armenia and Mesopotamia. When Western enterprise restores Assyria and Babylonia to their former level of agricultural prosperity, and when advantage has been taken of the mineral wealth of Armenia and the cheap fuel of Mesopotamia, then the Arabian centre will inevitably be transferred from Damascus eastward to Mosul Bagdad, or some new capital. Mesopotamia has three times the irrigable area of Egypt. Egypt now has a population of more than thirteen millions, while there are only five millions in Mesopotamia. In the near future Mesopotamia will increase to forty millions, and Syria, which now has a population of three million five hundred thousand, will have perhaps five millions. This is rather a bad outlook for Syria. But no matter where the centre of Arabian gravity may shift, nothing can change the Arabian Desert and the ideals of its people."

Despite Lawrence's desire to live in retirement, with only his books for companions, his countrymen would not listen to it. When Winston Churchill took up the Cabinet post of Colonial Secretary, one of the first things he did was to force Lawrence to come and help the Government straighten out the Near East tangle. He appointed Lawrence adviser on Near Eastern affairs, and the latter reluctantly agreed to remain at the Colonial Office for just one year. During this time the Mesopotamian problem was solved along the lines that Lawrence had originally suggested, and Emir Feisal was called to Bagdad and made King of Iraq, the modern successor to the great Caliph Harun al Rashid of Arabian Nights' fame. Thus Feisal, despite the fact that he had lost the throne of Syria, became the founder of a new Mesopotamian dynasty and the ruler of a far more important state than Syria. So Lawrence's ambition to see Emir Feisal rewarded for the part he had played in defeating Turkey and Germany was realized after all.

CHAPTER XXXI

THE SECRET OF LAWRENCE'S SUCCESS

AMONG the hundreds of questions we have been asked about Colonel Lawrence by Press and public in every part of the world, some of the most frequent have been: "What reward has Lawrence received? Does he intend to write a book? Where is he now? how does he earn his living? and what is to become of him? What are his hobbies? Will he ever marry? Is he a normal human being and has he a sense of humour? In fact just what was the secret of Lawrence's success, and how could a Christian and a European gain such influence over fanatical Mohammedans?"

Of course there have been a host of factors that have contributed to his success, that gained him his influence, and that enabled him to win not only the respect of the Arabs but their admiration and devotion as well. They respected him because, though a mere youth, he seemed endowed with the wisdom of their wise men. They admired him because of his personal prowess, his ability to outdo them at the things in which they excel, such as camel-riding and shooting, and because of his courage and modesty. He usually led them in battle, and under fire he was courageous to a fault. Wounded a number of times, his injuries fortunately were never serious enough to keep him out of action. Often he was too far from a base to get medical attention, so that his wounds were obliged to heal themselves. The Arabs became devoted to him because he gained them victories and then tactfully gave all the credit to his companions. That he was a Christian they considered unfortunate, and they decided that it was an accident and in some mysterious way "the will of Allah"; but some regarded him as having been sent from Heaven to help free them from the Turks.

West and East fraternize politely, if rather inharmoniously, in the more accessible towns of Arabia and Syria, for the West has money to spend, and the East is avaricious. But away in the desert and wild places it is otherwise. The nomads, whose ancestors have roamed the country for four thousand years and more, resist the inquisitive eyes and hungry note-books of foreigners who are not proved friends. They still regard stray Europeans with hostile suspicion—and as fair subjects for loot. But Lawrence's minute knowledge of their intricate customs and his apparent complete mastery of the Koran and complex Mohammedan law, caused them to regard him with a tolerance and respect which are exceedingly rare among the fanatical peoples of the Near East. And of course his knowledge of their customs and laws was of incalculable importance in enabling him to settle disputes between antagonistic factions.

To gain his ends it was necessary for Lawrence to be a consummate actor. He was obliged completely to submerge his European mode of living, even at the risk of winning the criticism and ridicule of his own countrymen, by appearing in cities like Cairo, where East and West meet, garbed as an Oriental. His critics scoffed and said that he did this merely to gain notoriety. But there was a far deeper reason. Lawrence knew that he was being watched constantly by shereefs, sheiks, and tribesmen, and he knew that they would regard it as a very great compliment to them if he went about, even among his own people, dressed in the costume of the desert. During those first days which I had spent with Lawrence in Jerusalem he wore nothing but Bedouin garb. Nor did he ever appear to be aware of the curiosity excited by his costume in the streets of the Holy City, for he always gave one the impression that he was engrossed in his own thoughts, hundreds of miles or hundreds of centuries away. And usually on occasions when he visited Palestine and Egypt in Arab kit, he was obliged to come in to Ramleh or Cairo direct from one of his desert expeditions. He was therefore obliged to turn up at headquarters just as he happened to be dressed for his work, without wasting the valuable days which would have been required for him to return all the way south to the base camp at Akaba for a uniform.

When in the desert he never wore anything but Arab garb, nor could he have succeeded in the amazing way he did had he offended the Arabs by wearing European costume. When off "in the blue" on his dromedary, it was not feasible for Lawrence to carry a wardrobe in his camel-bags. The speed with which he trekked obliged him to travel light. In fact, he usually carried nothing but a lump of unleavened bread, a bit of chocolate, his canteen, chlorine tablets, a toothbrush, a rifle, revolver and ammunition, and his little volume of Aristophanes.

The rifle which he carried through the whole campaign had a colourful history. It was one of the ordinary British Army variety which the Turks had captured at the Dardanelles. Then Enver Pasha had adorned it with a metal plate worked

with gold and inscribed, "To Feisal with Enver's regards."
Enver had given it to Emir Feisal early in 1916, before the
outbreak of the Shereefian Revolution, as evidence that the
Turks had already won the War. Later the Emir gave it to
Lawrence and it went with him on all of his raids. For every
Turk that he killed he cut a notch, a big one for an officer and
a little one for a soldier. The rifle is now in London in the
possession of the King.

Lawrence was no parlour conversationalist. He rarely said
anything to anyone unless it was necessary to give instructions
or ask advice or answer a question. Even in the heat of the
campaign he sought solitude. Frequently I found him in his
tent reading an archæological quarterly when the rest of the
camp was worked up to fever-pitch. He was so shy that
when General Clayton or some other officer sought to
compliment him he would get red as a schoolgirl and look
down at his feet.

Several years ago, in Calcutta, Colonel Robert Lorraine,
the actor-airman, said to me: "But if Lawrence is so modest
and shy, how did you get so many photographs of him?"
Out of justice to Lawrence this should be explained. We saw
considerable of Lawrence in the desert, and although he
arranged for us to get both "still" and motion pictures of
Emir Feisal, Auda Abu Tayi, and the other Arab leaders, he
would turn away when he saw the lens pointing in his own
direction. We got more pictures of the back of his kuffieh
than of his face. But after using all the artifices that one
learns as a reporter on a metropolitan newspaper, where it
is worth one's job to fail to bring back a photograph of the
lady involved in the latest scandal, I finally manœuvred
Lawrence into allowing Chase to take a "sitting shot" on two
different occasions. Then, while I distracted the colonel's
attention with questions regarding our proposed trip to the
"lost city" of Petra, which he believed to be the main object
of our visit to Arabia, Chase hurriedly took a dozen pictures
from as many different angles in less time than it usually
takes a studio photographer to set up and expose two plates.
Anyone familiar with the methods of newspaper photographers
will appreciate the simplicity of this where you are working
out-of-doors in good light. If you have a Graphlex, and are
not stricken with paralysis at the critical moment, you can get
photographs of St. Vitus himself. I realized that Lawrence
was one of the most romantic figures of the war, and that we
had a great scoop. So I had made up my mind that we would
not leave Arabia until we had the photographs we wanted.

Frequently Chase snapped pictures of the colonel without his knowledge, or just at the instant that he turned and found himself facing the lens and discovered our perfidy. When experienced hunters start out for game, one acting as the decoy and the other doing the shooting, the victim has less chance than the Bengal tiger selected as the target for visiting royalty.

But to get back to the topic of how Lawrence succeeded in obtaining such a wonderful hold over the Arabs by dressing like them and mastering the smallest details of their daily life, by his courage, his modesty, his physical prowess and his mature wisdom, there can hardly be any question that the way in which he gained the confidence not only of the more cosmopolitan descendants of the Prophet who rule over the cities of Holy Arabia, but also of the Bedouin tribes of the desert, will be regarded by historians of the future as one of the most amazing personal achievements of this age.

The phenomenal character of his accomplishment can be more accurately appraised if we keep in mind that for thirteen hundred years, since the days of Mohammed, fewer Europeans have explored Holy Arabia than have penetrated mysterious Tibet or Central Africa. The zealous Mohammedans who live around the sacred cities of Mecca and Medina prevent Christians, Jews and other non-Mohammedans from profaning that holy soil, and the Unbeliever who ventures into this part of Arabia is indeed lucky if he returns alive. So Lawrence's achievement seems all the more extraordinary when we remember that he admitted openly that he was a Christian. For even though he did wear the robes and accoutrements of a shereef of Mecca, he only actually posed as an Oriental when he slipped through the Turkish lines wearing the veil of a native woman.

Of course the seemingly inexhaustible supply of gold with which he paid his army was of great importance. But the Germans and Turks also tried using gold. They failed because they "had no Lawrence," declares Mr. Philby, who represented Britain in the Central Desert.

Colonel Lawrence played the part of a man of mystery endowed with the ability to do everything superlatively well, outvying the Arabs at everything from state-craft to camel-riding, and even to using the delicate shadings of their own language. In fact, language seems easy for him. In addition to his mother-tongue, he speaks French, Italian, Spanish, and German, some Dutch, Norwegian, and Hindustani, is a master of ancient Latin and Greek, and can manipulate many of the Arabic dialects of the Near East.

Lawrence was exceedingly careful never to enter into competition with the Bedouins unless he was quite certain of excelling them. He also gained a reputation as a man of deeds rather than words, which greatly impressed the desert-dwellers, who for the most part chatter as incessantly as the crows of India. When he did speak he had something of importance to say and knew whereof he spoke. He seldom made errors—and when he did he took care that the Arabs should ultimately regard it as a success. He was an indefatigable worker even under conditions of ever-insistent hospitality, and he would work far into the night when his Arab colleagues were asleep. It was late at night, or while trekking across the desert swaying in his camel-saddle, that he would plan his far-reaching policies of diplomacy and strategy. Small and wiry, he seemed made of steel. But the desert war left its indelible mark on him in more ways than one, for one of his brothers confided to me that ever since his return from Arabia he has suffered from severe heart strain.

Auda Abu Tayi, always sincere in his judgment of people, once said to me : "I have never seen anyone with such capacity for work, and he is one of the finest camel-riders that ever trekked across the desert." A Bedouin can pay no finer compliment. Then added Auda : "By the beard of the Prophet, he seems more than a man !"

CHAPTER XXXII

THE ART OF HANDLING ARABS

COLONEL LAWRENCE believed in the Arabs and the Arabs believed in him, but they would never have trusted him so implicitly had he not been such a complete master of their customs and all the superficial external features of Arabian life. I once asked him, when we were trekking across the desert, what he considered the best way of dealing with the wild nomad peoples of this part of the world. My motive was to try to get him to tell in his own words something about the methods that had enabled him to accomplish what few other men could do. I am confident that he thought I wanted the information merely for my own immediate use in dealing with the Bedouins with whom we were living. Had he suspected that I was attempting to make him talk about himself, he would have turned the conversation into other channels.

"The handling of Arabs might be termed an art, not a science, with many exceptions and no obvious rules," was his answer. "The Arab forms his judgment on externals that we ignore, and so it is vitally important that a stranger should watch every movement he makes, and every word he says during his first weeks of association with a tribe. Nowhere in the world is it so difficult to atone for a bad start as with the Bedouins. However, if you once succeed in reaching the inner circle of a tribe and actually gain their confidence, you can do pretty much as you please with them and at the same time do many things yourself that would have caused them to regard you as an outcast had you been too forward at the start. The beginning and end of the secret of handling Arabs is an unremitting study of them. Always keep on your guard; never speak an unnecessary word; watch yourself and your companions constantly; hear all that passes; search out what is going on beneath the surface; read the characters of Arabs, discover their tastes and weaknesses, and keep everything you find out to yourself. Bury yourself in Arab circles; have no ideas and no interests except the word in hand, so that you master your part thoroughly enough to avoid any of the little slips that would counteract the painful work of weeks. Your success will be in proportion to your mental effort."

To illustrate the importance the Bedouins place on

externals, Lawrence told me that on one occasion a British officer went up country, and the first night, as the guest of a Howeitat sheik, he sat down on the guest rug of honour with his feet stretched out in front of him instead of tucked under him in Arab fashion. That officer was never popular with the Howeitat. To the Bedouins it is as offensive to display the pedal extremities ostentatiously as it would be for us to put our feet on the table at a dinner-party. A short distance behind us in the caravan rode a chief of the Shammar Arabs who had a great scar across his face. Lawrence related this story:

"While that fellow was dining with Ibn Rashid, the ruler of North Central Arabia, he happened to choke. He felt so much humiliated that he jerked out his knife and slit his mouth right up to the carotid artery in his cheek, merely to show his host that a bit of meat had actually stuck in his back teeth."

The Arabs consider it a sign of very bad breeding for a man to choke over his food. Not only does it show that he is greedy, but it is believed that the devil has caught him. Other fine points of etiquette are bound up in the fact that the Bedouins never use forks and knives, but simply reach into the various dishes on the table with their hands. For instance, it is extremely bad form for anyone to eat with his left hand.

The dyed-in-the-wool nomad of Arabia never makes allowances for any ignorance of desert-customs in forming his judgment of a stranger. If you have not mastered desert etiquette, you are regarded as an alien and perhaps hostile outsider. Lawrence's understanding of the Arabs and his unfailing ability to do the right thing at the right moment was uncanny. Of course, he could not have lived as an Arab in Arabia if he had not learned the family history of all the prominent peoples of the desert, including the complete list of their friends and enemies. He was expected to know that a certain man's father had been hanged or that his mother was the divorced wife of some famous chieftain. It would be as awkward to inquire about an Arab's father if he had been a famous fighter as it would be to introduce a divorced woman to her former husband. If Lawrence desired any information he gained it by indirect means and by cleverly leading the conversation around the subject in which he was interested; he never asked questions. Fortunately for the Arab Nationalist movement and for the Allies, Lawrence had got beyond the stage of making mistakes before the War, and at one time was actually a sheik of a tribe in Mesopotamia.

"It is vitally important for anyone dealing with the desert

peoples to speak their local dialects, not the Arabic current
in some other part of the East," declared Lawrence. "The
safest plan is to be rather formal at first, to avoid getting too
deeply involved in conversation." Nearly all the officers sent
to co-operate with the Arabs in the revolt spoke the Egyptian-
Arabic dialect. The Arabs despise the Egyptians, whom they
regard as poor relations, therefore most of the Europeans sent
by the Allies to co-operate with the Hedjaz people found themselves coldly treated. The Allies succeeded in winning the
support of the Arabs because Lawrence was able to crystallize
the Arabian idea of winning independence from the Turks into
definite form and because he had attained the unusual
distinction of being taken into the bosom of most of their
tribes.

It was Colonel Lawrence who was mainly responsible for
the elevation of Hussein, and his sons Feisal and Abdullah,
to their respective thrones. Lawrence believed that the best
way to consolidate the desert peoples and wipe out their terrible
blood feuds would be to create an Arabian aristocracy. Nothing
of this kind had ever existed in Arabia before, because the
nomads of the Near East are the freest people on earth and
refuse to recognize any authority higher than themselves.
But all Arabs have for centuries accorded a little extra respect
to the direct descendants of the founder of their religion.
Lawrence, in his attempt to persuade the Arabs to recognize
shereefs as specially-chosen people, cleverly took advantage of
the fact that the family tree of Hussein towered higher, in fact,
than a eucalyptus—right up to the Prophet himself.

Since the beginning of time the sheiks of one tribe have
had absolutely no influence with members of other tribes.
Shereefs, who really do not belong to any tribe, were
recognized as superior leaders only by the people of Mecca,
Medina, and the larger towns. The word "shereef" or "shrf,"
as it is spelled in Arabic (a language without vowels) signifies
"honour." A shereef is supposed to be a man who displays
honour. In the holy cities of Mecca and Medina, Shereef
Hussein and Shereef Feisal had long stood high in the esteem
of the inhabitants, who were accustomed to refer to them as
"Sidi" or "Lord." The care-free Bedouins, unlike their city
cousins, merely addressed them as "Hussein" and "Feisal"
without bothering about titles. But Lawrence, with his usual
powers of persuasion, convinced even the Bedouins that they
should adopt the term "Sidi" in referring to all shereefs. So
successful was he, that within a few months, in spite of the
fact that he was a foreigner and a Christian, they honoured

even Lawrence with this title because of their deep and genuine admiration for him.

Lieutenant-Colonel C. E. Vickery, C.M.G., D.S.O., of the regular army, who played a prominent part in the campaign and afterward acted as British agent at Jeddah, gives us a vivid glimpse into the formality of a shereef's daily life. Colonel Vickery is one of the few Europeans who have ever visited Taif, the summer capital of the Hedjaz, a city that is not nearly so sacred as Mecca or Medina, but nevertheless a place about which the outside of the world knows nothing.

"It was quite dark when we arrived, very cold and stiff," relates Colonel Vickery. "We were asked into the guest-chamber—a fine apartment, its floor covered with priceless Persian carpets, and round the walls cushions and pillows. Courteously our host turned to us and, embracing us on each cheek, prayed Allah to bless us and murmured the graceful compliment that we were now in our own home. For an hour we sat in that room drinking coffee and highly-sugared tea and smoking, while we watched an Eastern scene that centuries have not changed. The shereef had only been absent a day, but such is the etiquette of the East, that it behoved all to pay their respects to him on his safe return from a journey. To the threshold of the door from time to time came relatives, friends, and slaves. All removed their slippers and entered the room—the door was open—according to their station. The slaves came in quickly, bent with due humility and hastily kissed the two fingers extended to them and as hastily withdrew. Dependents entered more leisurely and kissed the back of the shereef's hand. Turning it over, they then kissed the part between the first finger and thumb and withdrew quietly.

"Friends came in, and for these the shereef rose, showed a faint reluctance at having his hand kissed, and embraced them on one cheek with murmured salutations. For his relatives he rose, allowed his hand to be kissed with seeming reluctance, and then embraced them warmly on each cheek, straining them to his breast and murmuring many and heartfelt wishes for their long life and happiness."

The special deference paid to shereefs by the townsmen and villagers in particular had long ago developed in the city Arabs a sense of their own superior responsibility and honour. That, of course, was of great assistance to Lawrence in creating his Arabian aristocracy. In fact, it was by the sagacious use of this personal responsibility that Lawrence and his associates were able to unify the rival tribes and develop men capable of acting as subordinate leaders under King Hussein, Prince Feisal and his brothers. In order to carry out his plans for widening the influence of the shereefs and making Hussein the recognized ruler of the Hedjaz, Lawrence had first to win the confidence of all the rival tribes. Then, quietly, in such a manner as to make them think the idea entirely their own, he induced them to forget past tribal differences and unite under the leadership of Hussein and his sons and the other shereefs, in order to drive out the hated Turks in the hope of helping bring the War to a victorious conclusion for the Allies, and in the hope of restoring the Caliphate and the former splendour of their ancient empire.

King Hussein had to rely entirely on tribal loyalty for his military strength. His personal Bedouin following was drawn principally from two of the most numerous tribes of the desert, the Harb and the Ateibah, together with one tribe of inferior rank, the Juheinah. These three tribes occupy a great block of territory embracing three quarters of the Hedjaz and a strip of western Nejd. South and west of this block, but within the limits of the Hedjaz, dwell half a dozen small tribes: the Hudheil, Beni, Saad, Buqum, Muteir, Thaqif, and Juhadlah. Still farther south is a group of powerful tribes, the Dhaur, Hasan, Ghamid, Zahran, and Shahran, whose adhesion meant the favourable disposal of stouter fighting material than the Hedjaz itself could supply. All of them sent contingents to assist King Hussein.

From the country north of the central group he drew reinforcements from three of the smaller Anazeh tribes. The Billi, immediately north of the Juheinah, enrolled to a man, and they were followed by the Atiyah and Howeitat. The great Howeitat tribe, which roams the country between the head of the Gulf of Akaba and the lower end of the Dead Sea and Central Arabia, has more enemies, causes more trouble, and takes part in more blood-feuds than any other group of tent dwellers. One can meet no more obstinate, unruly and quarrelsome people. They seem to have no fear. The Howeitats find it impossible to unite even among themselves when attacked from without. About the only thing they possess in common are wounds and the same tribal marks on their camels. This great tribe has two sub-divisions, the Ibn Jazi and the Abu Tayi, of which old Auda Abu Tayi, the Bedouin Robin Hood, is the chieftain. But Auda is chieftain only by virtue of his daring and prowess, for no man in that spirited group cares to bow down before the authority of any sheik.

For fifteen years the two sections of the Howeitat waged relentless war upon each other until the mild-voiced Shereef Lawrence succeeded in getting them both to unite with Hussein and Feisal to drive out the Turks. But even then Lawrence found it advisable to keep the two sections attached to different parts of his army so that they could not leap at each other's throats. Both were willing to obey Lawrence's orders so long as they were kept apart, but in the event of their meeting they regarded themselves in honour bound to start a row. Auda Abu Tayi and his people consider the Druses, who wage the most merciless war in the desert, among their most bitter blood enemies, and Lawrence more than had his hands full to prevent them from killing each other instead of the Turks. In 1912, fifty of Auda's fighting men, mounted on camels, captured eighty Druse cavalrymen in battle. This is striking evidence of the fighting ability of the Howeitat warriors, since one horseman is usually worth two camelmen in a fight, due to the fact that a horse can be manœuvred so much more rapidly. Since that engagement the Druses have been continually on the alert, hoping to take the Howeitat by surprise and annihilate them. In spite of these minor insurgencies, the Howeitat, under Auda's leadership, became the finest fighting-force in Western Arabia, regarded by Colonel Lawrence as the backbone of his wild desert army.

Perhaps train-wrecking was Lawrence's most spectacular pastime, but nothing he did was more significant or remarkable than this consolidation of the Arab tribes. With them, raiding hostile neighbours was both their amusement and their business. To invite two enemy chieftains into Emir Feisal's tent to swear friendship and loyalty over the ghosts of stolen horses and camels was like asking a Wall Street magnate to turn over his fortune to Communists.

In order to illustrate the delicacy of the problem Lawrence manipulated, let me cite a particular instance. In June, 1917, we were attending a conference in the courtyard of Emir Feisal's palace at Akaba, a one-story structure resembling, with its extensive interior courtyard, a Spanish hacienda. The palace is situated in the little town, back of a fringe of waving palm trees, the only green splash of colour in this stretch of sand, where once was located the great seaport of King Solomon. In a circle round the Emir were seated thirty shereefs and sheiks, all heads of prominent tribes and among them six sheiks of the Ibn Jazi Howeitat. All of a sudden I saw a swift change come over the usually impassive countenance of the young Englishman. Jumping to his feet,

WARRIORS FROM JEBEL DRUZ WHO JOINED FEISAL AND LAWRENCE WHEN THE ARAB
FORCES INVADED SYRIA

A PART OF THE ARAB REGULAR ARMY CREATED BY COLONEL P. C. JOYCE, ANOTHER IRISHMAN

General Nuri Said in the foreground with Malud Bey to the left.

Lawrence slipped noiselessly to the doorway of the courtyard. I saw him speak to a group of Arabs who were about to enter and then lead them off in another direction. Later, when I asked him the reason for his speedy exit, he informed me that the warriors at the entrance were none other than the renowned Auda, his cousin, Mohammed, and some of the other leading fighting men of the Abu Tayi. He added that, if Auda and his companions had come on through into the palace courtyard, a bloody battle might have been fought right in front of Emir Feisal, possibly resulting in the total disruption of the Arabian forces.

Until he became an undisputed leader, Lawrence kept in constant touch with the king of the Hedjaz and his four sons, principally Emir Feisal. He lived with the leaders that he might be with them when they were dining or holding audiences in their tents. It was his theory that giving direct and formal advice was not nearly so effective as the constant dropping of ideas in casual talk. At his meals the Arab is off guard and at his ease, engaging in small talk and general conversation. Whenever Lawrence wanted to make a new move, start a raid, or capture a town, he would bring up the question casually and indirectly, and before half an hour had passed he usually succeeded in inspiring one of the prominent sheiks to suggest the plan. Lawrence would then seize his advantage, and before the sheik's enthusiasm had time to wane he would push him on to the execution of the plan.

On one occasion Lawrence was dining with Emir Feisal and some of his leaders, not far from Akaba. The Arab chieftains thought it would be a splendid plan to take Deraa, the important railway junction hundreds of miles farther north, just south of Damascus. Lawrence knew that Deraa could be captured, but he also realized that at that state of the campaign it could not be held for any length of time, so he said: "Oh, yes, that's a fine idea! But first, let's work out the details." A great council of war was held, but somehow the longer the matter was discussed the less enthusiasm manifested itself. In fact, the Arab leaders became so disheartened that they even suggested retreating from the position that they occupied at that moment. Then Lawrence delicately suggested that such a retreat would greatly anger King Hussein, and little by little he prevailed upon them to go through with the original plan for capturing Akaba, which was his first objective.

As Lawrence once remarked to me under his breath when we were attending a consultation of Arab leaders: "Everybody is a general in the Arab army. In British circles a

Q

general is allowed to make a mess of things by himself, whereas
here in Arabia every man wants a hand in it."

The Arab shereefs and sheiks are strong-minded and
obstinate men. Nothing hurts them more than to have someone point out their mistakes. If you say "rubbish" to an
Arab it is sure to put his back up, and he will ever afterward
decline to help you. Lawrence never refused to consider any
scheme that was put forward, even though he had the actual
power to do so. Instead, he always approved a plan and then
skilfully directed the conversation so that the Arab himself
modified it to suit Lawrence, who would then announce it
publicly to the other Arab leaders before the originator of
the scheme had time to change his point of view. All this
would be manipulated in such a delicate way that the Arab
would not for a moment be aware that he was acting under
pressure.

If Lawrence and his British associates had acted behind
the shereef's back they might have attained certain of their
objectives in half the time, but until Lawrence actually had
been raised to supreme command by the voluntary act of the
Arabs themselves and was regarded by them as a sort of
superman he was wise enough never to give direct orders.
Even his suggestions and advice to Emir Feisal he reserved
until they were alone. From the beginning of the campaign
Lawrence adopted the policy of trying not to do too much
himself, always remembering that it was the Arab's war. At
times, when it seemed necessary, he would even strengthen
the prestige of the Arab leaders with their subordinates at the
expense of his own position. The failure of the Turks and
Germans, on the other hand, was partly due to the fact that
they rushed at the Arabs blindly and attempted to deal with
them in a brutally direct manner.

Whenever a new shereef or sheik came for the first time
to offer his services to King Hussein, Lawrence and any other
British officer present made it a point to leave the Emir's tent
until the formality of swearing allegiance on the Koran and
touching Feisal's hand was over. They did this because the
strange sheik might easily become suspicious if his first
impression revealed foreigners in Feisal's confidence. At the
same time it was Lawrence's policy always to have his name
associated with those of the shereefs. Everywhere he went
he was regarded as Feisal's mouthpiece. "Wave a shereef
in front of you like a banner and hide your own mind and
person," was the maxim of this student of Bedouin tactics.
But Lawrence was careful not to identify himself too long or

too often with any one tribal sheik, for he did not want to lose prestige by being associated with any particular tribe and its inevitable feuds. The Bedouins are extremely jealous. When going on an expedition Lawrence would ride with everyone up and down the line, so that no one could criticize him for showing favouritism.

In every way Lawrence used his knowledge of desert psychology to the best possible advantage. For instance, he was constantly in need of detailed information regarding the topography of the country over which the Arabian forces were campaigning; but the Bedouins are always reluctant to reveal the location of wells, springs, and points of vantage. Lawrence convinced them that making maps was an accomplishment of every educated man. Auda Abu Tayi and many of the other sheiks became so keenly interested in maps that they often kept Lawrence up to all hours of the night helping them with maps that were not of the slightest military value and in which he was not in the least interested.

CHAPTER XXXIII

LAWRENCE THE MAN

ALTHOUGH he had been cited for nearly every decoration that the British and French Governments had to offer, Lawrence sedulously ran away from them by camel, aeroplane, or any available method of swift transportation.

The French Government sent word to its contingent in Arabia to bestow upon the dashing colonel the Croix de Guerre with palms. Captain Pisani, commandant of the French force at Akaba, was anxious to make the ceremony an impressive affair. He wanted to have all of the British, French, and Arab troops out on parade so that he could deliver an appropriate eulogistic address, present the decoration to Lawrence, and then kiss him on both cheeks. But Lawrence heard of the plan and vanished into the desert. Several times he gave the persistent Pisani the slip. In despair the commandant went to Major Marshall, Lawrence's tent-mate, who advised him to surround the mess-tent some morning when Lawrence happened to be in Akaba, and take him by surprise. So Pisani and his detachment waited until he returned, then turned up in full regalia, surrounded him just as he had reached the marmalade course, and read an impressive document relating how he had gone for days without food or water, and how he had outwitted and defeated the Turks.

At the end of the campaign, when Lawrence returned to Europe and left Marshall behind in Arabia, the colonel wrote asking his tent-mate to ship his things from Akaba to Cairo. Lawrence neither drank nor smoked, but was inordinately fond of chocolate, and there were dozens of empty tins piled in the corner of his tent together with books, bits of theodolites, a camel saddle, cartridge-drums, and odds and ends from machine-guns. In one of the empty chocolate-tins the major found the French decoration which Pisani had presented. He put it in his own bag, and when Lawrence came to meet Emir Feisal and the Arab delegates at Marseilles, Major Marshall "pulled his leg" by making another speech, reminding the colonel of his splendid work for France, and then presented him with the Croix de Guerre with palms.

When the Duke of Connaught visited Palestine to confer the Grand Cross of the Order of the Knights of St. John of Jerusalem on General Allenby, he intended to present a

decoration to Lawrence as well. The young leader of the
Arabian forces happened at the time to be out "in the blue,"
busily blowing up Turkish trains. Aeroplanes were sent to
scour the desert for him. Messages were dropped on various
Arab camps requesting anyone who saw Shereef Lawrence
to tell him to report to Jerusalem. One fine day Lawrence
came strolling in on foot through the Turkish lines, to show
his indifference of the enemy. In the meantime the ceremony
in Jerusalem had already taken place, and the Duke of
Connaught had gone to Egypt. Knowing Lawrence's peculiar
aversion to the acceptance of medals or military honours of
any kind, his associates of the intelligence staff succeeded in
seducing him to Cairo only by inventing some other plausible
pretext. Upon his arrival, a subaltern who was not acquainted
with Lawrence's eccentricities inadvertently tipped him off to
the fine affair that was to be staged for his benefit. Without
stopping to pick up his uniform and kit at Shepheard's Hotel,
Lawrence hurried out to the headquarters of the Flying Corps
at Heliopolis, an oasis a few miles from Cairo, jumped into
an aeroplane, and taxied back to Arabia.

Not only did he care nothing for decorations but he
avoided wearing what ribbons he possessed. Captain
Ferdinand Tuohy in his exploits of "The Secret Corps," says
of him: "Colonel Lawrence was given the Companionship
of the Bath for his services. He was actually recommended
for the Victoria Cross, but was not granted that supreme
decoration because there had never been a senior officer witness
of his exploits—a lame enough excuse seeing that there was
ample proof in a dozen ways that those exploits had well and
truly been carried out." As a matter of fact, although
Lawrence was posted for the "C.B.," he never attended any
ceremony in connection with receiving it, and he asked his
friends to sidetrack the recommendation for the Victoria Cross.
He also stood aside when he had an opportunity to become
a general at the time when his force was actually the right wing
of Allenby's army and when he was practically filling the role
of a lieutenant-general. He even declined knighthood. When
I asked him why he didn't want to be knighted, he replied:
"Well, if I become a knight my tailor will hear about it and
double my bills. I have trouble enough paying them as it is."

So far as I know there was only one thing that Lawrence
wanted out of the War, and that was something that he didn't
get. I asked him once if there was anything to be bought
with money that he couldn't afford but would like to have.
His answer, which he gave unhesitatingly, showed how human

and simple he is. He replied: "I should like to have a Rolls Royce car with enough tyres and petrol to last me all my life." The particular car that he would have liked to have had was the Rolls Royce tender called the "Blue Mist" which he used during some of his railway demolition raids around Damascus. But after the War it was overhauled and became Allenby's personal car at the Residency in Cairo.

Lawrence has often been criticized for refusing the various honours offered him. But the truth of the matter is that he did not decline them merely to be eccentric. For instance, before the War he was presented with the Order of the Medjidieh by the Sultan of Turkey for having saved the lives of some of the Germans at work on the Berlin-to-Bagdad Railway when the natives were going to mob them. Then, shortly before the outbreak of the Arabian Revolution, while still a subordinate in Cairo, he received and accepted a number of decorations including the Legion of Honour. But he refused the rewards offered to him for what he had accomplished in Arabia, because he had realized from the very beginning that the Allies, once victory was assured, would find it difficult not only to satisfy the claims of the Arabs, but even to fulfil their obligations to the Hedjaz leaders. He realized full well that the French were determined to have Syria, and he knew all along that they would never agree to the Arabs even keeping Damascus. Lawrence, therefore, felt that he did not care to accept anything in return for having conducted a campaign based on promises which the Allies could not fulfil to the extent to which he believed they ought to be fulfilled. Perhaps he would have felt differently had he known that his friend Emir Feisal would be crowned king of Bagdad after losing the Syrian throne, which Lawrence foresaw he would never be allowed to occupy for long. But at the end of the War no one dreamed that Feisal was going to be the founder of a new dynasty in the city of Harun al Rashid after first being driven out of Damascus by the French.

The only honour that Lawrence accepted was one perhaps more dear to his heart than any other, a fellowship at All Souls' College, Oxford. This fellowship is awarded to men of exceptional scholastic attainments. There are only a score or so of them, usually men past the prime of life who are completing important historical, literary or scientific works. For example, Lord Curzon is a fellow of All Souls. The distinction is an unusual one. It carries with it a modest honorarium and attractive quarters at the college; a delightful place for a distinguished scholar to retire. There is no prescribed work that goes with it, and Lawrence once told me that there were but three requirements for a fellowship at All Souls: to be a good dresser, to be adept at small conversation, and to be a good judge of port. And then he added: "My clothes are an abomination; as a parlour conversationalist I am hopeless, and I never drink. So how I came to receive this honour is a mystery to me."

After his election to All Souls, Lawrence divided his time between the college and the home of a friend in Westminster known as "the house with the green door," and a bungalow that he built for himself in Epping Forest. The porter at All Souls said they never knew when to expect him, that when he was in residence he rarely dined with the other fellows, and that the light in his studio usually burned all night. No doubt he was busy on his Arabian book. But he did the most of his writing at the "house with the green door," where he occupied a bare room that had been an architect's office. One of his friends had given him a fur-lined aviator's costume, and in the dead of winter when the cold in London is decidedly penetrating he would sit in that bleak room in his fur-lined suit writing the inside story of his experiences in far-off Araby.

On his frequent trips to Oxford he would carry his manuscript in a little black bag like those used by London bank messengers. On one such occasion, after he had gone through the gate to the platform at Paddington Station, he put the bag down for a moment and walked over to the news-stand for a paper. When he returned the bag was gone. It not only contained the only copy of his two-hundred-thousand-word manuscript, which he had written entirely in longhand, but it also contained the journal that he had kept faithfully through the desert campaign and many valuable original historical documents that can never be replaced. I saw him a few days later, and in telling me about the theft of the bag he referred to it jokingly and merely said: "I've been saved a lot of trouble, and after all, it's a good thing the bag was stolen. The world is simply spared another war-book." The bag and its contents were never seen or heard of again. Lawrence's theory was that they were probably thrown into the Thames by the disappointed thief, who had hoped for a better haul. But his friends finally prevailed upon him to re-write the book; and this time, in order to find solitude, away from the curious admirers who were constantly disturbing him at All Souls, and a solitude that carried with it a means of keeping body and soul together, he enlisted in the Royal Air Force under the name of "Private Ross." Even there he was unable to conceal

A/c SHAW.

his identity, and someone, for a consideration, tipped off a London newspaper, with the result that once more he found himself drawn into the limelight. A few weeks previous he had agreed to sell the publication rights for a large sum, but when this unexpected publicity appeared he turned down the contract, left the Air Force, called on the various London editors imploring them to allow him to live in peace and print nothing more about him, and then vanished again.

One of Colonel Lawrence's hobbies is printing books by hand. There are few things that he likes more than an attractive book, and he has a valuable library of rare hand-printed volumes. On the edge of Epping Forest, some ten miles out from London, he built himself a little cottage with an interior resembling a chapel. Here he installed a hand-press, and when he finally finished his Arabian book he made six copies. Several were presented to friends, and one copy went to the British Museum Library to be locked up in a vault for forty years; that is, unless someone can prevail upon him to release it for publication. Rudyard Kipling, George Bernard Shaw, and several of Lawrence's literary friends were among those to read it, and one of the most famous writers of the day declared that he considered it "a pyramid in English literature."

Lawrence has great literary ability and a style of his own. He is an individualistic in his writing as in everything else that he does. A number of brilliant articles have come from his pen since he put aside the curved gold sword of a shereef of Mecca; and he has written an introduction to a new edition of "Arabia Deserta," which all agree forms a valuable addition to that classic. Nor could he receive higher literary praise, for Orientalists concede that the foremost work ever published on Arabia is Charles Montagu Doughty's "Travels in Arabia Deserta." Lawrence says of it: "There is no sentiment, nothing merely picturesque, that most common failing of Oriental travel-books. Doughty's completeness is devastating. It is a book which begins powerfully, written in a style which has apparently neither father nor son, so closely wrought, so tense, so just in its words and phrases, that it demands a hard reader."

But Doughty's book had been out of print for many years, and copies of it were extremely rare. "We call the book 'Doughty' pure and simple," adds Lawrence, "for it is a classic, and the personality of Mr. Doughty hardly comes into question. Indeed, it is rather shocking to learn that he is a real and living person. The book has no date and can never

grow old. It is the first and indispensable work upon the
Arabs of the desert; and if it has not always been referred
to, or enough read, that has been because it was excessively
rare.''

So he set about to rectify this deficiency. He proposed
that a new two-volume edition be published to sell for nine
guineas, just half what dealers had been asking for secondhand copies of the original. Doughty, an old man, had for
years been devoting himself to poetry, and existing on a poet's
pittance. So Lawrence had at least three reasons for seeing
a new edition published; to get the public better acquainted
with a classic, to augment the income of his illustrious friend
and predecessor, and to pay personal tribute to one to whom
he felt deeply indebted.

In the preface Doughty says regarding Lawrence and the
new edition: ''A reprint has been called for, and is reproduced
thus, at the suggestion chiefly of my distinguished friend,
Colonel T. E. Lawrence, leader with Feisal, Meccan Prince,
of the nomad tribesmen; whom they, as might none other at
that time marching from Jedda, the port of Mecca, were able
(composing, as they went, the tribes' long-standing blood-feuds
and old enmities), to unite with them in victorious arms,
against the corrupt Turkish sovereignty in those parts: and
who greatly thus serving his Country's cause and her Allies,
from the Eastward, amidst the Great War, has in that
imperishable enterprise, traversed the same wide region of
Desert Arabia.''

No sooner was the edition off the press than it was
exhausted, and since then more editions have followed. So
Lawrence's ambition to do something for Doughty, and sign
for his classic a still wider circulation, was more than realized.
Unquestionably the sale of ''Arabia Deserta'' was stimulated
by the fact that Lawrence had written a special introduction
to it in which he paid glowing tribute to the great traveller
whose experiences in the desert had done so much to pave
the way for his own success. Lawrence's introduction to this
new edition also gives us a hint as to his own skill with the
pen, and as to what we may expect from his own volume on
Arabia. He writes:

''The realism of the book is complete. Doughty tries to
tell the full and exact truth of all that he saw. If there is a
bias it will be against the Arabs, for he liked them so much;
he was so impressed by the strange attraction, isolation and
independence of this people that he took pleasure in bringing
out their virtues by a careful expression of their faults. 'If

one live any time with the Arab he will have all his life after a feeling of the desert.' He had experienced it himself, the test of nomadism, that most deeply biting of all social disciplines, and for our sakes he strained all the more to paint it in its true colours, as a life too hard, too empty, too denying for all but the strongest and most determined men. Nothing is more powerful and real than this record of all his daily accidents and obstacles, and the feelings that came to him on the way. His picture of the Semites, sitting to the eyes in a cloaca, but with their brows touching Heaven, sums up in full measure their strength and weakness, and the strange contradictions of their thoughts which quicken curiosity at our first meeting with them.

"To try and solve their riddle many of us have gone far into their society, and seen the clear hardness of their belief, a limitation almost mathematical, which repels us by its unsympathetic form. Semites have no half-tones in their register of vision. They are a people of primary colours, especially of black and white, who see the world always in line. They are a certain people, despising doubt, our modern crown of thorns. They do not understand our metaphysical difficulties, our self-questionings. They know only truth and untruth, belief and unbelief, without our hesitating retinue of finer shades.

"Semites are black and white not only in vision, but in their inner furnishing; black and white not merely in clarity, but in apposition. Their thoughts live easiest among extremes. They inhabit superlatives by choice. Sometimes the great inconsistents seem to possess them jointly. They exclude compromise, and pursue the logic of their ideas to its absurd ends, without seeing incongruity in their opposed conclusions. They oscillate with cool head and tranquil judgment from asymptote to asymptote, so imperturbably that they would seem hardly conscious of their giddy flight."

Lawrence's command of English is amazing, the reason, of course, is his familiarity with the classics and his knowledge of both ancient and modern languages. His vocabulary is wider than that of most learned professors, and he has great descriptive powers, as we have observed from his description of the death of his friend Talal el Haredhin of Tafas.

Despite his scorn of money in private life, and his well-nigh complete lack of it, while in the desert he had almost unlimited credit and could draw on his Government up to many hundreds of thousands of pounds. It was by no means an uncommon sight to see him stuffing ten thousand pounds in gold sovereigns in one camel-bag and ten thousand in another. Then off he would go with it, accompanied only by ten or twelve Bedouins. On one occasion Lawrence drew a paltry six hundred pounds from Major Scott, "to do a bit of shopping." Major Scott kept the boxes of sovereigns in his tent at headquarters in Akaba. Major Maynard, who was in charge of some of the records, heard of this and asked for a receipt. When Scott informed Lawrence, the latter nearly doubled up with laughter and said: "He shall have it!" And so far as I could find out that was the only receipt he ever signed. As for the letters he received in the desert, he usually read them, then burned them and never bothered about answering.

His has indeed been a strange existence, full of individual experience. Fond of Oriental rugs, Lawrence picked up many rare ones during his wanderings. On the floor of his tent at Akaba were two beauties. Lawrence slept on one of them, while his companion, Major Marshall, used a camp-bed. One of the two rugs is now in the possession of Lady Allenby, while Marshall has the other. One day in the bazaar in Jedda, Lawrence saw a barber kneeling on a prayer-rug that he liked. It had two holes in it three or four inches in diameter. The barber offered it to him for two pounds, and Lawrence bought it. When he took it to Cairo and had it appraised by one of the leading rug-merchants of Egypt he found that it was worth about seventy pounds after being repaired. So Lawrence sent the barber a five-pound note. At his mother's home in Oxford he had a pile of Oriental rugs and carpets, still covered with the dust of the East. A friend of the family got married at a time when Lawrence was away, and his mother sent one of the rugs as a wedding-gift. When the colonel returned she told him about the incident, and said she presumed it was not worth much. "The one you gave away cost me 147 pounds," replied Lawrence. But he was not the least bit vexed and promptly forgot about it.

When the year was up during which he had promised to serve as Near Eastern adviser at the Colonel Office, Lawrence put on his hat and walked out. Since then he has found a new exhaust for his surplus energy. He met an army officer who had a high-power motor-cycle which was too much for the latter to handle. So Lawrence bought it, and streaks it about England much as he formerly raced across the North Arabian Desert in the "Blue Mist."

When an undergraduate at Oxford, he and another student made a solemn compact that if either ever did anything particularly noteworthy he would wire for the other to come so that they could celebrate. In 1920, Lawrence telegraphed his friend as follows: "Come at once. Have done something." This was the first word that had passed between the two since their pre-War college days. When the friend arrived this is what Lawrence had done that he thought worth celebrating: he had just finished his bungalow on the edge of Epping Forest, and was keeping cows!

Epping Forest is a semi-national preserve of some sort, and there is a law that forbids the erection of non-movable structures. After Lawrence had finished his bungalow the police came and pointed out to him that he had broken the law because his house was a stationary edifice. So Lawrence bought some paint and made four camouflage red wheels on the sides of the cottage. This so amused the authorities that they said no more about the law. But not long afterward a fire wiped out nearly everything he had.

As to what will happen to Lawrence in the future, only Allah knows. One thing is certain, that he will not permit his country to make a hero out of him. The maker of history has once more become the student of history. But Lawrence may live to see the effect of the wave that he rolled up out of the desert, in the form of an important new power in the East. As a result of the Arabian war of liberation, which was not a foolish dream on paper, and as a result of Allenby's smashing campaign in Palestine and Syria, three new Arabian states came into existence: the kingdom of the Hedjaz under Hussein I., of Mecca; the independent state of Transjordania under Hussein's second son, the Sultan Abdullah; and the kingdom of Iraq in Mesopotamia, where Hussein's third son, King Feisal I., ascended the throne. It is the dream of these three, assisted by Hussein's eldest son, King Ali, who succeeded his father to the throne in Mecca, one day to form a United States of Arabia.

Much depends on King Feisal. Colonel Lawrence played the dominant part in making him one of the greatest Arabs of his time. But the task before Feisal is stupendous. He has vision and high ideals for his people. Will he be strong enough to maintain his position in Bagdad and remain the leading figure in the Arabian world? Events are now moving swiftly in the Near East. If King Feisal can, through the quiet force of his personality, continue the work of wiping out the ancient quarrels between the tribes and cities of the desert, in which task he and his father and brothers were given such effective help by Lawrence, and if the nations of the West will send railway, sanitary, and irrigation engineers and disinterested military and political advisers; co-operate in the establishment of schools, and lend financial support, the glory that once was Babylon's may come again in Mesopotamia. The future of King Feisal and his brothers may be the future of Arabia. None may know the end of the story.

However, one thing is certain, that Feisal, like his romantic predecessor, Harun al Rashid of the Arabian Nights, is a just and merciful monarch; but had it not been for the youthful Lawrence, Feisal would not be ruling in Bagdad to-day, nor would his brother Abdullah be the Sultan of Transjordania, nor would the Arabs ever have had the opportunity to proclaim King Hussein as Caliph. For it was this youth who destroyed the thousand-year-old network of blood-feuds, who built up the Arabian army, who planned the strategy of the desert campaign and led the Arabs into battle, who swept the Turks from a thousand miles of country between Mecca and Damascus, who was the brains of the epic Arabian campaign, and rode in triumph through the bazaars of Damascus, and established a government for Prince Feisal in the capital of Omar and Saladin, the oldest surviving city in the world. But without a complete understanding of the mentality and instinct of Arabia, and without a sincere love for the peoples of the desert, this would never have been possible. Nor is it surprising that with such love and understanding from such a man, translated into successful policies and glorious deeds, he won the adoration of the Arab race.

Little did young Lawrence dream, when he was studying Hittite ruins, that it was his destiny to play a major role in building a new empire, instead of piecing together, for a scholar's thesis, the fragments of a dead-and-buried Kingdom. As Captain Tuohy has tersely said in his brief note in "The Secret Corps," "for romantic adventure his career has probably been unexampled in this or any other war."

This twenty-eight year old poet and scholar had started out across the Arabian Desert in February, 1916, to raise an army, accompanied by only three companions. I do not know of a more hopeless task than this that has been essayed during the last thousand years. They at first had no money, no means of transportation except a few camels, and no means of communication except camel-riders. They were trying to raise and equip an army in a country which has no manufacturing interests, which produces very little food and less water. In many parts of Arabia water-holes are a five days' camel-trek apart. They had no laws to help them, and they were trying to raise an army among the nomadic Bedouin tribes that had been separated from one another by blood-feuds for hundreds of years. They were trying to unify a people who quarrel over the possession of the water-holes and pasture-lands of Arabia and war with one another for the possession of camels; a people who, when they meet one another in the desert; usually substitute volleys of pot-shots for the conventional rules of Oriental courtesy.

In habit, instinct, and mental outlook Europe is utterly at variance with Asia, and it is rarely, perhaps once in hundreds of years, that there comes forward some brilliant Anglo-Saxon, Celt, or Latin, who, possessing an understanding that transcends race, religion, and tradition, can adopt the Eastern temperament at will. Such men were Marco Polo, the Venetian, and General Charles Gordon. Such a man is Thomas Edward Lawrence, the modern Arabian knight.

A few minutes after eight o'clock on the Sunday morning of the 19th May, 1935, Lawrence of Arabia died from injuries received in an accident whilst motor-cycling along a Dorset road. For 142 hours he had lain unconscious in Wool Military Hospital, Bovington Camp, and at the inquest which followed the fatality it was stated that, had death been averted, Lawrence would have lost the power of speech, his memory, and the partial use of his limbs. The following tribute to Colonel Lawrence's life and character was broadcast by Field-Marshal Viscount Allenby during the evening of the same Sunday.

IN T. E. Shaw, better known to the public as Colonel T. E. Lawrence, I have lost a good friend and a valued comrade. When first I met him—in the summer of 1917—he had just returned from a venturesome raid behind the Turkish front: thenceforward, until the Armistice, we were closely associated in the conduct of the campaigns of 1917 and 1918 in Palestine and Syria—closely, that is, in mind and purpose, though distance often separated us widely.

Lawrence was under my command, but, after acquainting him with my strategical plan, I gave him a free hand. His co-operation was marked by the utmost loyalty, and I never had anything but praise for his work which, indeed, was invaluable throughout the campaign. He was the mainspring of the Arab movement. He knew their language, their manners, their mentality; he understood and shared their merry, sly humour; in daring, he led them; in endurance, he equalled, if not surpassed, their strongest. Though in complete sympathy with his companions, and sharing to the full with them hardship and danger, he was careful to maintain the dignity of his position as Confidential Adviser to the Emir Feisal. Himself an Emir, he wore the robes of that rank, and kept up a suitable degree of state.

His own bodyguard—men of wild and adventurous spirit— were all picked by Lawrence personally. Mounted on thorough- bred camels, they followed him in all his daring rides; and among those reckless desert rangers there was none who would not wil- lingly have died for their chief. In fact, not a few lost their lives through devotion to him and in defence of his person. The shy and retiring scholar, archæologist, philosopher, was swept by the tide of war into a position undreamt of.

His well-balanced brain and disciplined imagination facilitated adaptation to the new environment; and there shone forth a brilliant tactician, with a genius for leadership. Such men win friends—such also find critics and detractors. But the highest reward for success is the inward knowledge that it has been rightly won. Praise or blame were regarded with indifference by Lawrence. He did his duty as he saw it before him. He has left, to us who knew and admired him, a beloved memory; and to all his countrymen, the example of a life well-spent in service.

Reprinted by kind permission of Field-Marshal Viscount Allenby, and "The Listener"